CHILTON'S
REPAIR & TUNE-UP GUIDE
RENAULT
1975-85

**All U.S. and Canadian models of R-12, R-15, R-17, R-18, R-18i •
Alliance • Encore • Fuego • Fuego Turbo •
Gordini • LeCar • Sport Wagon**

President LAWRENCE A. FORNASIERI
Vice President and General Manager JOHN P. KUSHNERICK
Executive Editor KERRY A. FREEMAN, S.A.E.
Senior Editor RICHARD J. RIVELE, S.A.E.

CHILTON BOOK COMPANY
Radnor, Pennsylvania
19089

SAFETY NOTICE

Proper service and repair procedures are vital to the safe, reliable operation of all motor vehicles, as well as the personal safety of those performing repairs. This book outlines procedures for servicing and repairing vehicles using safe, effective methods. The procedures contain many NOTES, CAUTIONS and WARNINGS which should be followed along with standard safety procedures to eliminate the possibility of personal injury or improper service which could damage the vehicle or compromise its safety.

It is important to note that repair procedures and techniques, tools and parts for servicing motor vehicles, as well as the skill and experience of the individual performing the work vary widely. It is not possible to anticipate all of the conceivable ways or conditions under which vehicles may be serviced, or to provide cautions as to all of the possible hazards that may result. Standard and accepted safety precautions and equipment should be used when handling toxic or flammable fluids, and safety goggles or other protection should be used during cutting, grinding, chiseling, prying, or any other process that can cause material removal or projectiles.

Some procedures require the use of tools specially designed for a specific purpose. Before substituting another tool or procedure, you must be completely satisfied that neither your personal safety, nor the performance of the vehicle will be endangered.

Although information in this guide is based on industry sources and is as complete as possible at the time of publication, the possibility exists that the manufacturer made later changes which could not be included here. While striving for total accuracy, Chilton Book Company cannot assume responsibility for any errors, changes, or omissions that may occur in the compilation of this data.

PART NUMBERS

Part numbers listed in this reference are not recommendations by Chilton for any product by brand name. They are references that can be used with interchange manuals and aftermarket supplier catalogs to locate each brand supplier's discrete part number.

SPECIAL TOOLS

Special tools are recommended by the vehicle manufacturer to perform their specific job. Use has been kept to a minimum, but where absolutely necessary, they are referred to in the text by the part number of the tool manufacturer. These tools can be purchased, under the appropriate part number from the tool manufacturer or an equivalent tool can be purchased locally from a tool supplier or parts outlet. Before substituting any tool for the one recommended, read the SAFETY NOTICE at the top of this page.

ACKNOWLEDGMENTS

The Chilton Book Company expresses its appreciation to the American Motors Corporation, Detroit, Michigan for their generous assistance in the preparation of this book.

Copyright © 1985 by Chilton Book Company
All Rights Reserved
Published in Radnor, Pennsylvania 19089, by Chilton Book Company

Manufactured in the United States of America
67890   43210987

Chilton's Repair & Tune-Up Guide: Renault 1975–85
ISBN 0-8019-7561-1 pbk.
Library of Congress Catalog Card No. 84-45489

CONTENTS

Quick Reference Specifications For Your Vehicle

Fill in this chart with the most commonly used specifications for your vehicle. Specifications can be found in Chapters 1 through 3 or on the tune-up decal under the hood of the vehicle.

 Tune-Up

Firing Order_____

Spark Plugs:

    Type_____

    Gap (in.)_____

Point Gap (in.)_____

Dwell Angle (°)_____

Ignition Timing (°)_____

    Vacuum (Connected/Disconnected)_____

Valve Clearance (in.)

    Intake_____   Exhaust_____

Capacities

Engine Oil (qts)

    With Filter Change_____

    Without Filter Change_____

Cooling System (qts)_____

Manual Transmission (pts)_____

    Type_____

Automatic Transmission (pts)_____

    Type_____

Front Differential (pts)_____

    Type_____

Rear Differential (pts)_____

    Type_____

Transfer Case (pts)_____

    Type_____

FREQUENTLY REPLACED PARTS

Use these spaces to record the part numbers of frequently replaced parts.

PCV VALVE

Manufacturer_____

Part No._____

OIL FILTER

Manufacturer_____

Part No._____

AIR FILTER

Manufacturer_____

Part No._____

General Information and Maintenance

HOW TO USE THIS BOOK

Chilton's Repair & Tune-Up Guide for the Renault is intended to teach you more about the inner workings of your car and save you money on its upkeep. The first two chapters will be used the most, since they contain maintenance and tune-up information and procedures. The following chapters concern themselves with the more complex systems of your Renault. Operating systems from engine through brakes are covered to the extent that we feel the average do-it-yourselfer should get involved. This book will not explain such things as rebuilding the differential for the simple reason that the expertise required and the investment in special tools make this task uneconomical. We will tell you how to change your own brake pads and shoes, replace points and plugs, and many more jobs that will save you money, give you personal satisfaction, and help you avoid problems.

A secondary purpose of this book is as a reference for owners who want to understand their car and/or their mechanics better. In this case, no tools at all are required.

Before removing any parts, read through the entire procedure. This will give you the overall view of what tools and supplies will be required.

The sections begin with a brief discussion of the system and what it involves, followed by adjustments, maintenance, removal and installation procedures, and repair or overhaul procedures. When repair is not considered feasible, we tell you how to remove the part and then how to install the new or rebuilt replacement. In this way, you at least save the labor costs. Backyard repair of such components as the alternator is just not practical.

Two basic mechanic's rules should be mentioned here. One, whenever the left side of the Renault or engine is referred to, it is meant to specify the driver's side of the Renault. Conversely, the right side of the Renault means the passenger's side. Secondly, most screws and bolts are removed by turning counterclockwise, and tightened by turning clockwise. Safety is always the most important rule. Constantly be aware of the dangers involved in working on an automobile and take the proper precautions. Use jackstands when working under a raised vehicle. Don't smoke or allow an exposed flame to come near the battery or any part of the fuel system. Always use the proper tool and use it correctly; bruised knuckles and skinned fingers aren't a mechanic's standard equipment. Always take your time and have patience. Once you have some experience, working on your Renault will become an enjoyable hobby.

TOOLS AND EQUIPMENT

It would be impossible to catalog each and every tool that you may need to perform all the operations included in this book. It would also not be wise for the amateur to rush out and buy an expensive set of tools on the theory that he may need one of them at some time. The best approach is to proceed slowly, gathering together a good quality set of those tools that are used most frequently. Don't be misled by the low cost of bargain tools. It is far better to spend a little more for quality, name brand tools. Forged wrenches, 10 or 12 point sockets and fine-tooth ratchets are by far preferable to their less expensive counterparts. As any good mechanic can tell you, there are few worse experiences than trying to work on a car or truck with bad tools. Your monetary savings will be far outweighed by frustration and mangled knuckles.

Begin accumulating those tools that are used most frequently; those associated with routine maintenance and tune-up. In addition to the normal assortment of screwdrivers and pliers, you should have the following tools for routine maintenance jobs:

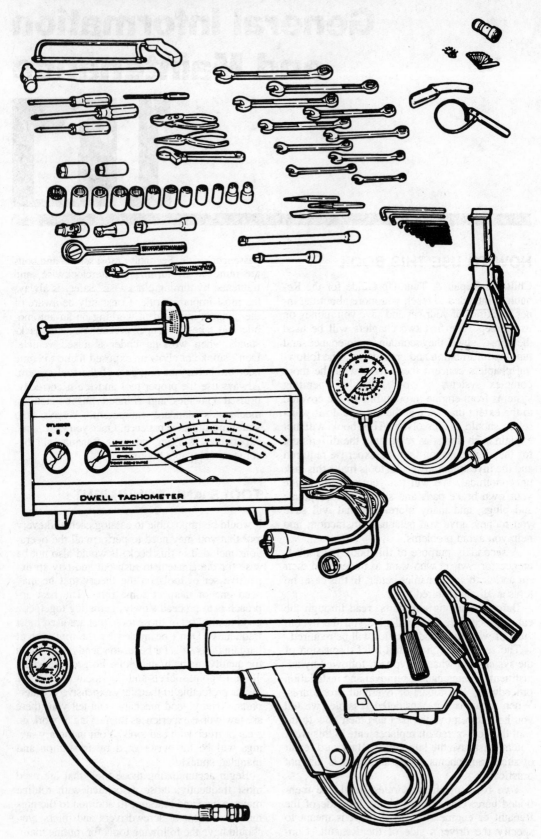

You need only a basic assortment of hand tools for most maintenance and repair jobs

1. SAE wrenches, sockets and combination open end/box end wrenches;
2. Jackstands—for support;
3. Oil filter wrench;
4. Oil filler spout or funnel;
5. Grease gun—for chassis lubrication;
6. Hydrometer—for checking the battery;
7. A low flat pan for draining oil;
8. Lots of rags for wiping up the inevitable mess.

In addition to the above items, there are several others that are not absolutely necessary, but are handy to have around. These include oil drying compound, a transmission funnel, and the usual supply of lubricants, antifreeze and fluids, although these can be purchased as needed. This is a basic list for routine maintenance, but only your personal needs can accurately determine your list of tools.

The second list of tools is for tune-ups. While the tools involved here are slightly more sophisticated, they need not be outrageously expensive. There are several inexpensive tach/dwell meters on the market that are every bit as good for the average mechanic as a $100.00 professional model. Just be sure that it goes to at least 12000–1500 rpm on the tach scale, and that it works on 4, 6, and 8 cylinder engines. A basic list of tune-up equipment could include:

1. Tach/dwell meter;
2. Spark plug wrench;
3. Timing light (preferably a DC light that works from the van's battery);
4. A set of flat feeler gauges;
5. A set of round wire spark plug gauges.

In addition to these basic tools, there are several other tools and gauges you may find useful. These include:

1. A compression gauge. The screw-in type is slower to use, but eliminates the possibility of a faulty reading due to escaping pressure;
2. A manifold vacuum gauge;
3. A test light;
4. An induction meter. This is used for determining whether or not there is current in a wire. These are handy for use if a wire is broken somewhere in a wiring harness. As a final note, you will probably find a torque wrench necessary for all but the most basic work. The beam type models are perfectly adequate, although the newer click type are more precise.

Special Tools

Normally, the use of special factory tools is avoided for repair procedures, since these are not readily available for the do-it-yourself mechanic. When it is possible to perform the job with more commonly available tools, it will be pointed out, but occasionally, a special tool was designed to perform a specific function and should be used. Before substituting another tool, you should be convinced that neither your safety nor the performance of the vehicle will be compromised.

SERVICING YOUR VEHICLE SAFELY

It is virtually impossible to anticipate all of the hazards involved with automotive maintenance and service but care and common sense will prevent most accidents.

The rules of safety for mechanics range from "don't smoke around gasoline," to "use the proper tool for the job." The trick to avoiding injuries is to develop safe work habits and take every possible precaution.

Do's

• Do keep a fire extinguisher and first aid kit within easy reach.
• Do wear safety glasses or goggles when cutting, drilling, grinding or prying. If you wear glasses for the sake of vision, then they should be made of hardened glass that can serve also as safety glasses, or wear safety goggles over your regular glasses.
• Do shield your eyes whenever you work around the battery. Batteries contain sulphuric acid; in case of contact with the eyes or skin, flush the area with water or a mixture of water and baking soda and get medical attention immediately.
• Do use safety stands for any under-car service. Jacks are for raising vehicles; safety stands are for making sure the vehicle stays raised until you want it to come down. Whenever the vehicle is raised, block the wheels remaining on the ground and set the parking brake.
• Do use adequate ventilation when working with any chemicals. Asbestos dust resulting from brake lining wear can cause cancer.
• Do disconnect the negative battery cable when working on the electrical system. The primary ignition system can contain up to 40,000 volts.
• Do follow manufacturer's directions whenever working with potentially hazardous materials. Both brake fluid and antifreeze are poisonous if taken internally.
• Do properly maintain your tools. Loose hammerheads, mushroomed punches and chisels, frayed or poorly grounded electrical cords, excessively worn screwdrivers, spread wrenches (open end), cracked sockets, slipping ratchets, or faulty droplight sockets can cause accidents.

• Do use the proper size and type of tool for the job being done.

• Do when possible, pull on a wrench handle rather than push on it, and adjust your stance to prevent a fall.

• Do be sure that adjustable wrenches are tightly adjusted on the nut or bolt and pulled so that the face is on the side of the fixed jaw.

• Do select a wrench or socket that fits the nut or bolt. The wrench or socket should sit straight, not cocked.

• Do strike squarely with a hammer to avoid glancing blows.

• Do set the parking brake and block the drive wheels if the work requires that the engine be running.

DON'TS

• Don't run an engine in a garage or anywhere else without proper ventilation—EVER! Carbon monoxide is poisonous; it is absorbed by the body 400 times faster than oxygen; it takes a long time to leave the human body and you can build up a deadly supply of it in your system by simply breathing in a little every day. You may not realize you are slowly poisoning yourself. Always use power vents, windows, fans or open the garage doors.

• Don't work around moving parts while wearing a necktie or other loose clothing. Short sleeves are much safer than long, loose sleeves. Hard-toed shoes with neoprene soles protect your toes and give a better grip on slippery surfaces. Jewelry such as watches, fancy belt buckles, beads or body adornment of any kind is not safe working around a car. Long hair should be hidden under a hat or cap.

• Don't use pockets for toolboxes. A fall or bump can drive a screwdriver deep into your body. Even a wiping cloth hanging from the back pocket can wrap around a spinning shaft or fan.

• Don't smoke when working around gasoline, cleaning solvent or other flammable material.

• Don't smoke when working around the battery. When the battery is being charged, it gives off explosive hydrogen gas.

• Don't use gasoline to wash your hands; there are excellent soaps available. Gasoline may contain lead, and lead can enter the body through a cut, accumulating in the body until you are very ill. Gasoline also removes all the natural oils from the skin so that bone dry hands will suck up oil and grease.

• Don't service the air conditioning system unless you are equipped with the necessary tools and training. The refrigerant, R-12, is extremely cold and when exposed to the air, will instantly freeze any surface it comes in contact with, including your eyes. Although the refrigerant is normally non-toxic, R-12 becomes a deadly poisonous gas in the presence of an open flame. One good whiff of the vapors from burning refrigerant can be fatal.

SERIAL NUMBER IDENTIFICATION

Vehicle

Renault vehicles are identified by two plates in the engine compartment. One plate, diamond shaped through 1979 and rectangular beginning in 1980, shows the model number, serial number, maximum gross vehicle weight (GVW), maximum gross axle weight rating, date of manufacture and vehicle class.

Vehicle identification plate through 1979

The other plate, oval in shape, as indicated by the illustration, shows:
• the model number
• the transmission type

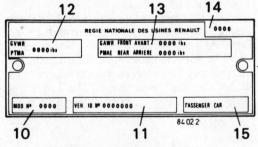

10. model number
11. serial number
12. maximum gross vehicle weight
13. maximum axle loading
14. date of manufacture
15. vehicle class

Vehicle identification plate, 1980 and later

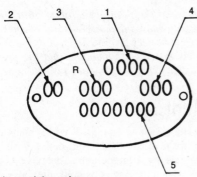

1. model number
2. transmission type and any special feature
3. basic equipment code
4. optional equipment code
5. manufacturing sequence number

Supplemental identification plate used on all years

- basic equipment code
- optional equipment code
- manufacturer's number

Engine

The engine identification plate is attached to the engine block on the left side at the rear, just below the head. On earlier models, all plates were uniformly rectangular on all engines. On later models, however, the size and shape of the plate was determined by available space. Through 1979 the plate showed the engine type, index and manufacturing sequence numbr. Beginning in 1980, the plate shows, as illustrated:

A. the engine type;

Engine ID plate through 1979

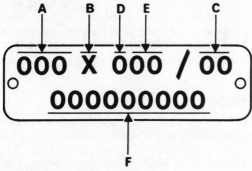

Engine ID plate 1980 and later

B. The French Ministry of Mines homologation number;
C. Engine equipment;
D. Manufacturer's identification number;
E. Engine index number;
F. the manufacturing sequence number;

Transaxle

The transaxle identification tag is located under a bolt on the transaxle at the end opposite the engine. The plate shows the type and the manufacturing sequence number.

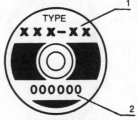

Transmission ID plate, 1 is the type code and 2 is the manufacturing number

ROUTINE MAINTENANCE

Air Cleaner

On all cars, the air cleaner housing is mounted on the fender liner and is connected to the carburetor inlet by a flexible hose and neck housing. To change air cleaner elements, simply unscrew the wing nut or remove the clip holding the housing end cap, remove the end cap, pull out and discard the old element, and install the new element.

Battery

The electrolyte level in the battery should be checked at least twice a month. Batteries should be filled to the bottom of the split ring liner in the filler hole. On later models, maintenance free batteries are used. These never need refilling and can be checked for state of charge by a charge indicator built into the top of the battery. For other batteries, the state of charge can be accurately tested with a simple and inexpensive tool called a hydrometer. The hydrometer measures the specific gravity of the electrolyte in a range of 1.100 to 1.300 and most good hydrometers have a built-in thermometer to allow you to correct for temperature.

CAUTION: *When working with batteries, please be careful. The electrolyte is sulfuric acid and can cause severe burns on contact*

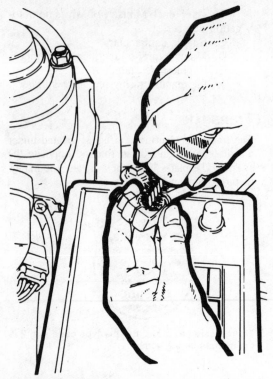

Clean the inside of the clamps with a wire brush, or the special tool

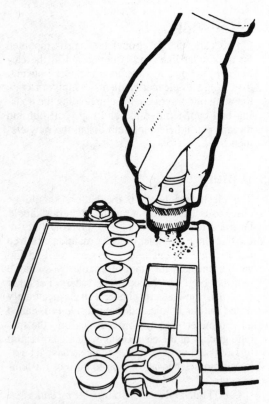

Clean the posts with a wire brush, or a terminal cleaner made for the purpose (shown)

with your skin. Any electrolyte gotten in the eyes can cause blindness. Also, the fumes given off by a battery are hydrogen sulfide gas. This gas is extremely flammable and the presence of a cigarette or cigar can cause an explosion.

Heat Riser

Some models are equipped witha shutter-type valve in the exhaust manifold outlet. This valve is operated by a temperature-sensivive bi-metal spring. When the engine is cold, the valve shuts, directing hot exhaust gases back upward to warm the carburetor and intake manifold. When the engine warms, the valve opens allowing the normal passage of exhaust gases. A special heat riser lubricant can be used to keep the valve working freely. This is important, since rust and scale can form on the valve, making it stick in either the closed or open position. If it sticks in the open position, hard starting and poor drive-ability will result until the engine warms up. If it sticks in the closed position, the engine will suffer from loss of power, overheating, poor performance and poor fuel mileage.

Belts

The maintaining of proper tension on belts is perhaps the most important thing in ensuring long life and the proper functioning of the components they drive.

If belts are installed too tightly, they put excess pressure on pulleys and bearings causing failure of such components as the water pump, alternator, power steering pump, air conditioning compressor, etc. Installing belts too loosely can cause slippage, which permits improper operation of the components that they drive, plus glazing and cracking of the belt.

A general rule for proper belt tensioning is simply this: find the longest straight run of the belt and depress it at its mid-point with your finger. You should be able to depress it about ½ inch; no more and not much less. Belts are tightened by loosening the components which they drive and moving it to increase tension. Some components are made of soft or brittle metals such as aluminum or magnesium, so don't pry on them with a metal prybar.

Hoses

Check the condition of the hoses at least twice a year; more frequent checking is a safety measure. A sure sign of impending hose failure is a swelling of the hose around clamps. Another obvious sign is cracking of the surface of the hose,

HOW TO SPOT WORN V-BELTS

V-Belts are vital to efficient engine operation—they drive the fan, water pump and other accessories. They require little maintenance (occasional tightening) but they will not last forever. Slipping or failure of the V-belt will lead to overheating. If your V-belt looks like any of these, it should be replaced.

This belt has deep cracks, which cause it to flex. Too much flexing leads to heat build-up and premature failure. These cracks can be caused by using the belt on a pulley that is too small. Notched belts are available for small diameter pulleys.

Cracking or weathering

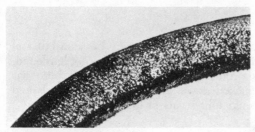

Oil and grease on a belt can cause the belt's rubber compounds to soften and separate from the reinforcing cords that hold the belt together. The belt will first slip, then finally fail altogether.

Softening (grease and oil)

Glazing is caused by a belt that is slipping. A slipping belt can cause a run-down battery, erratic power steering, overheating or poor accessory performance. The more the belt slips, the more glazing will be built up on the surface of the belt. The more the belt is glazed, the more it will slip. If the glazing is light, tighten the belt.

Glazing

The cover of this belt is worn off and is peeling away. The reinforcing cords will begin to wear and the belt will shortly break. When the belt cover wears in spots or has a rough jagged appearance, check the pulley grooves for roughness.

Worn cover

This belt is on the verge of breaking and leaving you stranded. The layers of the belt are separating and the reinforcing cords are exposed. It's just a matter of time before it breaks completely.

Separation

HOW TO SPOT BAD HOSES

Both the upper and lower radiator hoses are called upon to perform difficult jobs in an inhospitable environment. They are subject to nearly 18 psi at under hood temperatures often over 280°F., and must circulate nearly 7500 gallons of coolant an hour—3 good reasons to have good hoses.

Swollen hose

A good test for any hose is to feel it for soft or spongy spots. Frequently these will appear as swollen areas of the hose. The most likely cause is oil soaking. This hose could burst at any time, when hot or under pressure.

Cracked hose

Cracked hoses can usually be seen but feel the hoses to be sure they have not hardened; a prime cause of cracking. This hose has cracked down to the reinforcing cords and could split at any of the cracks.

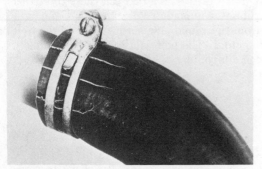

Frayed hose end (due to weak clamp)

Weakened clamps frequently are the cause of hose and cooling system failure. The connection between the pipe and hose has deteriorated enough to allow coolant to escape when the engine is hot.

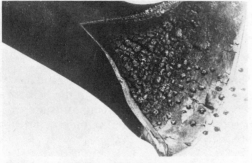

Debris in cooling system

Debris, rust and scale in the cooling system can cause the inside of a hose to weaken. This can usually be felt on the outside of the hose as soft or thinner areas.

due to age or chemical contamination. Check the illustrations for all hose failure signs. When replacing a hose, make sure that the replacement is the exact length as the original. An overly long or short replacement will fail in a short time. The engine does move on its mounts causing the hoses to flex. Original equipment hoses are sized to flex the correct amount with the engine movement. Also, make certain that the hose clamps are in good condition. A distorted clamp could cut a hose when tightened.

Cooling System

At least once every 2 years, the engine cooling system should be inspected, flushed, and refilled with fresh coolant. If the coolant is left in the system too long, it loses its ability to prevent rust and corrosion. If the coolant has too much water, it won't protect against freezing.

The pressure cap should be looked at for signs of age or deterioration. Fan belt and other drive belts should be inspected and adjusted to the proper tension.

Hose clamps should be tightened, and soft or cracked hoses replaced. Damp spots, or accumulations of rust or dye near hoses, water pump or other areas, indicate possible leakage, which must be corrected before filling the system with fresh coolant.

CHECK THE RADIATOR CAP

While you are checking the coolant level, check the radiator cap for a worn or cracked gasket. If the cap doesn't seal properly, fluid will be lost and the engine will overheat.

Worn caps should be replaced with a new one.

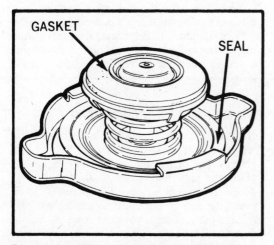

Be sure the rubber gasket makes a tight seal

CLEAN RADIATOR OF DEBRIS

Periodically clean any debris—leaves, paper, insects, etc.—from the radiator fins. Pick the large pieces off by hand. The smaller pieces can be washed away with water pressure from a hose.

Carefully straighten any bent radiator fins with a pair of needle nose pliers. Be careful—the fins are very soft. Don't wiggle the fins back and forth too much. Straighten them once and try not to move them again.

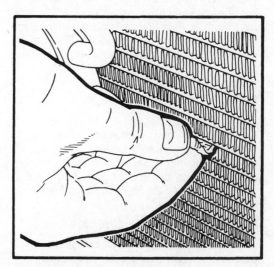

Remove debris from the radiator fins

Air Conditioning
SAFETY PRECAUTIONS

There are two particular hazards associated with air conditioning systems and they both relate to the refrigerant gas.

First, the refrigerant gas is an extremely cold substance. When exposed to air, it will instantly freeze any surface it comes in contact with, including your eyes. The other hazard relates to fire. Although normally non-toxic, refrigerant gas becomes highly poisonous in the presence of an open flame. One good whiff of the vapor formed by burning refrigerant can be fatal. Keep all forms of fire (including cigarettes) well clear of the air conditioning system.

Any repair work to an air conditioning system should be left to a professional. Do not, under any circumstances, attempt to loosen or tighten any fittings or perform any work other than that outlined here.

CHECKING FOR OIL LEAKS

Refrigerant leaks show up as oily areas on the various components because the compressor oil is transported around the entire system along with the refrigerant. Look for oily spots on all the hoses and lines, and especially on the hose and tubing connections. If there are oily deposits, the system may have a leak, and you should have it checked by a qualified repairman.

NOTE: *A small area of oil on the front of the compressor is normal and no cause for alarm.*

KEEP THE CONDENSER CLEAR

Periodically inspect the front of the condenser for bent fins or foreign material (dirt, bugs, leaves, etc.) If any cooling fins are bent, straighten them carefully with needlenosed pliers. You can remove any debris with a stiff bristle brush or hose.

OPERATE THE A/C SYSTEM PERIODICALLY

A lot of A/C problems can be avoided by simply running the air conditioner at least once a week, regardless of the season. Let the system run for at least 5 minutes a week (even in the winter), and you'll keep the internal parts lubricated as well as preventing the hoses from hardening.

REFRIGERANT LEVEL CHECK

There are two ways to check refrigerant level, depending on how your model is equipped.

With Sight Glass

The first order of business when checking the sight glass is to find the sight glass. It will either be in the head of the receiver/drier, or in one of the metal lines leading from the top of the receiver/drier. Once you've found it, wipe it clean and proceed as follows:

1. With the engine and the air conditioning system running, look for the flow of refrigerant through the sight glass. If the air conditioner is working properly, you'll be able to see a continuous flow of clear refrigerant through the sight glass, with perhaps an occasional bubble at very high temperatures.

2. Cycle the air conditioner on and off to make sure what you are seeing is clear refrigerant. Since the refrigerant is clear, it is possible to mistake a completely discharged system for one that is fully charged. Turn the system off and watch the sight glass. If there is refrigerant in the system, you'll see bubbles during the off cycle. If you observe no bubbles when the system is running, and the air flow from the unit in the car is delivering cold air, everything is OK.

3. If you observe bubbles in the sight glass while the system is operating, the system is low on refrigerant. Have it checked by a professional.

4. Oil streaks in the sight glass are an indication of trouble. Most of the time, if you see oil in the sight glass, it will appear as a series of streaks, although occasionally it may be a solid stream of oil. In either case, it means that part of the charge has been lost.

Without Sight Glass

On vehicles that are not equipped with sight glasses, it is necessary to feel the temperature difference in the inlet and outlet lines at the receiver/drier to gauge the refrigerant level. Use the following procedure:

1. Locate the receiver/drier. It will generally be up front near the condenser. It is shaped like a small fire extinguisher and will always have two lines connected to it. One line goes to the expansion valve and the other goes to the condenser.

2. With the engine and the air conditioner running, place one hand on the line between the receiver/drier and the expansion valve, and the other on the line from the compressor to the condenser. Gauge their relative temperatures. If they are both the same approximate temperature, the system is correctly charged.

3. If the line from the expansion valve to the receiver/drier is a lot colder than the line from the condenser to the compressor, then the system is overcharged. It should be noted that this is an extremely rare condition.

4. If the line that leads from the compressor to the condensor is a lot colder than the other line, the system is undercharged.

5. If the system is undercharged or overcharged, have it checked by a professional air conditioning mechanic.

Windshield Wipers

Intense heat from the sun, snow and ice, road oils and the chemicals used in windshield washer solvents combine to deteriorate the rubber wiper refills. The refills should be replaced about twice a year or whenever the blades begin to streak or chatter.

WIPER REFILL REPLACEMENT

Normally, if the wipers are not cleaning the windshield properly, only the refill has to be replaced. The blade and arm usually require replacement only in the event of damage. It is not necessary (except on new Tridon refills) to remove the arm or the blade to replace the refill (rubber part), though you may have to position the arm higher on the glass. You can do this turning the ignition switch on and operating the wip-

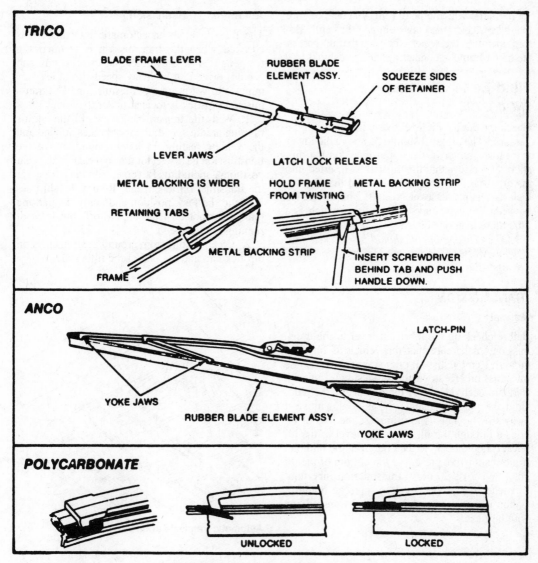

The three types of wiper blade retention

ers. When they are positioned where they are accessible, turn the ignition switch off.

There are several types of refills and your vehicle could have any kind, since aftermarket blades and arms may not use exactly the same refill as the original equipment.

Most Trico styles use a release button that is pushed down to allow the refill to slide out of the yoke jaws. The new refill slides in and locks in place. Some Trico refills are removed by locating where the metal backing strip or the refill is wider. Insert a small screwdriver blade between the frame and metal backing strip. Press down to release the refill from the retaining tab.

The Anco style is unlocked at one end by squeezing 2 metal tabs, and the refill is slid out of the frame jaws. When the new refill is installed, the tabs will click into place, locking the refill.

The polycarbonate type is held in place by a locking lever that is pushed downward out of the groove in the arm to free the refill. When the new refill is installed, it will lock in place automatically.

The Tridon refill has a plastic backing strip with a notch about an inch from the end. Hold the blade (frame) on a hard surface so that the frame is tightly bowed. Grip the tip of the backing strip and pull up while twisting counterclockwise. The backing strip will snap out of the retaining tab. Do this for the remaining tabs until the refill is free of the arm. The length of these refills is molded into the end and they should be replaced with identical types.

No matter which type of refill you use, be sure that all of the frame claws engage the refill. Before operating the wipers, be sure that no part of the metal frame is contacting the windshield.

Fluid Level Checks

ENGINE OIL

Check the engine oil level every time you fill the gas tank. The oil level should be above the lower mark and not above the upper mark on the dipstick. Make sure that the dipstick is inserted into the crankcase as far as possible and that the vehicle is resting on level ground. The difference between the two marks is one liter, which is a little more than one quart.

NOTE: *The engine oil should be checked only when warm with the engine off. (operating temperature).*

TRANSMISSION

Manual

Before checking the lubricant level in the transmission, make sure that the vehicle is on level ground. Remove the fill plug from the side of the transmission. Remove the plug slowly when it starts to reach the end of the threads on the plug. Hold the plug up against the hole and move it away slowly. This is to minimize the loss of lubricant through the fill hole. The level of the lubricant should be up to the bottom of the fill hole. If lubricant is not present at the bottom of the fill hole, add SAE 90 or 80 transmission lube until it reaches the proper level. A squeeze bottle or siphon gun is used to fill a manual transmission with lubricant.

Automatic Transmission

The fluid level in an automatic transmission is checked when the transmission is at operating temperatures. If the vehicle has been sitting and is cold, drive it at highway speeds for at least 20 minutes to warm up the transmission. The transmission dipstick is located under the hood.

1. With the transmission in Park, the engine running at idle speed, the foot brakes applied and the vehicle resting on level ground, move the transmission gear selector through each of the gear positions, including Reverse, allowing time for the transmission to engage. Return the shift selector to the Park position and apply the parking brake. Do not turn the engine off, but leave it running at idle speed.

2. Clean all dirt from around the transmission dipstick cap and the end of the filler tube.

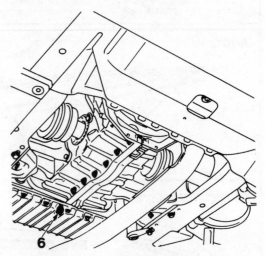

Automatic transaxle drain plug (6)

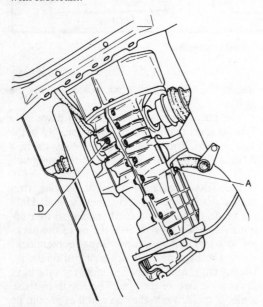

Manual transaxle drain (D) and refill (A) points

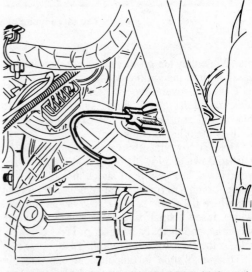

Automatic transaxle dipstick (7). Add fluid through the dipstick tube

3. Pull the dipstick out of the tube, wipe it off with a clean cloth, and push it back into the tube all the way, making sure that it seats completely.

4. Pull the dipstick out of the tube again and read the level of the fluid on the stick. The level should be between the ADD and FULL marks. If fluid must be added, add enough fluid through the tube to raise the level up to between the ADD and FULL marks. Do not overfill the transmission because this will cause foaming and loss of fluid through the vent and malfunctioning of the transmission. Use only Dexron® II fluid.

BRAKE MASTER CYLINDER

The master cylinder reservoir is located under the hood, on the left side firewall. Before removing the master cylinder reservoir cap, make sure the vehicle is resting on level ground and clean all dirt away from the top of the master cylinder. Pry off the retaining clip and remove the cap. The brake fluid level should be within ¼ in. of the top of the reservoir.

If the level of the brake fluid is less than half the volume of the reservoir, it is advised that you check the brake system for leaks. Leaks in a hydraulic brake system most commonly occur at the wheel cylinder.

There is a rubber diaphragm in the top of the master cylinder cap. As the fluid level lowers in the reservoir due to normal brake shoe wear or leakage, the diaphragm takes up the space. This is to prevent the loss of brake fluid out the vented cap and contamination by dirt. After filling the master cylinder to the proper level with brake fluid, but before replacing the cap, fold the rubber diaphragm up into the cap, then replace the cap on the reservoir and tighten the retaining bolt or snap the retaining clip into place.

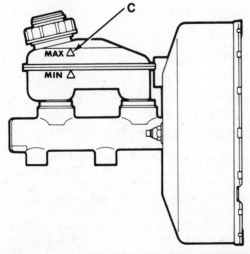

Master cylinder and reservoir. C is the maximum fill level

POWER STEERING RESERVOIR

Position the vehicle on level ground. Run the engine until the fluid is at normal operating temperature. Turn the steering wheel all the way to the left and right several times. Position the wheels in the straight ahead position, then shut off the engine. Check the fluid level on the dipstick which is attached to the reservoir cap. The level should be between the ADD and FULL marks on the dipstick. Add fluid accordingly. Do not overfill. Use power steering fluid.

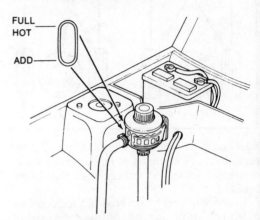

Typical power steering reservoir

Tires and Wheels

Tires should be rotated periodically. Follow the accompanying diagrams for the proper rotation pattern. Note that radial tires must be kept on the same side of the vehicle on which they were originally installed.

If uneven tire wear occurs before 6,000 miles, rotate the tires sooner and determine the cause of the uneven wear. Uneven wear and abnormal wear patterns may be caused by incorrect front end alignment, uneven tire pressures, unbalanced tires and worn or broken suspension parts. Tire balance should be checked at rotation.

Common sense and good driving habits will prolong the life of any tire. Hard cornering and spinning tires is a waste of money. Overloading and improper inflation also cut tire life.

Inspect the tires frequently for cuts, cracks, side wall bubbles or stones. Replace any tire with a deep cut or side wall bubble.

When replacing original equipment tires, remember that the replacement should be in, at least, a set of four. It is a bad idea to mix tire tread patterns or sizes. Tire construction types should never be mixed. The differences in handling characteristics can be hazardous.

When installing oversized tires, make sure that sufficient clearance exists at all points and angles. Oversized floatation tires will require wider

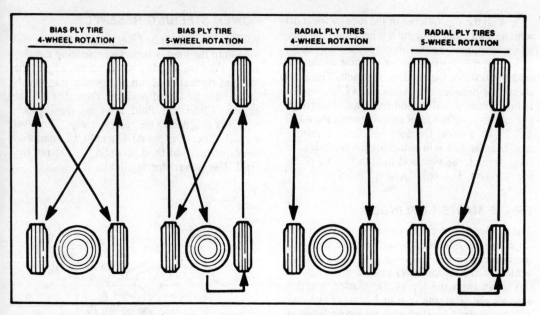

rims than those on a stock vehicle. Mud and snow tires should be operated at manufacturer's recommended pressures, and not at sustained high speeds.

In summary, select the type of tire according to the type of driving that will be done most of the time.

Fuel Filter

CARBURETED ENGINES

The filter is a wire mesh screen located under a nut in the inlet side of the carburetor. Periodically remove the nut and clean the screen. Always use a new gasket on the nut.

FUEL INJECTION

The filter is located next to the fuel pump on the right rear frame member. Before removing the filter clamps, clamp-off the lines on either side of the filter to avoid spills. Remove the filter clamps, install the new filter, noting the direction of flow stamped on the filter, and replace the clamps. Unclamp the lines.

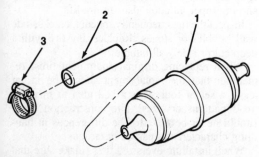

Fuel filter used with injected engines. 1 is the filter, 2 is the hose connector, 3 is the clamp

LUBRICATION

Oil and Fuel Recommendations

ENGINE

- 10W-40 or 10W-50 above 14°F
- 20W-40 or 20W-50 above 32°F
- 10W-30 below 14°F
- 5W-20 below −14°F

MANUAL TRANSAXLE

- SAE 80W, 90W or 80/90W

AUTOMATIC TRANSAXLE

- Dexron® II

BRAKE SYSTEM

- DOT 3 or 4

COOLING SYSTEM

- 50/50 mix of water and Ethylene Glycol

POWER STEERING

- Dexron® II

Fluid Changes

ENGINE OIL AND FILTER

The oil and filter should be changed at the same time, at least every 6,000 miles. The oil should be drained with the engine hot by removing the oil drain plug from the pan and draining the oil into a suitable container. Be very careful when removing the drain plug since hot oil can burn you! A good practice is to wear heavy rubber work gloves when removing the plug.

To remove the filter, use a filter wrench, available at all auto parts stores. Place the catch pan under the filter, since it holds about a quart.

When refilling the engine oil pan, install the plug securely and screw a new filter onto the engine. Before installing the filter, coat the rubber seal on the new filter with clean engine oil. Screw the filter onto the engine until the rubber seal makes contact, turn it ¼ additional turn, then loosen it. Using the filter wrench, turn the filter back until the seal again makes contact, then turn it an additional ½ to ¾ turn.

MANUAL TRANSAXLE

The manual transaxle fluid should be changed every 5 years or 50,000 miles. To drain the fluid, raise and support the car on jackstands. Remove the drain plug on the bottom of the transaxle and allow the fluid to drain. Replace the plug and fill the transaxle through the plug on the side of the case, until the fluid is level with the plug opening.

AUTOMATIC TRANSAXLE

The automatic transaxle fluid should be changed every two years or 25,000 miles. Drive the car for 10–20 minutes to heat the fluid. Drain the fluid immediately after shut-down. Be careful! The fluid will be very hot. It can burn the skin. A good practice is to wear heavy rubber gloves when removing the drain plug. Drain the fluid into a suitable container. Install the plug. Add 3¼ quarts of new fluid. Start the engine and let it idle in Park. Check the fluid level and add enough fluid to fill it.

COOLANT

Drain and Refill the Cooling System

Completely draining and refilling the cooling system every two years at least will remove accumulated rust, scale and other deposits. Coolant mixture is 50–50 ethylene glycol and water for year round use. Use a good quality antifreeze with water pump lubricants, rust inhibitors and other corrosion inhibitors along with acid neutralizers.

1. Drain the existing antifreeze and coolant. Open the radiator and engine drain petcocks, or disconnect the bottom radiator hose, at the radiator outlet.

NOTE: *Before opening the radiator petcock, spray it with some penetrating lubricant.*

2. Close the petcock or re-connect the lower hose and fill the system with water.

3. Add a can of quality radiator flush.

4. Idle the engine until the upper radiator hose gets hot.

5. Drain the system again.

6. Repeat this process until the drained water is clear and free of scale.

7. Close all petcocks and connect all the hoses.

8. If equipped with a coolant recovery system, flush the reservoir with water and leave empty.

9. Determine the capacity of your cooling system (see capacities specifications). Add a 50/50 mix of quality antifreeze (ethylene glycol) and water to provide the desired protection.

10. Run the engine to operating temperature.

11. Stop the engine and check the coolant level.

12. Check the level of protection with an antifreeze tester, replace the cap and check for leaks.

PUSHING AND TOWING

To push start your vehicle, (manual transmission only) follow the procedures below:

Check to make sure that the bumpers of both vehicles are aligned so that neither will be damaged. Be sure that all electrical system components are turned off (headlights, heater blower, etc.). Turn on the ignition switch. Place the shift lever in Third gear and push in the clutch pedal. Have the driver of the other vehicle push your vehicle at a gentle but steadily increased rate of speed. At about 15 mph, signal the driver of the pushing vehicle to fall back, slightly depress the accelerator pedal, and release the clutch pedal slowly. The engine should start.

When you are doing the pushing, make sure that the two bumpers match so that you won't damage the vehicle you are to push. Another good idea is to put an old tire between the two vehicles.

Whenever you are towing another vehicle, make sure that the tow chain or rope is sufficiently long and strong, and that it is securely attached to both vehicles. Attach the chain at a point on the frame or as close to it as possible. Once again, go slowly and tell the other driver to do the same. Warn the other driver not to allow too much slack in the line when he gains traction or can move under his own power. Otherwise, he may run over the tow line and damage both vehicles.

If your vehicle has to be towed by a tow truck, it can be towed forward tith the driveshaft connected no faster than 30 mph and no farther than 15 miles. Otherwise, disconnect the driveshaft and tie it up. If your vehicle has to be towed backward, make sure that the steering wheel is secured in the straight-ahead position.

JACKING

Fuego, LeCar, Alliance, Encore

When jacking at the front, you'll have to rig a support made of a length of 4x4 lumber bolted to the jack cradle to lift the car by means of the frame rails as illustrated. When lifting at the rear, use the same 4x4 rig under the rear axle spanning the rise in the axle. When lifting at the sides, use the same 4x4 rig under the rocker panels at the mid-point of the door. Jackstands must be placed only at the reinforced frame rail pads.

Lifting an Alliance or Encore at the side

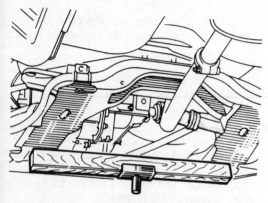

Lifting the front end of an Alliance or Encore

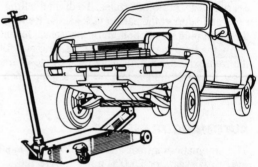

Lifting the front of the LeCar. Fuego and R-18 are similar

Lifting a LeCar at the side. Fuego and R-18 are similar

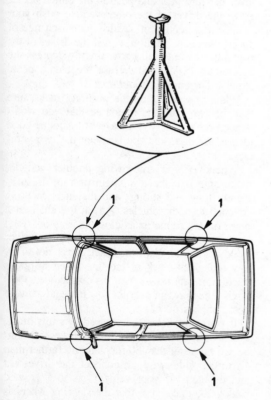

Jackstand support points for an Alliance or Encore

Lifting the rear of a LeCar. Fuego and R-18 are similar

JUMP STARTING A DEAD BATTERY

The chemical reaction in a battery produces explosive hydrogen gas. This is the safe way to jump start a dead battery, reducing the chances of an accidental spark that could cause an explosion.

Jump Starting Precautions

1. Be sure both batteries are of the same voltage.
2. Be sure both batteries are of the same polarity (have the same grounded terminal).
3. Be sure the vehicles are not touching.
4. Be sure the vent cap holes are not obstructed.
5. Do not smoke or allow sparks around the battery.
6. In cold weather, check for frozen electrolyte in the battery.
7. Do not allow electrolyte on your skin or clothing.
8. Be sure the electrolyte is not frozen.

Jump Starting Procedure

1. Determine voltages of the two batteries; they must be the same.
2. Bring the starting vehicle close (they must not touch) so that the batteries can be reached easily.
3. Turn off all accessories and both engines. Put both cars in Neutral or Park and set the handbrake.
4. Cover the cell caps with a rag—do not cover terminals.
5. If the terminals on the run-down battery are heavily corroded, clean them.
6. Identify the positive and negative posts on both batteries and connect the cables in the order shown.
7. Start the engine of the starting vehicle and run it at fast idle. Try to start the car with the dead battery. Crank it for no more than 10 seconds at a time and let it cool off for 20 seconds in between tries.
8. If it doesn't start in 3 tries, there is something else wrong.
9. Disconnect the cables in the reverse order.
10. Replace the cell covers and dispose of the rags.

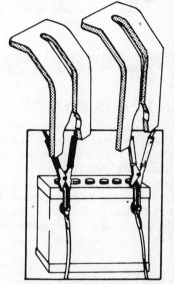

Side terminal batteries occasionally pose a problem when connecting jumper cables. There frequently isn't enough room to clamp the cables without touching sheet metal. Side terminal adaptors are available to alleviate this problem and should be removed after use.

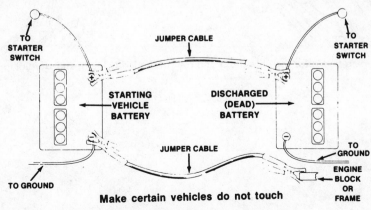

TO STARTER SWITCH

JUMPER CABLE

TO STARTER SWITCH

STARTING VEHICLE BATTERY

DISCHARGED (DEAD) BATTERY

TO GROUND

JUMPER CABLE

ENGINE BLOCK OR FRAME

TO GROUND

Make certain vehicles do not touch

This hook-up for negative ground cars only

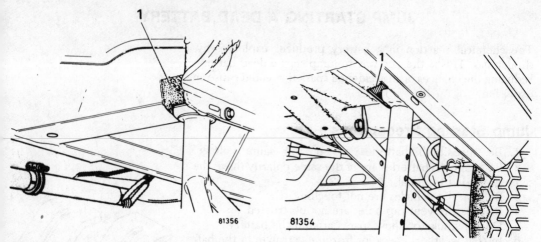

Support points on the R-18 and Fuego for jackstand use. Reinforcing blocks, supplied with the vehicle (1 in the illustration) must be used when using jackstands

R-12, R-15, R-17, Gordini, R-18i

When jacking at the front, you'll have to make a lifting rig out of a length of 4x4 lumber bolted to the floor jack cradle to support the car under the frame rails. When jacking at the rear, place the jack cradle at the center of the rear axle. When jacking at the sides, use the 4x4 mount at the mid-point of the floor panel, just inside the door. Jackstands should be placed only at the reinforced frame rail pads.

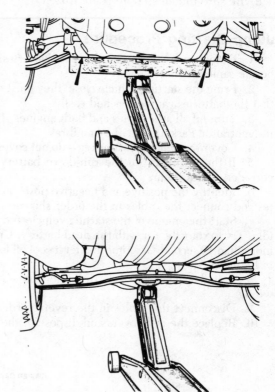

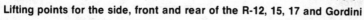

Lifting points for the side, front and rear of the R-12, 15, 17 and Gordini

Capacities

Model	Year	Crankcase Incl. Filter (qts.)	Pints to Refill After Draining		Fuel Tank (gal.)	Cooling System (qts.)	
			Manual	Automatic ●		With Heater	With A/C
LeCar	All	3.5	4.0	—	10.0	6.5	6.5
R-12	All	4.5	4.5	13.0	14.5	9.5	9.5
R-15	All	4.5	4.5	13.0	13.2	7.0	7.0
R-17	All	4.5	4.5	13.0	13.2	7.0	7.0
Gordini	All	4.5	4.5	—	12.5	8.0	8.0
R-18i, 18	1981–83	4.5	4.5	10.5	①	6.5	6.75
Fuego	1982–83	4.5	4.5	10.5	15.0	6.4	6.75
Alliance	1982–83	3.5	7.0	9.0	12.5	4.4	4.8
Alliance, Encore	1984–85	4.0	②	7.5	12.5	4.4	4.8
Sport Wagon, Fuego	1984–85				N.A.		
Fuego Turbo	1984–85	4.5	4.5	10.5	15.0	6.4	6.75

● includes converter
① Sedan: 14
   Sta. Wgn.: 15

② 4 sp: 6.4
  5 sp: 6.8

Tune-Up and Performance Maintenance

T2

TUNE-UP PROCEDURES

Spark Plugs

A typical spark plug consists of a metal shell surrounding a ceramic insulator. A metal electrode extends downward through the center of the insulator and protrudes a small distance. Located at the end of the plug and attached to the side of the outer metal shell is the side electrode. The side electrode bends in at a 90° angle so that its tip is even with, and parallel to, the tip of the center electrode. The distance between these two electrodes (measured in thousandths of an inch) is called the spark plug gap. The spark plug in no way produces a spark but merely provides a gap across which the current can arc. The coil produces anywhere from 20,000 to 40,000 volts which travels to the distributor where it is distributed through the spark plug wires to the spark plugs. The current passes along the center electrode and jumps the gap to the side electrode, and, in so doing, ignites the air/fuel mixture in the combustion chamber.

SPARK PLUG HEAT RANGE

Spark plug heat range is the ability of the plug to dissipate heat. The longer the insulator (or the farther it extends into the engine), the hotter the plug will operate; the shorter the insulator the cooler it will operate. A plug that absorbs little heat and remains too cool will quickly accumulate deposits of oil and carbon since it is not hot enough to burn them off. This leads to plug fouling and consequently to misfiring. A plug that absorbs too much heat will have no deposits, but, due to the excessive heat, the electrodes will burn away quickly and in some instances, preignition may result. Preignition takes place when plug tips get so hot that they glow sufficiently to ignite the fuel/air mixture before the actual spark occurs. This early ignition will usually cause a pinging during low speeds and heavy loads.

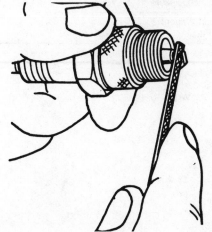

Plugs that are in good condition can be filed and re-used

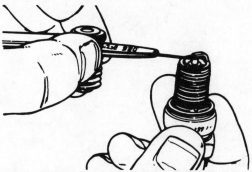

Always use a wire gauge to check the electrode gap

The general rule of thumb for choosing the correct heat range when picking a spark plug is: if most of your driving is long distance, high speed travel, use a colder plug; if most of your driving is stop and go, use a hotter plug. Original equipment plugs are compromise plugs, but most people never have occasion to change their plugs from the factory-recommended heat range.

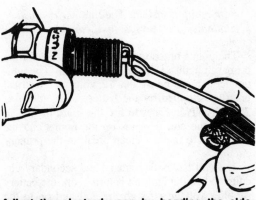

Adjust the electrode gap by bending the side electrode

REPLACING SPARK PLUGS

A set of spark plugs usually requires replacement after about 10,000 miles on cars with conven-

tional ignition systems and after about 20,000 to 30,000 miles on cars with electronic ignition, depending on your style of driving. In normal operation, plug gap increases about 0.001 in. for every 1,000–2,500 miles. As the gap increases, the plug's voltage requirement also increases. It requires a greater voltage to jump the wider gap and about two to three times as much voltage to fire a plug at high speeds than at idle.

When you're removing spark plugs, you should work on one at a time. Don't start by removing the plug wires all at once, because unless you number them, they may become mixed up. Take a minute before you begin and number the wires with tape. The best location for numbering is near where the wires come out of the cap.

1. Twist the spark plug boot and remove the boot and wire from the plug. Do not pull on the wire itself as this will ruin the wire.

2. If possible, use a brush or rag to clean the area around the spark plug. Make sure that all

Engine Tune-Up Specifications

Year	Engine Displacement cu in. (cc)	Spark Plug Type	Spark Plug Gap (in.)	Distributor Point Dwell (deg)	Distributor Point Gap (in.)	Ignition Timing (deg) MT	Ignition Timing (deg) AT	Intake Valve Opens (deg)	Fuel Pump Pressure (psi)	Idle Speed (rpm) MT	Idle Speed (rpm) AT	Valve Clearance (in.) In	Valve Clearance (in.) Ex
1975–76	78.6 (1289)	L-92Y	.026–.029	57	.016–.020	0	—	22B	2.5–3.5	775①	—	.006	.008
1977–79	78.6 (1289)	②	③	57	.016–.020	0	—	22B	2.5–3.5	775④	—	.006	.008
1980–81	85.2 (1397)	WD9DS	.022–.026	Electronic		3B⑧	—	12B	2.5–3.5	700⑤	—	.006	.008
1982–85	85.2 (1397)	RN-12Y	.032	Electronic		8B	8B	12B	28–36	700	700	.006	.008
1975⑨	95.5 (1565)	N-3	.025–.028	57	.016–.020	12B	12B	24B	28–36	1000	1000	.010	.012
1975	100.5 (1647)	N-94	.025–.028	57	.016–.020	10B⑥	10B	10B	2.5–4.0⑦	850	650	.008	.010
1976	100.5 (1647)	N-9Y	.025–.028	57	.016–.020	7B⑥	10B	10B	2.5–4.0⑦	850	650	.008	.010
1977–78	100.5 (1647)	N-9Y	.025–.028	57	.016–.020	7B⑥	7B	22B	2.5–40⑦	850	650	.008	.010
1981–84	100.5 (1647)	WR7DS	.024–.028	Electronic		10B	10B	22B	28–36	800	650	.008	.010
1984–85	132.0 (2165)	— See underhood sticker —											

① w/air pump: 800
② 1977–78 exc. Calif.: L-874
   1977 exc. Calif.: L-92Y
   1977–79 Calif.: L-92Y
③ 1977–78 exc. Calif.: .026–.029
   All others: .022–.026
④ w/air pump: 850

⑤ w/air pump: 750
⑥ Gordini: 12B
⑦ Gordini: 28.5–29.2 in 1975
           25–35 in 1976–78
⑧ Canada: 0
⑨ Canadian Gordini only

the dirt is removed so that none will enter the cylinder after the plug is removed.

3. Remove the spark plug using the proper size socket. Turn the socket counterclockwise to remove the plug. Be sure to hold the socket straight on the plug to avoid breaking the plug, or rounding off the hex on the plug.

4. Once the plug is out, check it against the plugs shown in the "Color" section of chapter four to determine engine condition. This is crucial since plug readings are vital signs of engine condition.

5. Use a round wire feeler gauge to check the plug gap. The correct size gauge should pass through the electrode gap with a slight drag. If you're in doubt, try one size smaller and one larger. The smaller gauge should go through easily while the larger one shouldn't go through at all. If the gap is incorrect, use the electrode bending tool on the end of the gauge to adjust the gap. When adjusting the gap, always bend the side electrode. The center electrode is non-adjustable.

6. Squirt a drop of penetrating oil on the threads of the new plug and install it. Don't oil the threads too heavily. Turn the plug in clockwise by hand until it is snug.

7. When the plug is finger tight, tighten it with a wrench. If you don't have a torque wrench, tighten the plug as shown.

8. Install the plug boot firmly over the plug. Proceed to the next plug.

CHECKING AND REPLACING SPARK PLUG CABLES

Visually inspect the spark plug cables for burns, cuts, or breaks in the insulation. Check the spark plug boots and the nipples on the distributor cap and coil. Replace any damaged wiring. If no physical damage is obvious, the wires can be checked with an ohmmeter for excessive resistance. (See the tuneup and troubleshooting section.)

When installing a new set of spark plug cables, replace the cables one at a time so there will be no mixup. Start by replacing the longest cable first. Install the boot firmly over the spark plug. Route the wire exactly the same as the original. Insert the nipple firmly into the tower on the distributor cap. Repeat the process for each cable.

Breaker Points and Condenser

NOTE: *Some 1980 and 1981 and later models are equipped with a breakerless, solid-state ignition system. The breakerless system eliminates the points and condenser completely.*

The points function as a circuit breaker for the primary circuit of the ignition system. The ignition coil must boost the 12 volts of electrical pressure supplied by the battery to as much as 25,000 volts in order to fire the spark plugs. To do this, the coil depends on the points and the condenser to make a clean break in the primary circuit.

The coil has both primary and secondary circuits. When the ignition is turned on, the battery supplies voltage through the coil and on to the points. The points are connected to ground, completing the primary circuit. As the current passes through the coil, a magnetic field is created in the iron center core of the coil. As the cam in the distributor turns, the points open and the primary circuit is interrupted. The magnetic field in the primary circuit of the coil collapses and cuts through the secondary circuit windings around the iron core. Because of the scientific phenomenon called "electromagnetic induction," the battery voltage is at this point increased to a level sufficient to fire the spark plugs.

When the points open, the electrical charge in the primary circuit jumps the gap created between the two open contacts of the points. If this electrical charge were not transferred elsewhere, the metal contacts of the points would melt and the gap between the points would start to change rapidly. If this gap is not maintained, the points will not break the primary circuit. If the primary circuit is not broken, the secondary circuit will not have enough voltage to fire the spark plugs.

The function of the condenser is to absorb excessive voltage from the points when they open and thus prevent the points from becoming pitted or burned.

The cycle must be completed by the ignition system every time a spark fires. So, when the engine is at an idle speed of 800 rpm, the points are opening and closing 1,600 times a minute.

There are two ways to check the breaker point gap: It can be done with a feeler gauge or a dwell meter. Either way you set the points, you are basically adjusting the amount of time that the points remain open. The time is measured in degrees of distributor rotation. When you measure the gap between the breaker points with a feeler gauge, you are setting the maximum amount the points will open when the rubbing block on the points is on a high point of the distributor cam. When you adjust the points with a dwell meter, you are adjusting the number of degrees that the points will remain closed before they start to open as a high point of the distributor cam approaches the rubbing block of the points.

When you replace a set of points, always replace the condenser at the same time.

When you change the point gap or dwell, you will also have changed the ignition timing. So, if the point gap or dwell is changed, the ignition timing must be adjusted also. Changing the ignition timing, however, does not affect the dwell.

INSPECTION OF THE POINTS

1. Disconnect the high-tension wire from the top of the distributor and the coil.

2. Remove the distributor cap by prying off the spring clips on the side of the cap.

3. Remove the rotor from the distributor shaft by pulling it straight up. Examine the condition of the rotor. If it is cracked or the metal tip is excessively worn or burned, it should be replaced.

4. Pry open the contacts of the points with a screwdriver and check the condition of the con-

tacts. If they are excessively worn, burned or pitted, they should be replaced.

5. If the points are in good condition, adjust them, and replace the rotor and the distributor cap. If the points need to be replaced, follow the replacement procedure given below.

REPLACEMENT OF THE BREAKER POINTS AND CONDENSER

1. Remove the coil high-tension wire from the top of the distributor cap. Remove the distributor cap from the distributor and place it out of the way. Remove the rotor from the distributor shaft.

2. Loosen the screw which holds the condenser lead to the body of the breaker points and remove the condenser lead from the points.

3. Remove the screw which holds and grounds the condenser to the distributor body. Remove the condenser from the distributor and discard it.

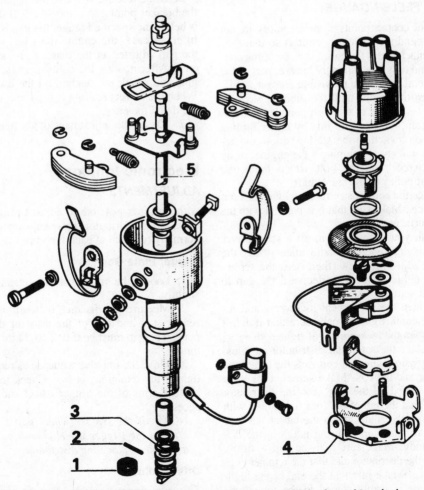

Point type distributor. LeCar uses a distributor cap with horizontal terminals

4. Remove the points assembly attaching screws and adjustment lockscrews. A screwdriver with a holding mechanism will come in handy here so that you don't drop a screw into the distributor and have to remove the entire distributor to retrieve it.

5. Remove the points by lifting them straight up and off the locating dowel on the plate. Wipe off the cam and apply new cam lubricant. Discard the old set of points.

6. Slip the new set of points onto the locating dowel and install the screws that hold the assembly onto the plate. Do not tighten them all the way.

7. Attach the new condenser to the plate with the ground screw.

8. Attach the condenser lead to the points at the proper place.

9. Apply a small amount of cam lubricant to the shaft where the rubbing block of the points touches.

ADJUSTMENT OF THE BREAKER POINTS WITH A FEELER GAUGE

1. If the contact points of the assembly are not parallel, bend the stationary contact so that they make contact across the entire surface of the contacts. Bend only the stationary bracket part of the point assembly; not the moveable contact.

2. Turn the engine until the rubbing block of the points is on one of the high points of the distributor cam. You can do this by either turning the ignition switch to the start position and releasing it quickly ("bumping" the engine) or by using a wrench on the bolt which holds the crankshaft pulley to the crankshaft.

3. Place the correct size feeler gauge between the contacts. Make sure that it is parallel with the contact surfaces.

4. With your free hand, insert a screwdriver into the notch provided for adjustment or into the eccentric adjusting screw, then twist the screwdriver to either increase or decrease the gap to the proper setting.

5. Tighten the adjustment lockscrew and recheck the contact gap to make sure that it didn't change when the lockscrew was tightened.

6. Replace the rotor and distributor cap, and the high-tension wire that connects the top of the distributor and the coil. Make sure that the rotor is firmly seated all the way onto the distributor shaft and that the tab of the rotor is aligned with the notch in the shaft. Align the tab in the base of the distributor cap with the notch in the distributor body. Make sure that the cap is firmly seated on the distributor and that the retainer clips are in place. Make sure that the end of the high-tension wire is firmly placed in the top of the distributor and the coil.

ADJUSTMENT OF THE BREAKER POINTS WITH A DWELL METER

1. Adjust the points with a feeler gauge as described earlier.

2. Connect the dwell meter to the ignition circuit according to the manufacturer's instructions. One lead of the meter is connected to a ground and the other lead is to be connected to the distributor post on the coil. An adapter is usually provided for this purpose.

3. If the dwell meter has a set line on it, adjust the meter to zero the indicator.

4. Start the engine.

NOTE: *Be careful when working on any vehicle while the engine is running. Make sure that the transmission is in Neutral or Park and that the parking brake is applied. Keep hands, clothing, tools, and the wires of the test instruments clear of the rotating fan blades.*

5. Observe the reading on the dwell meter. If the reading is within the specified range, turn off the engine and remove the dwell meter.

6. If the reading is above the specified range, the breaker point gap is too small. If the reading is below the specified range, the gap is too large. In either case, the engine must be stopped and the gap adjusted in the manner previously covered. After making the adjustment, start the engine and check the reading on the dwell meter. When the correct reading is obtained, disconnect the dwell meter.

7. Check the adjustment of the ignition timing.

Electronic Ignition
ADJUSTMENTS

Although it is possible to adjust certain components of the distributor, these adjustments are not normally required at each tune-up.

Trigger Plate Gap

1. Loosen the impulse sender retaining screws slightly.

2. Measure the distance between an impulse sender stud and one of the arms of the trigger plate. The gap must be 0.012–0.24 in. (0.3–0.6 mm).

3. Move the impulse sender(s) as required and tighten the retaining screws. Check the gap for all four arms of the trigger wheel and adjust as necessary.

NOTE: *If the trigger wheel gap for certain arms of the trigger wheel cannot be correctly adjusted, replace the distributor.*

Offset Adjustment

This adjustment is made after the trigger plate adjustment.

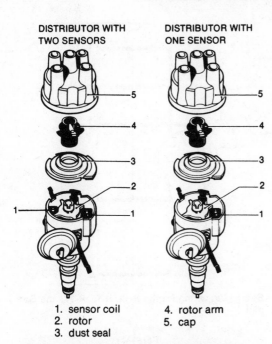

DISTRIBUTOR WITH
TWO SENSORS

DISTRIBUTOR WITH
ONE SENSOR

1. sensor coil
2. rotor
3. dust seal

4. rotor arm
5. cap

Breakerless distributor. Some R-18 models have a distributor with one sensor; some have two.

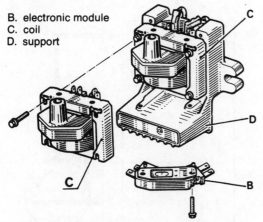

B. electronic module
C. coil
D. support

Ignition control unit for breakerless distributors

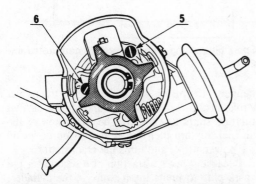

Loosen these two screws for air gap adjustment

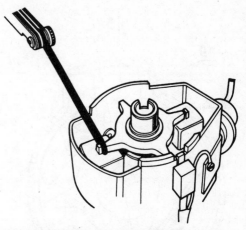

Measuring the air gap adjustment with a non-magnetic feeler gauge (plastic or brass)

1. Loosen the screws 6 & 7.
2. Line up the rotor cam 11, opposite the pickup tip 10.
3. For coil offset more than 3°, move the coil B1, so that the center of tip 9, is opposite rotor tip 8.
4. For coils offset more than 5°, move the coil B, so that point 12 on tip 9, is opposite point 8 of the rotor tip opposite tip 11.
5. Tighten screws 6 & 7.

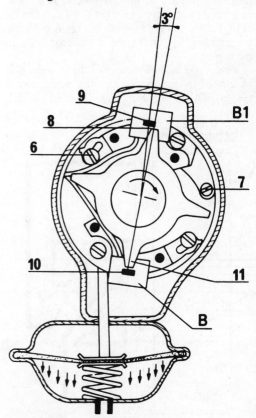

Adjustment for coils offset 3 degrees

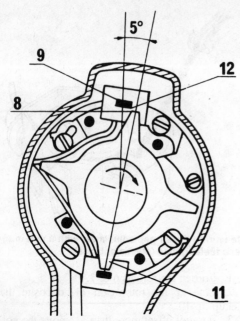

Adjustment for coils offset 5 degrees

Ignition Timing

Ignition timing is the measurement, in degrees of crankshaft rotation, of the point at which the spark plugs fire in each of the cyclinders. It is measured in degrees before or after Top Dead Center (TDC) of the compression stroke. Ignition timing is controlled by turning the distributor body in the engine.

Ideally, the air/fuel mixture in the cylinder will be ignited by the spark plug just as the piston passes TDC of the compression stroke. If this

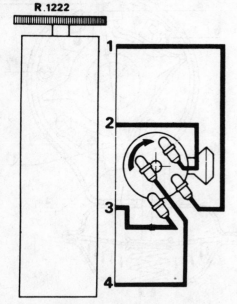

Spark plug wiring for Alliance, Encore and LeCar

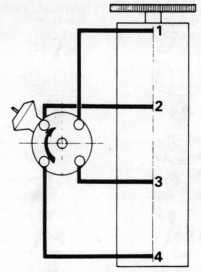

Spark plug wiring for the R-12, R-15, R-17, and Gordini

FRONT

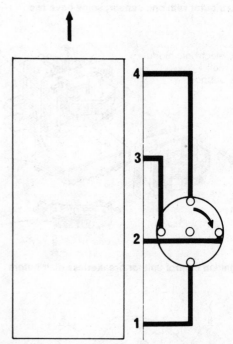

Spark plug wiring diagram for R-18 carbureted engines

happens, the piston will be beginning the power stroke just as the compressed and ignited air/fuel mixture starts to expand. The expansion of the air/fuel mixture then forces the piston down on the power stroke and turns the crankshaft.

Because it takes a fraction of a second for the spark plug to ignite the mixture in the cylinder, the spark plug must fire a little before the piston

FRONT

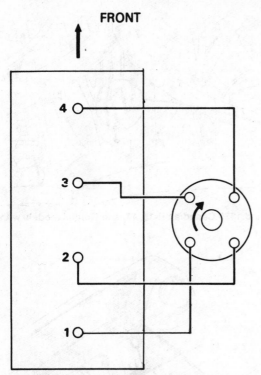

Spark plug wiring diagram for R-18 fuel injected engines and all Fuego models

of its travel. This will result in poor engine performance and lack of power.

The timing is best checked with a timing light. This device is connected in series with the No. 1 spark plug. The current that fires the spark plug also causes the timing light to flash.

There is a notch on the flywheel. A scale of degrees of crankshaft rotation is attached to the flywheel housing in such a position that the notch will pass close by the scale. When the engine is running, the timing light is aimed at the mark on the flywheel and the scale.

IGNITION TIMING ADJUSTMENT

1. Locate the timing marks on the flywheel and the flywheel housing.

2. Clean the timing marks so that you can see them.

3. Mark the timing marks with a piece of chalk or with paint. Color the mark on the scale that will indicate the correct timing when it is

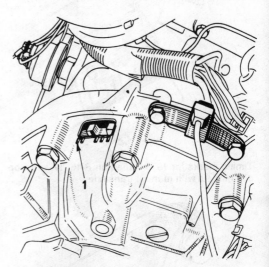

Timing marks for the Alliance and Encore. LeCar is similar. Each gradation is 2 degrees

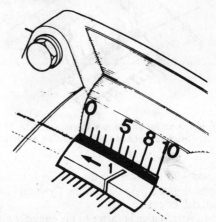

Timing marks for the R-12 with manual transaxle

reaches TDC. Otherwise, the mixture will not be completely ignited as the piston passes TDC and the full power of the explosion will not be used by the engine.

The timing measurement is given in degrees of crankshaft rotation before the piston reaches TDC (BTDC). If the setting for the ignition timing is 5° BTDC, each spark plug must fire 5° before each piston reaches TDC. This only holds true, however, when the engine is at idle speed.

As the engine speed increases, the pistons go faster. The spark plugs have to ignite the fuel even sooner if it is to be completely ignited when the piston reaches TDC. To do this, the distributor has a means to advance the timing of the spark as the engine speed increases. This is accomplished by centrifugal weights within the distributor and a vacuum diaphragm mounted on the side of the distributor. It is necessary to disconnect the vacuum lines from the diaphragm when the ignition timing is being set.

If the ignition is set too far advanced (BTDC), the ignition and expansion of the fuel in the cylinder will occur too soon and tend to force the piston down while it is still traveling up. This causes engine ping. If the ignition spark is set too far retarded after TDC (ATDC), the piston will have already passed TDC and started on its way down when the fuel is ignited. This will cause the piston to be forced down for only a portion

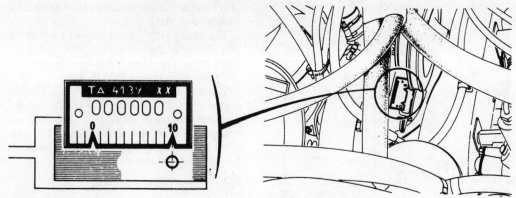

Timing marks for the R-12 with automatic transaxle, and 1975 Canadian R-15, 17, and Gordini models with automatic transaxle

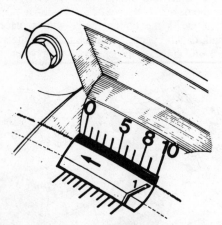

Timing marks for 1975 Canadian R-15, 17 and Gordini models with manual transaxle

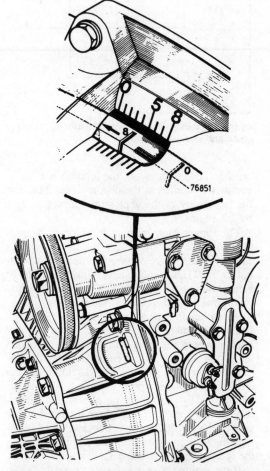

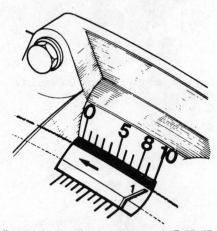

Timing marks for all manual transaxle R-15, 17 and Gordini models, except 1975 Canadian models

Timing marks for all automatic transaxle R-15, 17 and Gordini models except 1975 Canadian models

aligned with the mark on the flywheel. It is also helpful to mark the notch in the flywheel with a small dab of color.

4. Attach a tachometer to the engine.
5. Attach a timing light according to the manufacturer's instructions. If the timing light has three wires, one is attached to the No. 1 spark plug with an adapter. The other wires are connected to the battery. The red wire goes to the positive side of the battery and the black wire is connected to the negative terminal of the battery.

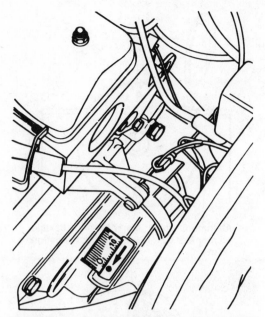

Timing marks for R-18 and Fuego with automatic transaxle

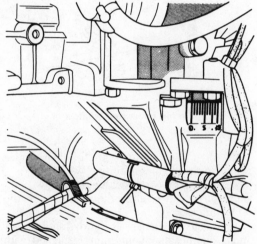

Timing marks for R-18 and Fuego with manual transaxle

6. Disconnect the vacuum line to the distributor at the distributor and plug the vacuum line. A golf tee does a fine job.

7. Check to make sure that all of the wires clear the fan and then start the engine.

8. Adjust the idle to the correct setting.

9. Aim the timing light at the timing marks. If the marks that you put on the flywheel and the flywheel housing are aligned when the light flashes, the timing is correct. Turn off the engine and remove the tachometer and the timing light. If the marks are not in alignment, proceed with the following steps.

10. Turn off the engine.

11. Loosen the distributor lockbolt just enough so that the distributor can be turned with a little effort.

12. Start the engine. Keep the wires of the timing light clear of the fan.

13. With the timing light aimed at the pulley and the marks on the engine, turn the distributor in the direction of rotor rotation to retard the spark, and in the opposite direction of rotor rotation to advance the spark. Align the marks on the pulley and the engine with the flashes of the timing light.

14. When the marks are aligned, tighten the distributor lockbolt and recheck the timing with the timing light to make sure that the distributor did not move when you tightened the lockbolt.

15. Turn off the engine and remove the timing light.

Valve Clearance
ADJUSTMENT

All except 2.2L Engine

NOTE: *Valve adjustment should be done through manual maintenance or when the cylinder head bolts are retorqued.*

1. Rotate the engine in correct rotation until the exhaust valve for the No. 1 cylinder is fully open.

2. Adjust the rocker arms of the intake valve for the No. 3 cylinder and the exhaust valve for the No. 4 cylinder.

3. Rotate the engine in correct rotation until the No. 3 cylinder exhaust valve is fully open. Adjust the rocker arms of the intake valve for the No. 4 cylinder and the exhaust valve for the No. 2 cylinder.

4. Rotate the engine in correct rotation until the No. 4 cylinder exhaust valve is fully open. Adjust the rocker arms of the intake valve for the No. 2 cylinder and the exhaust valve for the No. 1 cylinder.

5. Rotate the engine in correct rotation until the No. 2 cylinder exhaust valve is fully open. Adjust the rocker arms of the intake valve for the No. 1 cylinder and the exhaust valve for the No. 3 cylinder.

6. Rotate the engine in the correct rotation, and recheck the rocker arm adjustments for proper specification clearances.

2.2L OHC Engine 1984–85 Fuego

NOTE: *If the engine is equipped with a rear window in the timing belt cover, use Procedure A. If there is no rear window in the cover, use Procedure B.*

PROCEDURE A

1. Rotate the crankshaft clockwise and align the number one piston TDC mark with the notch in the FRONT cover window. Remember, #1 piston is at the flywheel end.

2. Rotate the crankshaft clockwise until the first mark appears in the REAR cover window. Align that mark with the cover notch. Loosen the locknut and adjust the #2 intake and #4 exhaust valves to give a clearance of .004–.008 in. for intakes and .008–.010 in. for exhaust. Repeat the procedure as follows:
- 2nd mark: #1 intake & #2 exhaust
- 3rd mark: #3 intake & #1 exhaust
- 4th mark: #4 intake & #3 exhaust

PROCEDURE B

NOTE: *A special tool is needed for this procedure.*

1. Remove the distributor cap and rotor.

2. Rotate the crankshaft clockwise and align the #1 piston TDC mark with the notch in the timing cover window.

3. Position Alignment Rotor Ms.1774 on the distributor shaft. Position flexible pointer Mot.591 on the #10 head bolt (nearest the distributor on the left).

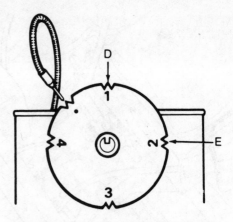

Alignment rotor Ms.1774 and flexible pointer Mot.591. D & E are piston location points

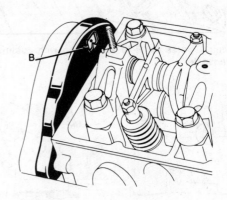

Timing cover rear window

4. Align the pointer with the TDC index (hole) on the alignment rotor.

5. Rotate the crankshaft clockwise two complete turns and re-align the pointer with the TDC index.

6. Rotate the crankshaft, slowly, until the #1 index on the alignment rotor is aligned with the pointer. Loosen the locknut and adjust the #2 intake and #4 exhaust valves to provide a clearance of .004–.006 in. for intakes and .008–.010 in. for exhausts. Tighten the locknuts. Rotate the crankshaft to each cylinder number in turn and adjust the valves as follows:
- mark #2: #1 intake & #2 exhaust
- mark #3: #3 intake & #1 exhaust
- mark #4: #4 intake & #3 exhaust

Carburetor

NOTE: *This section contains only idle speed adjustments. For all other fuel system services, see Chapter 4.*

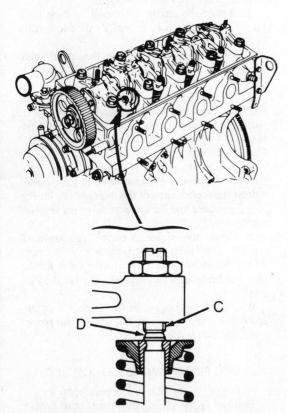

Valve adjustment point. C is the adjusting screw; D is the valve stem

IDLE SPEED AND MIXTURE ADJUSTMENT

NOTE: *1977 California models and all 1978–83 models must be adjusted with the use of a CO meter to obtain the correct emissions reading and idle speed. It is advised that these procedures be performed only by a qualified service person. Previous models may be adjusted by the lean drop method.*

Without a CO Meter (1977 and Earlier Except California)

1. Clamp off the air injection hose between the diverter valve and the engine, using the appropriate special tool.

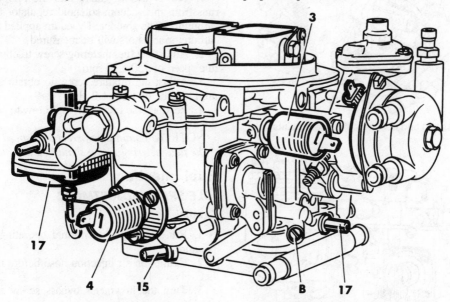

3. anti-dieseling solenoid
4. mixture control solenoid
15. 3-way thermovalve tube
17. fast idle throttle control

V. fast idle adjustment screw
A. idle speed adjustment screw
B. mixture adjustment screw

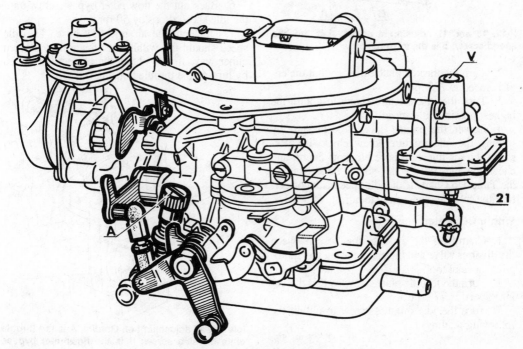

Canadian R-18 carburetor adjustment points

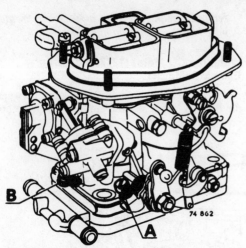

LeCar speed and mixture adjustment points

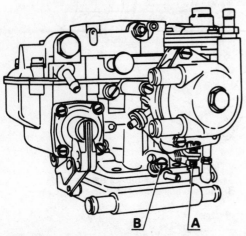

R-12, 15 and 17 adjustment points. A is the idle speed screw; B is the mixture screw

2. Turn the throttle plate screw so that the engine speed is 775 rpm.

3. Turn the idle mixture screw to obtain the highest possible idle speed.

4. Lower the engine speed 20–25 rpm by turning the idle mixture screw clockwise. Remove the air injection hose blockoff clamp and check the idle speed which should be as listed in the Tune-Up Chart. If the idle speed is incorrect, turn the throttle plate screw to adjust.

With a CO Meter

1. Clamp off the air injection hose between the diverter valve and the engine using the appropriate special tool.

2. Turn the throttle plate screw so that the engine speed is 775 rpm.

3. Turn the idle mixture screw to obtain the following readings:

- 1976–79   2.5% + .5%
  −2%

- 1980–85 Federal   2.0% + .5%
  −2%

4. Remove the air injection hose blockoff clamp and recheck the idle speed. Idle speeds are given in the Tune-Up Chart.

5. Repeat Steps 2–4 if necessary.

With a Vacuum Gauge

1. Tee a vacuum gauge into the line which runs from the vacuum solenoid regulator to the carburetor. The amount of vacuum applied to the carburetor actuators will be measured.

2. Adjust the fuel metering screw to obtain an idle speed of 750 ± 50 rpm.

3. Adjust the mixture screw to obtain a vacuum reading of 1.5 ± 1.2 Hg.

4. Readjust the fuel metering screw to correct the idle speed.

NOTE: *To obtain the correct idle speed, only the fuel metering screw should be adjusted.*

Fuel Injection

IDLE SPEED ADJUSTMENT

Gordini

1. Run the engine to normal operating temperature.

2. Clamp the air injection hose before the relief valve.

3. Turn the flowmeter bypass screw all the way in.

4. Connect a tachometer to the engine.

5. Turn the throttle plate housing screw to obtain an idle speed of 850 rpm.

6. Back out the flowmeter bypass screw until the idle speed drops by 50 rpm.

7. Unclamp the air injection hose. The idle speed should fall within specification by 50 rpm either way. If not, obtain the correct idle speed by turning the throttle housing screw.

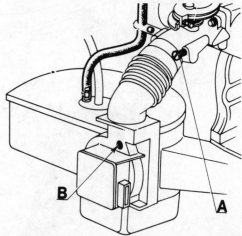

Idle speed adjustment on Gordini. A is the throttle plate housing screw; B is the flowmeter bypass screw

18i, Fuego, and California Alliance

1. Start the engine and allow it to come to operating temperature.

2. Connect a tachometer to leads D1–1 and D1–3 of the diagnostic connector.

3. Turn all accessories off. Wait for the electric fan to shut off.

4. Turn the throttle plate bypass screw to obtain the correct idle speed.

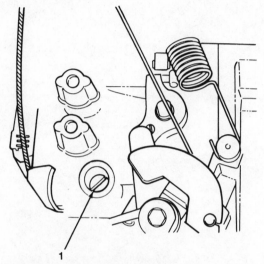

Idle speed adjustment on the 18i, Fuego and California Alliance. Point 1 is the idle speed screw located on top of the throttle plate housing

Alliance, except California

These cars use Throttle Body Injection. Idle speed adjustment is necessary only if the Idle Speed Control motor (ISC) has been replaced.

1. Remove the air cleaner.

2. Start the engine and allow it to reach normal operating temperature. Make sure that the A/C control is off.

3. Connect a tachometer to terminals D1–1 and D1–3 of the diagnostic connector.

4. Turn the engine off. The ISC plunger should move to the fully extended position.

5. Disconnect the ISC motor wire connector and start the engine.

6. Engine speed should be 3300–3700 rpm. If not, turn the hex head bolt on the end of the plunger to obtain 3500 rpm.

7. Fully retract the ISC motor plunger by holding the closed throttle switch plunger with the throttle open. The closed throttle switch plunger should not be touching the throttle lever when the throttle is returned to the closed posi-

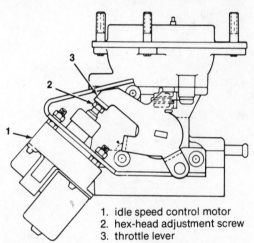

1. idle speed control motor
2. hex-head adjustment screw
3. throttle lever

Idle speed adjustment points for non-California Alliance

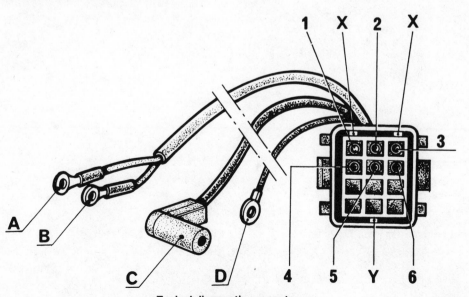

Typical diagnostic connector

tion. If contact is noted, check the throttle linkage and/or cable for binding.

8. Connect the ISC wire.

9. Turn the engine off for 10 seconds. The ISC motor plunger should move to the fully extended position.

10. Start the engine. The engine should speed up to 3500 rpm, stay there for a brief time, then drop off to normal idle speed as shown on the underhood sticker, and in the Tune-Up Chart.

11. Shut off the engine, disconnect the tachometer and apply a penetrating thread sealant to the adjustment screw threads.

ENGINE ELECTRICAL

Distributor

REMOVAL

1. Remove the coil wire from the distributor cap terminal.

2. Remove the distributor cap.

3. Disconnect the vacuum advance line at the distributor.

4. Note the position of the rotor and scribe a mark on the distributor body, indicating its position. Scribe two more marks, one on the body of the distributor and another on the engine block, indicating the position of the distributor body in relation to the engine block. All of the scribe marks should be made in line with each other, starting with the metal tip of the rotor and ending with the mark on the engine block. These marks will be used as guides when installing the distributor in the correctly timed engine (not disturbed).

5. Remove the retaining bolt and lockwasher which hold the distributor in the engine.

6. Lift the distributor out of the engine block.

INSTALLATION (ENGINE NOT DISTURBED)

1. Insert the distributor shaft into the engine. Align the marks on the distributor body with the metal tip of the rotor and the mark made on the engine block. Make sure that the vacuum advance diaphragm is pointed in the same direction as it was pointed originally. This will be done automatically if the marks on the engine and the distributor are aligned properly.

2. Install the distributor lockbolt and clamp. Leave the screw loose enough that you can turn the distributor with your hand.

3. Connect the distributor primary wire and install the distributor cap. Secure the distributor cap with the spring clips.

4. Install the spark plug wires. Make certain

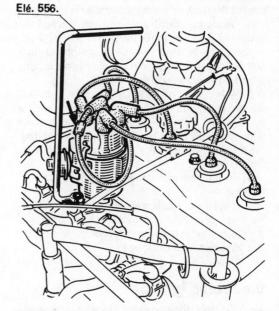

Elé. 556.

Removing the distributor holddown bolt

that the wires are pressed all the way into the top of the distributor cap and firmly onto the spark plugs.

5. Adjust the point dwell and set the ignition timing. Refer to the "Tune-Up" Section (Chapter 2).

INSTALLATION (ENGINE DISTURBED)

If the engine has been disturbed, (i.e., crankshaft turned) while the distributor has been removed or the alignment marks were not drawn, it will be necessary to initially time the engine. Follow the procedure given below:

1. Place the No. 1 piston at TDC of the compression stroke. To determine this, remove the spark plug from the No. 1 cylinder and the high-tension coil wire from the distributor cap. Place your thumb over the spark plug hole while

the engine is cranked. You will feel air being forced out of the cylinder as the piston comes up on its compression stroke. As soon as you feel this, stop cranking the engine. The final positioning adjustment for the No. 1 piston is to align the TDC timing mark with the pointer or notch in the crankshaft pulley.

2. Lightly oil the distributor housing, where the distributor mounts on the cylinder block.

3. Install the distributor so that the rotor, which is mounted on the shaft, points toward the No. 1 spark plug terminal of the distributor cap. To facilitate this operation, place the distributor cap on the distributor body in its normal position and make a mark on the body of the distributor just below the No. 1 spark plug terminal tower. Make sure that the metal tip of the rotor is pointing toward the mark when the distributor is installed.

4. When the distributor shaft has reached the bottom of the hole, move the rotor back and forth slightly until the drive gears of the distributor shaft and the camshaft mesh and the distributor assembly slides down into place.

5. When the distributor is correctly installed, the breaker point contacts should be in such a position that they are just ready to break contact with each other. This is accomplished by rotating the distributor body after it has been installed in the engine.

6. Install the distributor retaining plate and lockbolt.

7. Install the spark plug into the No. 1 cylinder spark plug hole and continue from Step 3 of the distributor installation procedure for engines that have not been disturbed.

Electronic Ignition

Renault calls their system IEI (Integral Electronic Ignition). The major parts of the system are an inductive distributor, an electronic control module and an ignition coil. Inside the distributor are a rotor, dust seal, rotor arm and sensor coil. Note that some cars have two sensor coils.

TROUBLESHOOTING

The Engine Does Not Start

Before assuming that the fault lies in the ignition system (coil, distributor, module), check the electrical system (relays, wires, and connections).

CHECK TEST

• Turn the ignition switch on.
• Remove the distributor cap.
• Disconnect the ignition coil wire from the distributor cap and hold it a few millimeters (⅛ to 3/16 in.) from a ground using insulated pliers.

NOTE: *The ground must not be next to the coil or the electronic module.*

Move a magnet (A) quickly in and out above the B1 or B sensor coils (for double sensor distributors) or above the sensor coil (for single sensor distributors). An electrical spark to ground should result.

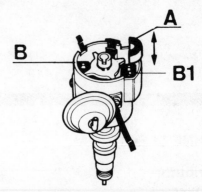

Electronic ignition spark test. A is the magnet; B & B1 are the sensors

If there is no spark, the components of the ignition system must be checked in the following order.

CHECKING THE COMPONENTS

Before checking the components, check to see that the ignition coil input lead is not broken.

CHECKING THE SENSOR COIL (DISTRIBUTOR)

• Connect an ohmmeter across the terminals of the sensor coil.

The needle should move.

If the needle does not move, change the sensor coil.

• Connect an ohmmeter to one of the sensor coil terminals and to the distributor ground.

The needle should move.

If the needle moves, change the sensor coil.

WARNING: *Do not use a test lamp to check*

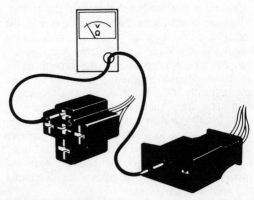

Checking the sensor coil

the distributor coil; it cannot withstand the current.

CHECKING THE IGNITION COIL AND THE ELECTRONIC MODULE

• Turn the ignition switch on.
• Connect a voltmeter across the two terminals of the ignition coil.
• Move a magnet quickly toward and away from the sensor coil (the distributor).

If the needle moves, change the coil (3).
If the needle does not move, change the electronic module (4).

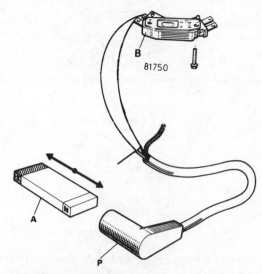

Checking the distributor body. A is a magnet; B is the module; P is the TDC sensor

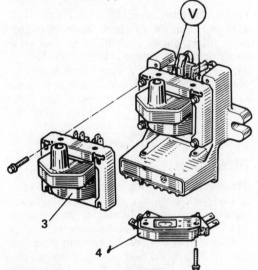

Checking the coil and module. 3 is the coil; 4 is the module

CHECKING THE DISTRIBUTOR

If the distributor seems faulty, it can be checked out in the following way:
• Disconnect the distributor connector and connect the two leads of a top dead center sensor (P) to the connecting pins of the electronic module (B).
• Move a magnet (A) quickly toward and away from the top dead center sensor (P).
If an electrical spark is produced, the distributor must be repaired or replaced.

Ignition Problems While the Engine is Running

Before assuming that the fault lies in the electronic module, check the condition of the spark plugs and the high-voltage wires.

If the vehicle runs roughly or misfires due to the ignition, after the spark plugs and the high-voltage wires have been checked out, change the electronic module.

IMPORTANT: *Do NOT disconnect a spark plug lead with the engine running. If this is* *done, the extremely high voltage produced will be grounded through the body of the distributor and will damage the distributor rotor arm.*

AIR GAP ADJUSTMENT

After the sensor coils have been changed, the air gap must be adjusted for proper ignition and engine operation.

The air gap must be between 0.3 and 0.6 mm (0.012 and 0.024 in.).

ADJUSTMENT

• Loosen the two screws (5) and (6).
• Place a feeler gauge between the top of the sensor coil and one of the rotor cams.
• Adjust the coil base on the screw (6) side so as to bring the coil tip into contact with the feeler gauge.
• Retighten the two screws (5) and (6).
• Check the air gap for all four cams of the rotor.

NOTE: *If the air gap is outside the acceptable range of 0.3 to 0.6 mm (0.012 to 0.024 in.) for any cam and it is impossible to adjust this air gap properly, change the distributor.*

DIAGNOSTIC CONNECTOR

The diagnostic connector is used to perform the following operations:

a. Checking the primary ignition circuit
b. Setting the ignition timing
c. Checking the centrifugal and vacuum advance
d. Setting the engine speed

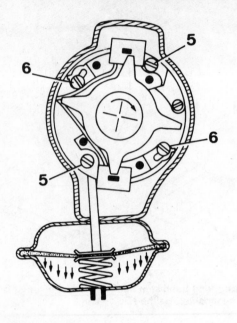

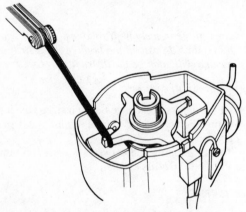

Air gap adjustment

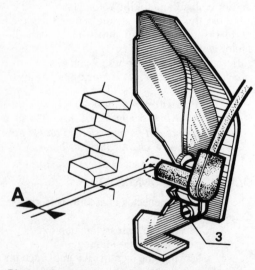

Diagnostic connector installation. A is the gap; 3 is the holddown screw

REMOVAL AND INSTALLATION

1. Disconnect the battery.
2. Remove the diagnostic connector. Do not remove the support plate.
3. Disconnect the wiring, tagging all wires for easy identification.
4. Unscrew the sensor attaching bolt and remove the sensor.
5. Unscrew the support plate, taking care not to bend it when removing.
6. Installation is the reverse of removal.

SENSOR ADJUSTMENT

The sensor must be between .5–1 mm (.020–.039 in.) from the flywheel. When installing a new sensor, simply bring the three pegs on the sensor into light contact with the flywheel and tighten the screws. If a used sensor is being installed and the pegs are worn, it will be necessary to measure the sensor-to-flywheel gap before tightening the screws.

Alternator

The alternator charging system is a negative ($-$) ground system which consists of an alternator, a regulator, a charge indicator, a storage battery and wiring connecting the components.

The alternator is belt-driven from the engine. Energy is supplied from the alternator/regulator system to the rotating field through two brushes to two slip-rings. The slip-rings are mounted on the rotor shaft and are connected to the field coil. This energy supplied to the rotating field from the battery is called excitation current and is used to initially energize the field to begin the generation of electricity. Once the alternator starts to generate electricity, the excitation current comes from its own output rather than the battery.

The alternator produces power in the form of alternating current. The alternating current is rectified by 6 diodes into direct current. The direct current is used to charge the battery and power the rest of the electrical system.

ALTERNATOR PRECAUTIONS

To prevent damage to the alternator and regulator, the following precautions should be taken when working with the electrical system.

1. Never reverse the battery connections.
2. Booster batteries for starting must be connected properly—positive-to-positive and negative-to-negative.
3. Disconnect the battery cables before using a fast charger; the charger has a tendency to force current through the diodes in the opposite

direction for which they were designed. This burns out the diodes.

4. Never use a fast charger as a booster for starting the vehicle.

5. Never disconnect the voltage regulator while the engine is running.

6. Avoid long soldering times when replacing diodes or transistors. Prolonged heat is damaging to AC generators.

7. Do not use test lamps of more than 12 volts (V) for checking diode continuity.

8. Do not short across or ground any of the terminals on the AC generator.

9. The polarity of the battery, generator, and regulator must be matched and considered before making any electrical connections within the system.

10. Never operate the alternator on an open circuit. Make sure that all connections within the circuit are clean and tight.

11. Disconnect the battery terminals when performing any service on the electrical system. This will eliminate the possibility of accidental reversal of polarity.

12. Disconnect the battery ground cable if arc welding is to be done on any part of the car.

REMOVAL AND INSTALLATION

While internal alternator repairs are possible, they require specialized tools and training. Therefore, it is advisable to replace a defective alternator, or have it repaired by a qualified shop.

1. Open the hood and disconnect the battery ground cable.

2. Remove the adjusting arm bolt.

3. Remove the alternator through-bolt. Remove the drive belt from the alternator pulley and lower the alternator.

4. Label all of the leads to the alternator so that you can install them correctly and disconnect the leads from the alternator.

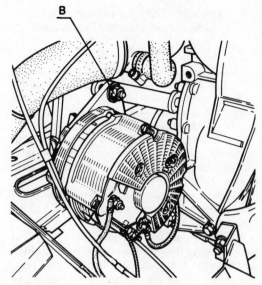

Typical alternor adjusting screw

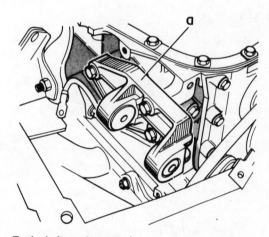

Typical alternator mount

Alternator and Regulator Specifications

Alternator		Voltage Regulator					
		Charge Indicator Relay		Voltage Regulator			
Manufacturer and/or Part Number	Output Amps @ Generator rpm	Back Gap (in.)	Point Gap (in.)	Back Gap (in.)	Air Gap (in.)	Point Gap (in.)	Regulated Voltage
A13R154	50 @ 3500	integral—not adjustable					13.8–14.8
A14-30	30 @ 3000	integral—not adjustable					13.3–14.8
71228312/ 71227702	30 @ 3000	integral—not adjustable					13.3–14.8

5. Remove the alternator from the vehicle.

6. To install, reverse the above procedure.

Belt Tension Adjustment

The fan belt drives the alternator and water pump. If the belt is too loose, it will slip and the alternator will not be able to produce its rated current. Also, the water pump will not operate efficiently and the engine could overheat.

Check the tension of the belt by pushing your thumb down on the longest span of the belt, midway between the pulleys. Belt deflection should be approximately ½ in.

To adjust belt tension, proceed as follows:

1. Loosen the alternator mounting bolt and the adjusting arm bolts.

2. Apply pressure on the alternator front housing only, moving the alternator away from the engine to tighten the belt. Do not apply pressure to the rear of the cast aluminum housing of an alternator; damage to the housing could result.

3. Tighten the alternator mounting bolt and the adjusting arm bolts when the correct tension is reached.

Regulator

On or about 1978, Renault phased in alternators with built-in regulators. Prior to that time the regulators were externally mounted. However, in either case, the regulators are not adjustable. Repairs are limited to replacement only. When replacing an external regulator, be sure to tag the wires to aid in correct installation.

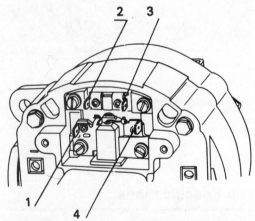

Typical alternator-mounted regulator. The wiring colors are: 1 black, 2 orange, 3 violet, 4 green

Starter

REMOVAL AND INSTALLATION

R-12

1. Remove the air cleaner.

2. Disconnect the battery.

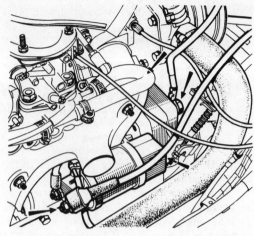

R-12 starter mounting

3. Disconnect the exhaust pipe from the manifold.

4. Disconnect and tag the wires at the starter.

5. Remove the three starter mounting bolts. Turn the starter sideways and pull it out.

6. Installation is the reverse of removal.

R-15, R-17, and Gordini

1. Disconnect the battery.

2. Disconnect the wires from the starter and tag them for installation.

3. Unbolt and remove the heat shield from the manifold.

4. Remove the heater hose support clip.

5. Remove the three starter mounting bolts and pull the starter out.

6. Installation is the reverse of removal.

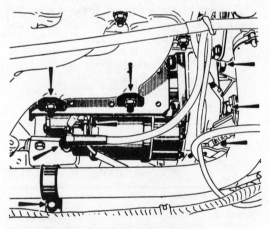

R-15, 17 and Gordini starter mounting

R-18, Sport Wagon and Fuego

1. Disconnect the battery. Remove the air cleaner. Raise and support the car on jackstands.

2. Disconnect the heater hoses, if they interfere.

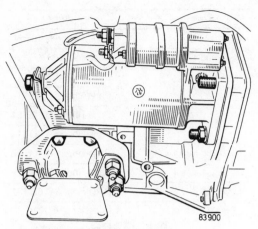

R-18 and Fuego starter mounting

3. Remove the catalytic converter shield and the converter.

4. Remove the starter heat shield.

5. Disconnect and tag the starter wires.

6. Remove the upper left starter mount bolt and loosen the upper right bolt.

7. Loosen the rear support bracket bolt.

8. Remove the spacer.

9. Remove the three mounting bolts and remove the starter.

10. Installation is the reverse of removal. Note that you must tighten the three starter mounting bolts before tightening the rear support bolt.

LeCar

1. Remove the air cleaner.

2. Clamp the carburetor heater hoses.

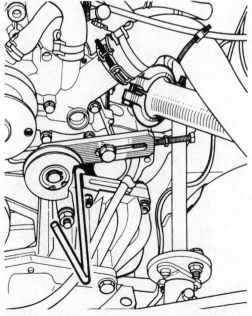

LeCar starter mounting. The starter is pretty well buried

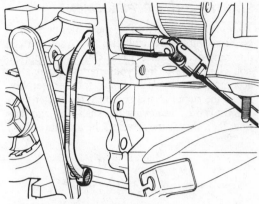

LeCar starter bolt removal

3. Disconnect the battery.

4. Disconnect the accelerator linkage.

5. Remove the exhaust manifold.

6. Disconnect and tag the starter wires.

7. Remove the lower starter bolt using a ⅜ inch drive ratchet and 13mm socket, holding the nut with a 13mm box wrench. Remove the upper bolt with special tool Ele. 565 or its equivalent.

8. Remove the starter.

9. Installation is the reverse of removal.

Alliance, Encore

1. Disconnect the battery.

2. Disconnect and tag the starter wires.

3. Remove the starter support bracket.

4. Remove the three starter mount bolts and remove the starter.

5. Installation is the reverse of removal. Note that the three mounting bolts must be tightened before tightening the support bolt.

CAUTION: *To avoid cross-threading the bolts, make certain that the starter motor locating dowel is centered in its hole.*

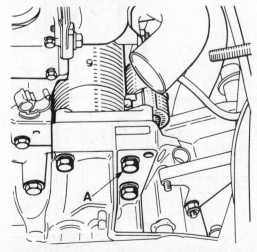

Alliance starter mounting bolts. A is the bolt that's especially easy to crossthread

STARTER DRIVE REPLACEMENT

To replace the starter drive, the starter body must be disassembled. Renault cars have used thirteen different starters since 1975. Check the application chart below, find your starter and use the accompanying exploded view for disassembly. When the starter is disassembled, the starter drive is removed by removing the snap-ring and stop ring, then sliding the drive off the armature shaft.

Car Line	Starter
R-12	Paris-Rhone D 10E 54
R-15 and 17	Ducellier 6183
	Ducellier 6187
	Paris-Rhone D 8E 71
	Paris-Rhone D 10E 54
	Paris-Rhone D 8E 81
R-18 and Fuego	Paris-Rhone D 10E 63
	Paris-Rhone D 10E 79
LeCar	Paris-Rhone D 8E 121
Alliance, Encore	Ducellier 534 019
	Ducellier 534 031
	Paris-Rhone D 9E 39
	Paris-Rhone D 9E 52

Typical starter drive disassembly

STARTER DRIVE ADJUSTMENT

Take out the plug at the end of the solenoid opposite the electrical terminals. Apply current to the solenoid as shown in the accompanying illustration. Check the clearance between the starter drive end and the end frame. The clearance should be .059 in. If not, turn the adjusting screw, uncovered by removing the end plug, until the proper clearance is obtained.

NOTE: *On the Paris-Rhone D 10E 79, clearance is adjusted with an eccentric screw which passes through the starter drive fork.*

ENGINE MECHANICAL

Engine Removal and Installation

R-12, R-15, R-17, Gordini

1. Disconnect the battery.
2. Remove the hood.
3. Remove the air cleaner.
4. Drain the cooling system.
5. Disconnect and tag all hoses, wires and cables attached to the engine.
6. Remove the radiator.
7. Remove the starter.

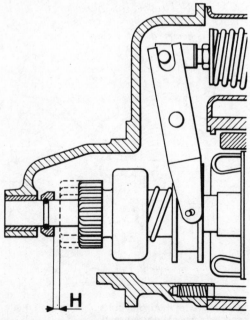

Starter drive adjustment. The gap is measured at H

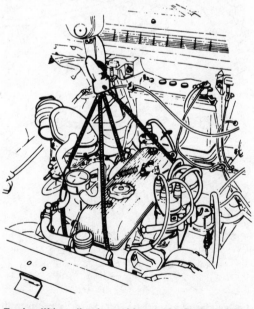

Engine lifting sling in position on the R-12, 15, 17 or Gordini

8. Remove the drive belts.

9. Remove the camshaft pulley.

10. Remove the top engine-transmission bolt.

11. Remove the fan and pulley.

12. Remove the crankshaft pulley.

13. Disconnect the exhaust pipe at the manifold and the rear crossmember.

14. Remove the clutch shield.

15. Install a shop crane or hoist on the engine and take up its weight.

16. Remove the two right side engine mount bolts at the block.

17. Remove the three engine mounting bracket bolts at the right side frame rail.

18. Remove the left side engine mount nut at the bracket.

19. Unbolt the mount bracket from the left side frame rail.

20. Raise the engine slightly and remove the engine support bracket.

21. Continue to raise the engine until the top of the transmission contacts the underside of the steering crossmember.

22. Support the transmission on a jack or jackstand.

23. Remove the two engine-transmission lower bolts.

24. Pull the engine forward and lift it out.

25. Installation is the reverse of removal. Coat the clutch shaft splines lightly with chassis lube. Place a few drops of Loctite on the crankshaft pulley bolt.

R-18, Sport Wagon and Fuego

1. Disconnect the battery.

2. Remove the engine under-pan.

3. Drain the cooling system.

4. Drain the engine oil.

5. Remove the grille.

6. Remove the grille upper crossmember.

7. Remove the radiator and cooling fan. Vehicles with air conditioning have two fans. Both must be removed. On these vehicles, the air conditioning system should not be discharged. The condenser can be set aside without disconnecting any lines.

8. Remove the battery.

9. Remove the starter.

10. Remove the exhaust heat shields.

11. Remove the air cleaner.

12. Disconnect the exhaust pipe at the manifold.

13. Remove the catalytic converter.

14. Remove the clutch cable and its bracket on cars with manual transmission.

15. Disconnect and remove the alternator.

16. Remove the power steering pump from its bracket without disconnecting the hoses. Place it out of the way.

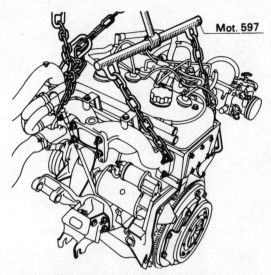

Mot. 597

Engine lifting sling in position on the R-18 or Fuego

17. Remove the air conditioning compressor from its bracket without disconnecting the refrigerant lines. Place it out of the way.

18. Disconnect and tag all hoses, wires and cables connected to the engine.

19. Attach a shop crane or hoist to the engine and just barely take up the engine weight.

20. Remove the upper engine-transmission bolts.

21. Remove the flywheel cover plate.

22. Remove the lower engine-transmission bolts.

23. Remove the side engine-transmission bolts.

24. Unbolt the automatic transmission torque converter from the flywheel. The flywheel will have to be turned by hand to reach all the bolts.

25. Raise the engine until the transmission just touches the steering crossmember.

26. Support the transmission with a jack or jackstand.

27. Pull the engine forward to clear the transmission and raise it clear of the car. Be careful not to pull the converter off of the transmission.

28. Installation is the reverse of removal. Note the following points:

a. On cars with manual transmission, coat the input shaft splines with chassis lube.

b. Adjust the clutch cable.

c. On cars with automatic transmission, coat the crankshaft recess with chassis lube.

d. The painted mark on the torque converter (automatic transmission) must be aligned with the sharp-edged spoke on the flywheel. New bolts of equal grade must be used to attach the torque converter to the flywheel.

e. Adjust the automatic speed control cable, the accelerator cable and adjust the upper grille crossmember as shown.

LeCar

NOTE: *The engine must be removed together with the transaxle.*

1. Raise the front of the car and support it on jackstands under the frame rails.

2. Disconnect and remove the battery.

3. Drain the cooling system at the radiator and block.

4. Drain the transaxle.

5. Remove the grille, the hood and the two cowl-to-inner fender support braces.

6. Remove the air cleaner.

7. Disconnect and tag all hoses, wires and cables attached to the engine, except for air conditioning and power steering hoses.

8. Remove the windshield washer bottle.

9. Remove the transaxle cover.

10. Remove the air cleaner support rod.

11. Disconnect the exhaust pipe at the manifold.

12. Remove the radiator, cooling fan and expansion tank.

13. Remove the steering column flexible coupling bolts.

14. Remove the front wheels.

15. Remove the brake calipers, but do not disconnect the brake lines. Support the calipers out of the way.

16. Disconnect the steering arms at the rack ends.

17. Disconnect the ball joints and tilt the spindles out of the way.

18. Unbolt and remove the steering gear box. Mark the right and left shims so that they can be installed properly to maintain steering box height.

19. Remove the air pump, filter and bracket.

20. An engine lifting frame is available which bolts under the two top engine-to-transaxle bolts. If one cannot be obtained, attach a shop crane or hoist in a manner which will maintain engine-transaxle balance while lifting. If the lifting frame (part # Mot.498) is used, the bolts must be replaced with 1⅜ in. long bolts to adequately support the weight.

21. Take up the weight of the engine with the hoist or lifting device. Remove the engine mount bolts.

22. Unbolt the transaxle shift rod support.

23. Disconnect the clutch cable at the fork.

24. Remove the front transaxle mount.

25. Push the transaxle left and right to free the driveshaft ends.

26. Gradually lift the engine/transaxle assembly clear of the car.

27. Installation is the reverse of removal. Note the following points:

    a. Lightly grease the driveshaft ends with chassis lube.

    b. When installing the driveshaft ends, take care not to damage the seal lips. Make certain that the driveshaft ends fully engage the differential side gears.

    c. Adjust the clutch.

    d. Make sure to replace the rubber bushing at the steering flexible coupling.

    e. Adjust the accelerator and choke cables.

Alliance, Encore

1. Remove the hood.

2. Disconnect the battery.

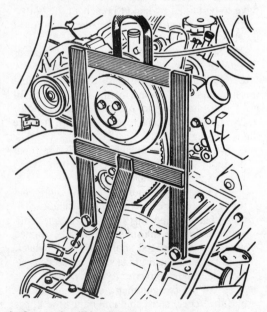

LeCar engine lifting fixture

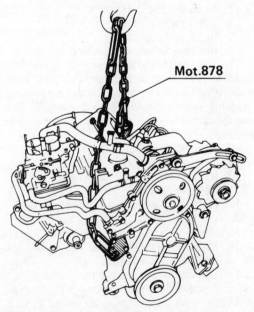

Mot.878

Alliance and Encore engine lifting sling

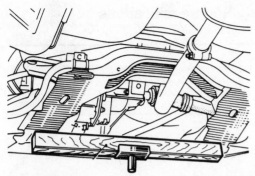

4 × 4 attached to the jack cradle for support on the Alliance

cables attached to the engine, except for air conditioning and power steering hoses. Raise and support the car on jackstands.

7. Drain the engine oil.

8. Remove the exhaust pipe clamp.

9. Remove the engine-to-transaxle support rod.

10. Remove the flywheel cover.

11. Remove all drive belts from the engine.

12. Remove the water pump.

13. Remove the crankshaft pulley and hub.

14. Remove the torque converter-to-flywheel bolts.

15. On cars with air conditioning, remove the compressor from its mounts without disconnecting the hoses, and place it out of the way.

16. Place a jack under the engine cradle, using a length a 4 × 4 lumber attached to the jack as shown.

17. Disconnect the clutch cable at the fork.

3. Remove the air cleaner.

4. Drain the cooling system.

5. Remove the radiator.

6. Disconnect and tag all wires, hoses and

General Engine Specifications

Engine Displacement cc (cu. in.)	Fuel System	Advertised Horsepower @ rpm	Advertised Torque @ rpm (ft. lbs.)	Bore and Stroke (in.)	Advertised Compression Ratio	Oil Pressure psi @ 4000 rpm
1289 (78.6)	2-bbl	①	66 @ 3000	2.874 x 3.031	②	50
1397 (85.2)	2-bbl/F.I.	③	67 @ 2500	2.992 x 3.031	8.8:1 ⑥	50
1565 (95.5) ⑦	F.I.	120 @ 6250	105 @ 5000	3.032 x 3.307	10.25:1	50
1647 (100.5)	2-bbl	72 @ 5500	84 @ 2500	3.110 x 3.307	8.0:1	50
1647 (100.5)	F.I.	④	86 @ 2500	3.110 x 3.307	⑤	50
1647 (100.5)	F.I. Turbo	107 @ 5500	120 @ 2500	3.110 x 3.307	8.0:1	50
2165 (132.1)	F.I.	91 @ 5000	98 @ 2500	3.464 x 3.897	8.7:1	50

① 1975–76: 58 @ 6000
  1977–79: 60 @ 6000
② 1975–76: 8.5:1
  1977–79: 9.5:1
③ Le Car Calif.: 53 @ 5000
  U.S.: 51 @ 5000
  Alliance, Encore Calif.: 72 @ 5500
    U.S.: 65 @ 5000

④ Gordini: 95 @ 6000
  18i and Fuego: 81.5 @ 5500
⑤ Gordini: 9.3:1
  18i and Fuego: 8.6:1
⑥ Encore, Alliance: 9.0:1
⑦ 1975 Canadian Gordini

Valve Specifications

Engine Displacement cc (cu in.)	Seat Angle (deg)	Face Angle (deg)	Spring Test Pressure (lbs. @ in.)		Stem-to-Guide Clearance (in.)		Stem Diameter (in.)	
			Outer	Inner	Intake	Exhaust	Intake	Exhaust
1289 (78.6)	45	45	80 @ 1.00	—	.0010	.0010	.276	.276
1397 (85.2)	①	①	81 @ .984	—	.0010	.0010	.276	.276
1565 (95.5)	45	45	114 @ 1³⁄₁₆	35 @ 1³¹⁄₃₂	.0010	.0010	.315	.315
1647 (100.5)	45	45	99 @ 1.140 ②	20 @ .750	.0010 ③	.0010 ③	.315	.315
2165 (132)	④	④	N.A.	—	.0040	.0040	.315	.315

① Intake: 60
  Exhaust: 45
② 18i and Fuego: 47 @ 1.173
③ 18i and Fuego: .0016
④ Intake: 60
  Exhaust: 45

Crankshaft and Connecting Rod Specifications
(All measurements given in inches)

| Engine Displacement cc (cu in.) | Crankshaft | | | | | Connecting Rod | | |
	Main Brg Journal Dia	Main Brg Oil Clearance	Shaft End-Play	Thrust on No.	Journal Dia	Oil Clearance	Side Clearance
1289 (78.6)	2.157	.0004–.0014	.002–.009	3	1.732	.0010–.0026	.012–.023
1397 (85.2)	2.157	.0004–.0014	.002– ① .009	3	1.732	.0010–.0026	.012–.023
1565 (95.5)	2.157	.0006–.0015	.002–.009	3	1.890	N.A.	.002–.009
1647 (100.5)	2.157	.0006–.0015	.002–.009	3	1.890	N.A.	.012–.023
2165 (132)	2.476	N.A.	.0005–.0011	3	2.215	N.A.	N.A.

① 1981–85: .004–.009
N.A.: Information not available

Piston and Liner Specifications
(Measurement in inches)

Engine cc (cu. in.)	Bore	Base Locating Diameter	Liner Protrusion	Base Seal Thickness	Piston Pin Length	Piston Pin Diameter
1289 (78.6)	2.874	3.091	.0016–.005	②	2.385	.787
1397 (85.2)	2.992	3.173	.001–.004 ③	.045–.053	2.520	.790
1565 (95.5)	3.032	3.248	.006–.008	①	2.685	.787
1647 (100.5)	3.110	3.307	.004–.007 ③	.045–.053	2.717	.827
2165 (132)	3.460	3.685	.003–.006	.029–.049	2.952	.905

① blue spot: .003
   red spot: .004
   green spot: .0047
② blue spot: .003
   red spot: .004
   green spot: .005
③ figure is without O-ring

Torque Specifications
(All readings in ft. lbs. unless noted)

| Engine Displacement cc (cu. in.) | Cylinder Head Bolts | Rod Bearing Bolts | Main Bearing Bolts | Crankshaft Pulley Bolts | Flywheel to Crankshaft Bolts | Manifolds | |
						Intake	Exhaust
1289 (78.6)	40 ①	35	50	65	40	25	25
1397 (85.2)	40 ①	35	50	81	40	25	25
1565 (95.5) 1647 (100.5)	60 ②	30	45	67	35	20	20
2165 (132)	72	46	69	96	44	20	20

① Run engine until hot, let cool for 50 minutes, then retorque to 45 ft. lb.
② Run engine until hot, let cool for 50 minutes, then retorque to 65 ft. lb.

18. Remove the 5 engine-to-transaxle bolts.

19. Attach a shop crane or hoist to the engine and take up the weight.

20. Position a jack or jackstand under the transaxle and lift the engine, first forward, then up and out.

21. Installation is the reverse of removal. Note the following points:

a. Bleed the cooling system of air after filling.

b. Exhaust pipe clamp bolt spring length should be 1.7 in. at a bolt torque of 33 ft. lb.

Rocker Arm Cover

REMOVAL AND INSTALLATION

1. Disconnect the battery ground cable.

2. Remove the air cleaner.

3. Remove any hoses or cables interfering with cover removal.

4. Remove the cover holddown bolts and carefully lift off the cover. The cover may stick. If it does, do not pry it off! Gently tap around the cover with a rubber mallet to break it free.

5. Clean the gasket surfaces after removing and discarding the old gasket. No trace of old gasket material should remain.

6. Coat the gasket surfaces with a non-hardening gasket sealer and install the cover using the new gasket. Never reuse an old gasket.

7. Torque the cover bolts to 3–5 ft. lb.

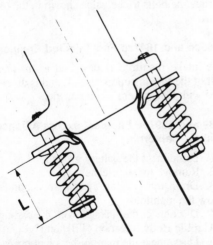

Measuring exhaust pipe clamp spring length. L is the area for measurement

Rocker Arms and/or Rocker Shaft

REMOVAL AND INSTALLATION

1289cc and 1397 cc

1. Remove the rocker arm cover as described above.

2. Loosen the rocker arm shaft retaining bolts a little at a time each working alternately from the ends towards the center. When the bolts are loose, remove them and the rocker shaft.

3. Place the shaft on a clean work surface.

4. Remove the retaining clips from the shaft ends.

5. Remove the spring, rocker arm, pedestal, etc., in turn. Keep all parts in the same order of which they were removed! Make sure you know

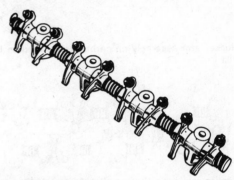

1289 and 1397cc rocker arm assembly

which side of the shaft is up! The oil holes must face downward!

NOTE: *If some of the pedestals are stuck, do not hammer them off. Use a penetrating oil to free them.*

6. Clean the shaft of deposits. Clean the inside surfaces of the rocker arms and make certain that all oil passages are clear. Check the bearing surface of each rocker arm for wear, scratches or other damage.

7. Freely lubricate the parts with clean engine oil.

8. Install the parts in reverse order of disassembly so that all parts are in their original places.

9. Place the shaft on the head, install the bolts and tighten them a little at a time, in turn, from the center toward the ends, to 10–15 ft. lb.

1565cc and 1647cc

1. Remove the rocker arm cover as described above.

2. Remove the rocker shaft attaching bolts from the pedestals and lift off the rocker arm assembly.

3. Using a thin punch, drive the roll pins from opposite ends of the shaft assemblies.

4. Slide the parts off of the shafts, keeping them in the same order in which they were on the shafts.

5. Clean all the parts in a safe solvent.

6. Check the bearing surfaces of the rocker arms for wear, scratches or other damage. Re-

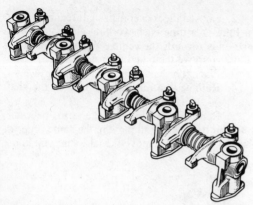

Rocker arm assembly on carbureted Canadian R-18s

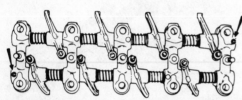

Rocker arm assembly on all 1565 and 1647cc engines, except Canadian carbureted engines. The arrows point to the roll pins

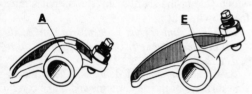

On engines with dual rocker arm shafts, the intake, A, and the exhaust, E, arms are different

place them if they are badly damaged. Check the rocker arms for signs of cracking. Check the shafts, at the point where the rocker arms ride, for wear or scratches. Check that the springs are in good condition.

7. Coat all parts liberally with clean engine oil.

8. Assemble all parts in exactly the same place that they originally were.

NOTE: *The oil holes in the shafts must face downward.*

9. Place the rocker arm shaft assembly on the head. Install the bolts and tighten them a little at a time each starting at the center and working toward the ends. Final tightening torque should be 25 ft. lb.

1984–85 Fuego 2.2L

Note: *The rocker shaft assembly retaining bolts are also the head bolts.*

1. Remove the rocker cover.

2. Remove the head bolts and lift off the rocker shaft assembly.

3. Remove the end plug and filter from one end and the roll pin from the other.

4. Slide the components from the shaft, keeping them in order.

NOTE: *Never hammer the components from the shaft. If they won't come off, use liberal amounts of gum-dissolving compound on the shaft.*

5. Installation is the reverse of removal. See the Cylinder Head Bolt Torque illustration and read the last step of the Cylinder Head procedure.

Intake/Exhaust Manifold
REMOVAL AND INSTALLATION
1647cc Carburetted Engines

1. Disconnect the battery ground.

2. Remove the air cleaner.

3. Drain the cooling system to a level below the manifold.

4. Disconnect the linkage at the carburetor.

5. Disconnect the manifold coolant hoses.

6. Remove the carburetor.

7. Unbolt and remove the manifold.

8. Clean the old gasket material from the mating surfaces. Always use a new gasket.

9. Installation is the reverse of removal. Torque the bolts to the value shown in the torque chart.

1565cc and 1647cc Fuel Injected Engines

The intake manifold is designed as an integral part of the fuel injection system, and is disassembled with that system's components.

1289 and 1397cc Engines, except Alliance Built for California

1. Disconnect the battery ground.

2. Remove the air cleaner.

3. Drain the cooling system to a point just below the manifold.

4. Disconnect the linkage from the carburetor or Throttle Body Injection (TBI) unit.

5. Disconnect the manifold coolant hoses.

6. Remove the carburetor or TBI unit.

7. Unbolt and remove the manifolds.

8. Installation is the reverse of removal. Make sure that the mating surfaces are clean and that a new gasket is used. Torque the bolts to the value shown in the Torque Specification chart.

Alliance Built for Sale in California

The intake manifold and exhaust manifold are integral with the fuel injection system and may be disassembled with that system's components.

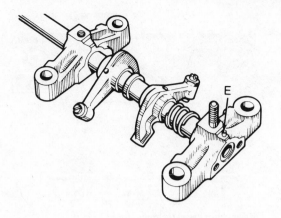

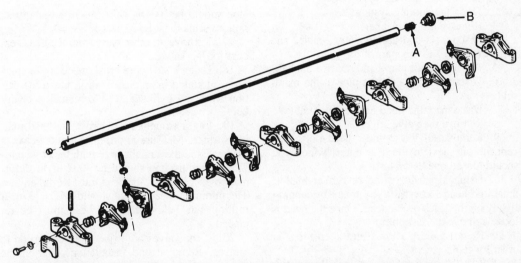

2.2L OHC rocker arm shaft assembly. E is the retaining pin, B is the end cap and A is the filter

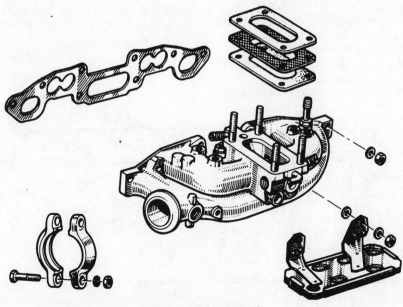

LeCar manifold assembly

Exhaust Manifold
REMOVAL AND INSTALLATION
1565cc and 1647cc Fuel Injected Engines

1. Remove the air cleaner.
2. Unbolt the exhaust pipe from the manifold.
3. Unbolt the manifold from its bracket and the head. Lift off the manifold.
4. Installation is the reverse of removal.

Cylinder Head
REMOVAL, INSPECTION AND INSTALLATION
1289 and 1397cc

1. Disconnect the battery.
2. Drain the cooling system.
3. Remove the air cleaner.
4. Disconnect and tag all wires, cables and hoses connected to any part of the head.
5. Loosen the air pump and remove the belt.
6. Disconnect the exhaust pipe at the manifold.
7. Disconnect the hood lock control cable.
8. Remove the valve cover.
9. Remove all the cylinder head bolts, except the one next to the distributor, which you should loosen one half a turn.
10. Using a plastic, wood or rubber mallet, break the head loose from the liners by tapping lightly on the sides of the head. Once the head is loose, remove the last bolt.
11. Remove the pushrods and keep them in order for replacement.
12. Lift the head off the engine. Be careful, it's heavy.
13. Clean the mating surface of the head and block thoroughly.
14. Remove the manifolds, carburetor or fuel injection assemblies. Remove the spark plugs. Remove the rocker arm assembly.
15. Clean the threaded holes in the head with compressed air.
16. Check the liner protrusion. Liner protru-

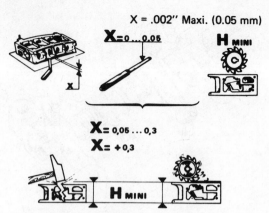

Measuring head flatness, head height

sion should be .0016–.0050 in. If not, the liner bottom seals must be replaced.
17. Remove all other parts from the head, except for the valves.
18. Using a stiff wire brush made for the purpose, mounted in an electric drill, clean the carbon from the cylinder head combustion chambers.
19. Lay a straight-edge across the head mating surface. Measure at different points between the head and the straight-edge with feeler gauges. The maximum gap should be .002 in. If deformation exceeds this, the head must be milled flat. The minimum head height should be 2.870 in. If milling cuts below this, the head must be replaced.
20. If the valves are to be replaced, go on to Valves, Removal and Installation, later in the text.
21. If you'd like to decarbon the tops of the pistons at this time, or do anything which will result in the turning of the crankshaft, you'll need a special tool (Mot.521) to hold the liners in place.

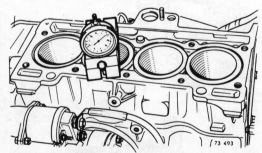

Checking liner protrusion on 1289 and 1397cc engines

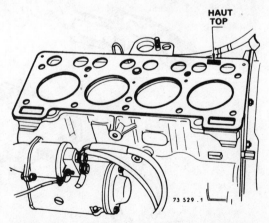

Head gasket installation on 1289 and 1397cc engines

ENGINE OVERHAUL

Most engine overhaul procedures are fairly standard. In addition to specific parts replacement procedures and complete specifications for your individual engine, this chapter also is a guide to accepted rebuilding procedures. Examples of standard rebuilding practice are shown and should be used along with specific details concerning your particular engine.

Competent and accurate machine shop services will ensure maximum performance, reliability and engine life. Procedures marked with the symbol shown above should be performed by a competent machine shop, and are provided so that you will be familiar with the procedures necessary to a successful overhaul.

In most instances it is more profitable for the do-it-yourself mechanic to remove, clean and inspect the component, buy the necessary parts and deliver these to a shop for actual machine work.

On the other hand, much of the rebuilding work (crankshaft, block, bearings, pistons, rods, and other components) is well within the scope of the do-it-yourself mechanic.

Tools

The tools required for an engine overhaul or parts replacement will depend on the depth of your involvement. With a few exceptions, they will be the tools found in a mechanic's tool kit (see Chapter 1). More indepth work will require any or all of the following:
• a dial indicator (reading in thousandths) mounted on a universal base
• micrometers and telescope gauges
• jaw and screw-type pullers
• scraper
• valve spring compressor
• ring groove cleaner
• piston ring expander and compressor
• ridge reamer
• cylinder hone or glaze breaker

• Plastigage®
• engine stand

Use of most of these tools is illustrated in this chapter. Many can be rented for a one-time use from a local parts jobber or tool supply house specializing in automotive work.

Occasionally, the use of special tools is called for. See the information on Special Tools and the Safety Notice in the front of this book before substituting another tool.

Inspection Techniques

Procedures and specifications are given in this chapter for inspecting, cleaning and assessing the wear limits of most major components. Other procedures such as Magnaflux and Zyglo can be used to locate material flaws and stress cracks. Magnaflux is a magnetic process applicable only to ferrous materials. The Zyglo process coats the material with a flourescent dye penetrant and can be used on any material. Check for suspected surface cracks can be more readily made using spot check dye. The dye is sprayed onto the suspected area, wiped off and the area sprayed with a developer. Cracks will show up brightly.

Overhaul Tips

Aluminum has become extremely popular for use in engines, due to its low weight. Observe the following precautions when handling aluminum parts:
• Never hot tank aluminum parts (the caustic hot-tank solution will eat the aluminum)
• Remove all aluminum parts (identification tag, etc.) from engine parts prior to hot-tanking.
• Always coat threads lightly with engine oil or anti-seize compounds before installation, to prevent seizure.
• Never over-torque bolts or spark plugs, especially in aluminum threads.

Stripped threads in any component can be repaired using any of several commercial repair kits (Heli-Coil, Microdot, Keenserts, etc.)

When assembling the engine, any parts that will be in frictional contact must be pre-lubed to provide lubrication at initial start-up. Any product specifically formulated for this purpose can be used, but engine oil is not recommended as a pre-lube.

When semi-permanent (locked, but removable) installation of bolts or nuts is desired, threads should be cleaned and coated with Loctite® or other similar, commercial non-hardening sealant.

Repairing Damaged Threads

Several methods of repairing damaged threads are available. Heli-Coil® (shown here), Keenserts® and Microdot® are among the most widely used. All involve basically the same principle—drilling out stripped threads, tapping the hole and installing a pre-wound insert—making welding, plugging and oversize fasteners unnecessary.

Two types of thread repair inserts are usually supplied—a standard type for most Inch Coarse, Inch Fine, Metric Coarse and Metric Fine thread sizes and a spark plug type to fit most spark plug port sizes. Consult the individual manufacturer's catalog to determine exact applications. Typical thread repair kits will contain a selection of pre-wound threaded inserts, a tap (corresponding to the outside diameter threads of the insert) and an installation tool. Spark plug inserts usually differ because they require a tap equipped with pilot threads and a combined reamer/tap section. Most manufacturers also supply blister-packed thread repair inserts separately in addition to a master kit containing a variety of taps and inserts plus installation tools.

Before effecting a repair to a threaded hole, remove any snapped, broken or damaged bolts or studs. Penetrating oil can be used to free frozen threads; the offending item can be removed with locking pliers or with a screw or stud extractor. After the hole is clear, the thread can be repaired, as follows:

Drill out the damaged threads with specified drill. Drill completely through the hole or to the bottom of a blind hole

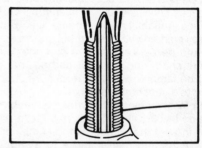

With the tap supplied, tap the hole to receive the thread insert. Keep the tap well oiled and back it out frequently to avoid clogging the threads

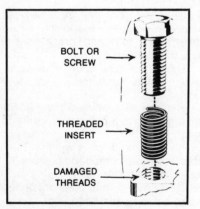

BOLT OR SCREW

THREADED INSERT

DAMAGED THREADS

Damaged bolt holes can be repaired with thread repair inserts

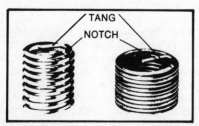

TANG
NOTCH

Standard thread repair insert (left) and spark plug thread insert (right)

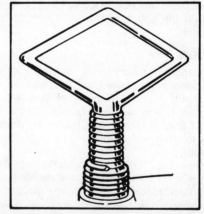

Screw the threaded insert onto the installation tool until the tang engages the slot. Screw the insert into the tapped hole until it is ¼–½ turn below the top surface. After installation break off the tang with a hammer and punch

Standard Torque Specifications and Fastener Markings

In the absence of specific torques, the following chart can be used as a guide to the maximum safe torque of a particular size/grade of fastener.

- There is no torque difference for fine or coarse threads.
- Torque values are based on clean, dry threads. Reduce the value by 10% if threads are oiled prior to assembly.
- The torque required for aluminum components or fasteners is considerably less.

U.S. Bolts

SAE Grade Number	1 or 2			5			6 or 7		
Number of lines always 2 less than the grade number.									
Bolt Size (Inches)—(Thread)	Maximum Torque			Maximum Torque			Maximum Torque		
	Ft./Lbs.	Kgm	Nm	Ft./Lbs.	Kgm	Nm	Ft./Lbs.	Kgm	Nm
¼ — 20	5	0.7	6.8	8	1.1	10.8	10	1.4	13.5
— 28	6	0.8	8.1	10	1.4	13.6			
⁵⁄₁₆ — 18	11	1.5	14.9	17	2.3	23.0	19	2.6	25.8
— 24	13	1.8	17.6	19	2.6	25.7			
⅜ — 16	18	2.5	24.4	31	4.3	42.0	34	4.7	46.0
— 24	20	2.75	27.1	35	4.8	47.5			
⁷⁄₁₆ — 14	28	3.8	37.0	49	6.8	66.4	55	7.6	74.5
— 20	30	4.2	40.7	55	7.6	74.5			
½ — 13	39	5.4	52.8	75	10.4	101.7	85	11.75	115.2
— 20	41	5.7	55.6	85	11.7	115.2			
⁹⁄₁₆ — 12	51	7.0	69.2	110	15.2	149.1	120	16.6	162.7
— 18	55	7.6	74.5	120	16.6	162.7			
⅝ — 11	83	11.5	112.5	150	20.7	203.3	167	23.0	226.5
— 18	95	13.1	128.8	170	23.5	230.5			
¾ — 10	105	14.5	142.3	270	37.3	366.0	280	38.7	379.6
— 16	115	15.9	155.9	295	40.8	400.0			
⅞ — 9	160	22.1	216.9	395	54.6	535.5	440	60.9	596.5
— 14	175	24.2	237.2	435	60.1	589.7			
1 — 8	236	32.5	318.6	590	81.6	799.9	660	91.3	894.8
— 14	250	34.6	338.9	660	91.3	849.8			

Metric Bolts

Relative Strength Marking	4.6, 4.8			8.8		
Bolt Markings						
Bolt Size Thread Size x Pitch (mm)	Maximum Torque			Maximum Torque		
	Ft./Lbs.	Kgm	Nm	Ft./Lbs.	Kgm	Nm
6 x 1.0	2–3	.2–.4	3–4	3–6	.4–.8	5–8
8 x 1.25	6–8	.8–1	8–12	9–14	1.2–1.9	13–19
10 x 1.25	12–17	1.5–2.3	16–23	20–29	2.7–4.0	27–39
12 x 1.25	21–32	2.9–4.4	29–43	35–53	4.8–7.3	47–72
14 x 1.5	35–52	4.8–7.1	48–70	57–85	7.8–11.7	77–110
16 x 1.5	51–77	7.0–10.6	67–100	90–120	12.4–16.5	130–160
18 x 1.5	74–110	10.2–15.1	100–150	130–170	17.9–23.4	180–230
20 x 1.5	110–140	15.1–19.3	150–190	190–240	26.2–46.9	160–320
22 x 1.5	150–190	22.0–26.2	200–260	250–320	34.5–44.1	340–430
24 x 1.5	190–240	26.2–46.9	260–320	310–410	42.7–56.5	420–550

CHECKING ENGINE COMPRESSION

A noticeable lack of engine power, excessive oil consumption and/or poor fuel mileage measured over an extended period are all indicators of internal engine wear. Worn piston rings, scored or worn cylinder bores, blown head gaskets, sticking or burnt valves and worn valve seats are all possible culprits here. A check of each cylinder's compression will help you locate the problems.

As mentioned in the "Tools and Equipment" section of Chapter 1, a screw-in type compression gauge is more accurate than the type you simply hold against the spark plug hole, although it takes slightly longer to use. It's worth it to obtain a more accurate reading. Follow the procedures below for gasoline and diesel-engined cars.

Gasoline Engines

1. Warm up the engine to normal operating temperature.
2. Remove all spark plugs.

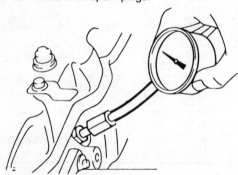

The screw-in type compression gauge is more accurate

3. Disconnect the high-tension lead from the ignition coil.
4. On carbureted cars, fully open the throttle either by operating the carburetor throttle linkage by hand or by having an assistant "floor" the accelerator pedal. On fuel-injected cars, disconnect the cold start valve and all injector connections.
5. Screw the compression gauge into the No. 1 spark plug hole until the fitting is snug.
NOTE: *Be careful not to crossthread the plug hole. On aluminum cylinder heads use extra care, as the threads in these heads are easily ruined.*
6. Ask an assistant to depress the accelerator pedal fully on both carbureted and fuel-injected cars. Then, while you read the compression gauge, ask the assistant to crank the engine two or three times in short bursts using the ignition switch.

7. Read the compression gauge at the end of each series of cranks, and record the highest of these readings. Repeat this procedure for each of the engine's cylinders. Compare the highest reading of each cylinder to the compression pressure specifications in the "Tune-Up Specifications" chart in Chapter 2. The specs in this chart are maximum values.

A cylinder's compression pressure is usually acceptable if it is not less than 80% of maximum. The difference between each cylinder should be no more than 12–14 pounds.

8. If a cylinder is unusually low, pour a tablespoon of clean engine oil into the cylinder through the spark plug hole and repeat the compression test. If the compression comes up after adding the oil, it appears that that cylinder's piston rings or bore are damaged or worn. If the pressure remains low, the valves may not be seating properly (a valve job is needed), or the head gasket may be blown near that cylinder. If compression in any two adjacent cylinders is low, and if the addition of oil doesn't help the compression, there is leakage past the head gasket. Oil and coolant water in the combustion chamber can result from this problem. There may be evidence of water droplets on the engine dipstick when a head gasket has blown.

Diesel Engines

Checking cylinder compression on diesel engines is basically the same procedure as on gasoline engines except for the following:

1. A special compression gauge adaptor suitable for diesel engines (because these engines have much greater compression pressures) must be used.
2. Remove the injector tubes and remove the injectors from each cylinder.
NOTE: *Don't forget to remove the washer underneath each injector; otherwise, it may get lost when the engine is cranked.*

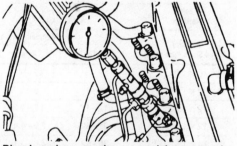

Diesel engines require a special compression gauge adaptor

3. When fitting the compression gauge adaptor to the cylinder head, make sure the bleeder of the gauge (if equipped) is closed.
4. When reinstalling the injector assemblies, install new washers underneath each injector.

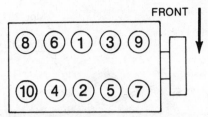

FRONT

1289 and 1397cc head bolt torque sequence

22. When you're ready to install the head, make sure you use a new gasket. Do not use sealer on the head gasket or on the water pump or end plate gaskets. The head gasket is positioned with the stamped word HAUTE-Top up. Place the gasket on the block and place the head in position. Make sure the gasket is still in alignment. Install the head bolts and hand tighten all of them. Torque the bolts to 40 ft. lb. in a circular pattern beginning at the middle and working towards the ends. All other parts should be installed in reverse order of removal.

1565cc and 1647cc

1. Disconnect the battery.
2. Drain the cooling system.
3. Remove the air cleaner.
4. On the 18i and Fuego, remove the grille and the grille upper crossmember.
5. Disconnect all wires, cables and hoses connected to any part on the head. Tag these for easy installation. On fuel injected cars, clamp off the injection hoses after removal to prevent fuel spillage.
6. Remove the valve cover.
7. Remove the water pump and alternator drive belts.
8. Remove the distributor.
9. Disconnect the exhaust pipe at the manifold. On cars with catalytic converters, remove the converter.
10. On the 18i and Fuego, remove the diagnostic connector.
11. Remove the alternator on R-12, 15, 17, and Gordini.
12. Remove the rocker arm shaft assembly.
13. Remove the pushrods, keeping them in order for replacement in their original positions.
14. Remove the rubber washers and cups in the spark plug recesses.
15. Remove the head bolts.
16. The head will stick to the cylinder liners. DO NOT ATTEMPT TO LIFT OFF THE HEAD BEFORE IT IS BROKEN LOOSE FROM THE LINERS! To break the head loose, tap around the head with a plastic, wood or rubber mallet, gently, and rotate the head using the built-in locating dowel in the block, near the distributor, as a pivot point.
17. Lift the head slightly, and remove the valve lifters, keeping them in order for replacement in their original locations.
18. Remove the head.
19. Remove the valve lifter housing gasket.
20. Using a special tool, Mot.521-01, secure the cylinder liners in place. Keep this tool in place the whole time the head is off. This tool prevents dislodgment of, or damage to the liner seals.
21. Clean the mating surface of the head and block thoroughly. There must be no trace of old gasket material or other debris. Do not scrape the surfaces! If necessary, use a gasket disolver, available in most auto parts stores.
22. Take care that no debris enters the oil,

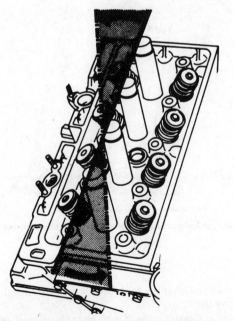

Breaking loose the 1565 or 1647cc engine head using the locating dowel, near the distributor as a pivot point

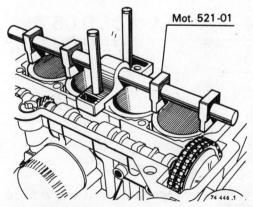

Mot. 521-01

Liner retaining clamp installed

coolant or bolt holes. Clean these holes thoroughly.

23. All bolt holes must be free of any oil. Use a kitchen baster for this operation.

24. Decarbon the combustion chambers using brushes made for this purpose mounted in an electric drill. Remove all traces of carbon from the chambers and valve faces.

25. If the valves are being removed, skip on to Valves, Removal and Installation, later.

26. Lay a straight-edge across the face of the head. Using feeler gauges, check between the straight-edge and the head's gasket surface. There should be no gap, ideally, but a gap of up to .002 in. is acceptable. Resurface the head if necessary. Most automotive machine shops perform this operation.

27. Check the head for any sign of cracks. Auto machine shops have ultraviolet crack detectors for this purpose.

28. Check the liner protrusion above the block surface. Protrusion should be .004–.007 in. If not, the liner seals must be replaced.

29. Head installation is the reverse of removal. Note the following points:

    a. Never reuse a gasket.

    b. Cylinder head positioning is vitally important since it can effect alignment of the distributor shaft with its drive pinion. Renault recommends using an alignment gauge, Mot.

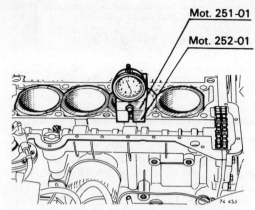

Checking liner protrusion on 1565 or 1647cc engines

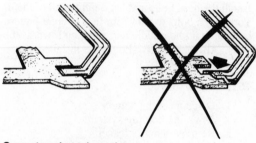

Correct gasket tab mating

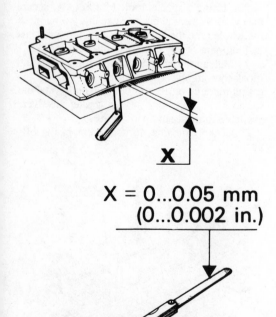

$$X = 0...0.05 \text{ mm}$$
$$(0...0.002 \text{ in.})$$

Checking head flatness. A gap of up to .002 in. is acceptable

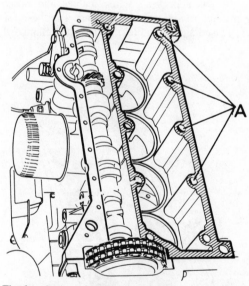

The four longest head bolts go in the holes marked A

446 and aligning tool, Mot.451, when installing the head.

    c. Once the head has been positioned on the block, the head gasket cannot be reused, if it is necessary to lift the head for any reason.

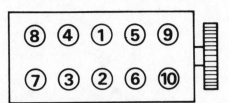

Head bolt torque sequence for the 1565, 1647 and 2200cc engines

d. When installing the head, be careful not to move the valve lifter chamber gasket.

e. Make sure that the lifters are firmly seated in the head so they won't drop out during head installation.

f. Lubricate the head bolts with a light coating of clean engine oil prior to insertion. Hand tighten all the bolts, then torque them to the valve shown in the Torque Specifications Chart, in the sequence shown.

g. When assembly is complete, start the engine, allow it to reach normal operating temperature. Shut it off and allow it to cool for 50 minutes, then back off the bolts ½ turn in sequence and tighten each, in sequence to 60–65 ft. lb. Check rocker arm adjustment.

1984–85 Fuego 2.2L

1. Disconnect the battery ground.
2. Remove the drive belts from the accessories.
3. Remove the alternator and AIR pump.
4. Remove the air conditioning compressor from its mounts, but do not disconnect the refrigerant lines. Wire it securely out of the way.
5. Drain the coolant from the engine.
6. Remove the crankshaft balancer.
7. Remove the manifolds.
8. Remove the timing belt cover.
9. Release the timing belt tensioner and remove the belt.
10. Remove the rocker cover.
11. Hold the camshaft sprocket firmly. There are tools made for the purpose.
12. Remove the sprocket nut and lift off the sprocket.
13. Remove all the cylinder head bolts except the front right one.
14. Loosen the remaining bolt and pivot the head on it to break the head loose from the liners. It may be necessary to get the head moving by tapping it with a wood mallet.
15. Install cylinder liner clamp #588 on the block.
16. Installation is the reverse of removal. Make sure that all gasket material is removed from the mating surfaces. Always use a new gasket. The dowel at the right front of the head will help you in aligning the head during installation. Use the sequence illustrated when tightening the head bolts. Tighten the bolts first to 37 ft. lb., then 59 ft. lb., then back them off ½ turn and retorque them to 64–72 ft. lb.

Valves
REMOVAL
All Engines

1. Remove the cylinder head, as described earlier.
2. Remove the rocker arm shaft assembly as described earlier.
3. Using a valve spring compressor, available in most auto parts stores, compress the valve springs, remove the keepers (they are also called keys or locks), remove the spring retaining collars and release the springs. Remove the springs and the base collars.
4. Some engines have rubber valve stem seals. If so remove these and discard them. Slide the valve from the valve guide.

INSPECTION, CLEANING AND REFACING

1. Using a stiff wire, drill-mounted brush, remove all traces of carbon and other deposits from the valve.
2. Check the valves for cracks, excessive

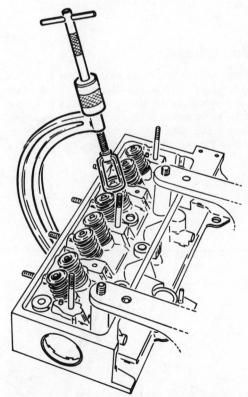

Typical valve spring compressor tool for valve removal

scoring or pitting and other damage. If cracked or excessively damaged, especially in the face area, replace them.

3. Check the valve stems for bending. If at all bent, replace the valve. Check the stem for wear; if the stem is worn beyond the diameter shown in the Valve Specifications Chart, replace it.

4. Using a valve grinding tool, reface the valves to the degree shown in the Valve Specifications Chart.

5. Coat the valve face with a dye such as Prussian Blue and insert it into the head. Holding the stem, turn the valve in its seat and carefully remove it. The dye should be distributed evenly on the valve face and seat. If not, check the angle ground on the seat. It may need regrinding. If no good contact can be established by grinding, replace the valve.

INSTALLATION

1. Coat the face of each valve with lapping compound and insert them into the head. Using a lapping tool, turn the valves in the seat to establish a finely honed and polished fit. Remove any left-over lapping compound.

2. Assembly is the reverse of removal. Make sure that the keepers are firmly seated. Make sure that the closer coils of the springs are at the bottom.

Valve Seats

The seats are not replaceable. Repair is limited to recutting of the seats to the angle shown in the valve specifications charts. All traces of carbon must be removed from the seat before cutting. Follow the cutter manufacturer's instructions on use of the tool when doing the cutting. Check

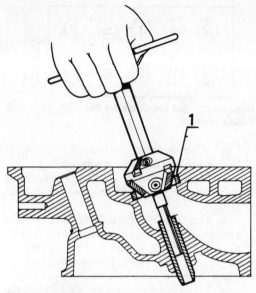

Cutting the valve seat

valve contact using a dye such as Prussian Blue, as described under Valves, Cleaning, Inspection and Refacing.

Valve Guides
ALL ENGINES

The guides are replaceable. However, a press is needed for this job.

1. Press the old guide out from the top side of the head.

2. Check the guide to see if it is original equipment or an oversize replacement. The outside diameter of the replacement guide must be one size larger than the one it is replacing. Oversize guides are available in two sizes and are identified by grooves cut in the outside diameter. Use the chart below to determine the oversize guide that you need:

3. Ream the valve guide hole in the head to accept the new guide.

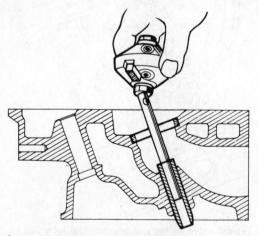

Assembling the valve seat cutting tool

Engine	Original OD	One Groove	Two Grooves
1289cc	.433 (11mm)	.437 (11.1mm)	.443 (11.25mm)
1397cc	.433 (11mm)	.437 (11.1mm)	.443 (11.25mm)
1565cc	.512 (13mm)	.516 (13.1mm)	.522 (13.25mm)
1647cc	.512 (13mm)	.516 (13.1mm)	.522 (13.25mm)
2165cc	.512 (13mm)	.521 (13.25mm)	—

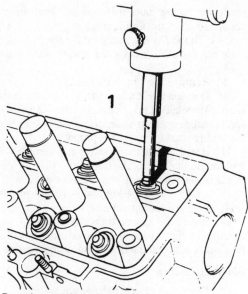

Pressing out the valve guide

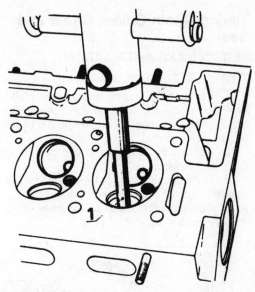

Reaming the guide bore

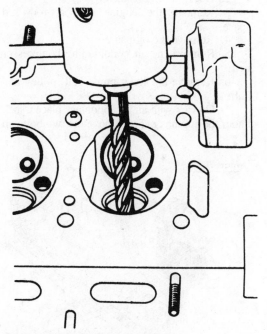

Reaming the guide locating hole

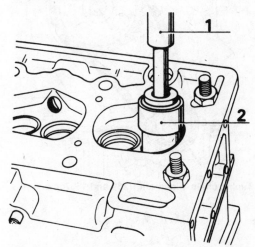

Installing a new guide. 1 is the mandrel shoulder; 2 is the stop sleeve

4. Press the new guide into place. Check the distance between the valve seat and the end of the guide.

Engine	Intake	Exhaust
1289, 1397cc	1.043 in.	1.032 in.
1565cc	1.260 in.	1.220 in.
1647cc	1.437 in.	1.161 in.
2165cc	1.220 in.	1.290 in.

5. Ream the guide bore to the proper ID as shown in the Valve Specifications Chart.

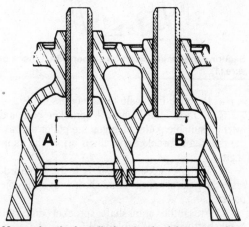

Measuring the installation depth of the new guides. A is intake; B is exhaust

Timing Chain Cover, Chain and Seal

REMOVAL AND INSTALLATION

1289cc, 1397cc LeCar

1. Remove the engine/transaxle assembly from the vehicle according to the "Engine Removal and Installation" procedure in the beginning of this section.

2. Remove the timing cover and clean all of the gasket surfaces.

3. If the timing chain is to be replaced, secure the shoe of the tensioner (component that actually contacts the chain) to the body of the tensioner with a piece of wire.

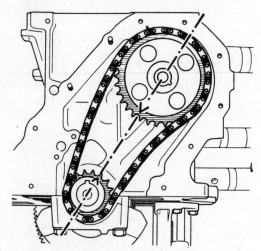

Timing chain alignment, 1289 and 1397cc engines

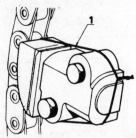

Securing the timing chain tensioner with a piece of wire (1)

4. Remove the chain tensioner assembly.

5. Remove the camshaft sprocket bolt and install a suitable puller. Tighten the puller to draw the camshaft sprocket and chain off of the camshaft.

6. If the crankshaft gear is to be replaced, draw the gear off of the crankshaft with a suitable puller.

7. Press the crankshaft sprocket onto the crankshaft using a suitable tool.

8. Temporarily install the camshaft sprocket (marking facing outward) without the timing chain and align the timing marks.

CAUTION: *Do not rotate either the camshaft or the crankshaft once the timing marks are aligned.*

9. Remove the camshaft sprocket.

10. Position the timing chain onto the camshaft sprocket and reinstall the camshaft sprocket/timing chain assembly, making sure that the timing marks are aligned properly.

11. Install the camshaft sprocket retaining bolt and torque the bolt to 20 ft. lbs.

12. Install the timing chain tensioner.

13. Using a new gasket and cover-to-oil pan seal, install the timing cover.

14. Install the engine/transaxle assembly according to the "Engine Removal and Installation" procedure in the beginning of this section.

Alliance, Encore

1. Disconnect the battery ground.

2. Drain the engine oil.

3. Remove the engine support rod and spacer.

4. Remove the oil pan.

5. Remove the air conditioning compressor belt.

6. Remove the water pump belt, pulley and hub.

7. On cars with air conditioning, place a jack under the engine cradle, remove the two bolts on

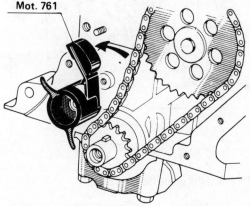

Using a special tool to move the tensioner on the Alliance

the right side of the cradle and lower the jack until the pulley clears the crossmember.

8. Remove the timing chain cover. Crank the engine until the V shaped timing marks on the sprockets are aligned.

9. Move the chain tensioner as far as possible from the chain and secure it out of the way.

10. Remove the tensioner.

11. Remove the camshaft sprocket bolt, pull the sprocket loose with a three-jawed puller and remove the sprocket and chain.

12. To pull the crankshaft sprocket, you must machine a large depression into the head of a bolt that will fit into the nose of the crankshaft. Use this bolt as a center point for a puller.

13. Installation is the reverse of removal. Some later models have a timing cover assembled with RTV silicone gasket material in place of a paper gasket. Use only this material when assembling. The camshaft sprocket bolt is torqued to 22 ft. lb. Make sure that the timing marks are aligned.

1565cc and 1647cc

1. Disconnect the battery cables at the battery.

2. Remove the cylinder head, distributor and distributor drive gear.

3. Remove the radiator.

4. Remove the crankshaft pulley retaining bolt. Using a suitable puller, remove the crankshaft pulley.

5. Remove the timing cover; raise the engine if necessary to gain working clearance.

6. Remove the timing chain guide shoes and chain tensioner.

7. Remove the two camshaft retaining bolts.

8. Using a suitable puller, remove the crankshaft sprocket and key along with the timing chain.

9. Position the timing chain onto the camshaft sprocket. Position the camshaft sprocket

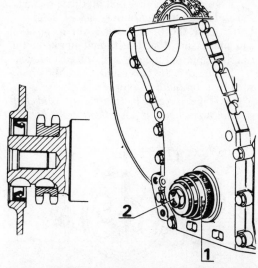

Timing cover seal installation on the 1565 or 1647cc engines. 1 is the seal sleeve; 2 is the installing bolt used to press the seal into place

timing mark so that the mark points toward the crankshaft centerline.

10. Install the crankshaft key and rotate the crankshaft so that the key faces up.

11. Place the crankshaft sprocket inside the timing chain to simulate installation. Make sure that the timing marks align properly.

12. After the marks have been aligned as necessary, install the crankshaft sprocket and timing chain.

13. Install the following items:

    a. Camshaft retaining bolts

    b. Timing chain tensioner

    c. Timing chain guide shoes—push the chain guides against Renault gauge Mot. 420 (or its equivalent) and tighten the guide bolts.

    d. Timing cover, using a new gasket and seal

    e. Radiator

    f. Crankshaft pulley

    g. Cylinder head, distributor drive gear and distributor. Time engine.

14. Reconnect the battery cable.

Timing Belt and Cover
REMOVAL AND INSTALLATION
2.2L OHC Engines

1. Follow steps 1–9 of Cylinder Head Removal & Installation, omitting step 5.

2. For installation, position the camshaft sprocket timing mark in line with the static timing mark as shown in the illustration.

3. Position the crankshaft so that #1 piston is at TDC on the compression stroke as shown in the illustration.

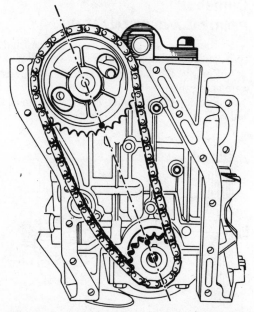

Timing gear alignment on the 1565 and 1647cc engines

4. Install the timing belt on the sprockets.

5. Tighten the tensioner.

6. Place the timing belt cover in position and make sure that the timing mark on the camshaft sprocket indexes with the cover notch.

7. Remove the cover and rotate the crankshaft two complete revolutions clockwise.

CAUTION: *NEVER rotate the crankshaft counterclockwise when adjusting the belt.*

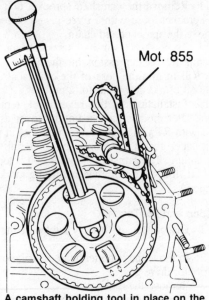

A camshaft holding tool in place on the 2.2L engine

8. Loosen the tensioner bolts ¼ turn, maximum.

9. The tensioner should automatically adjust the belt to the proper tension.

10. Tighten the bottom tensioner bolt first, then the top, to 18 ft. lb.

11. Timing belt deflection, mid-point along it longest straight run, should be 7mm.

12. Install the cover and make sure the belt doesn't rub.

Camshaft

REMOVAL AND INSTALLATION

1. Remove the timing cover, camshaft sprocket and timing chain as previously outlined.

2. Remove the valve cover (and the pushrods were applicable).

3. Remove the cylinder head as previously outlined.

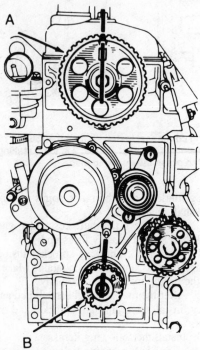

B

2.2L timing belt installation. A is the camshaft sprocket; B is the crankshaft sprocket

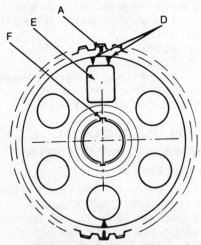

The camshaft sprocket on the 2.2L engine has a timing index (A), two bosses (D), a rectangular hole (E) and a keyway (F) all of which are used for valve adjustments

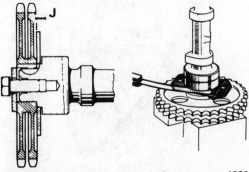

Checking the camshaft flange clearance on 1289 and 1397cc engines

Camshaft oil seal installation tool for the 1289 or 1397cc engine

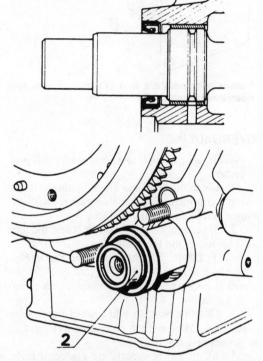

Camshaft oil seal in position on the 1289 or 1397cc engine. 2 is the seal sleeve

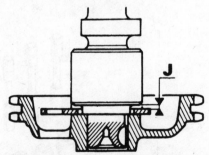

Checking the camshaft flange clearance on the 1565 or 1647cc engine

4. Remove the air injection pump sprocket where applicable.

5. Remove the camshaft flange screws.

6. Temporarily reinstall the camshaft sprocket (to assist in removal as a handle) and carefully withdraw the camshaft from the engine.

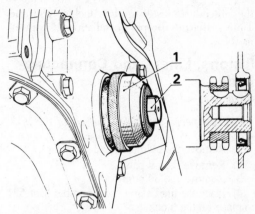

Camshaft oil seal installation tool in place on the 1565 or 1647cc engine

7. Remove the camshaft oil seal.

8. Installation is the reverse of the removal procedure. Take note of the following:

   a. On LeCar and Alliance models, check the clearance between the camshaft and the flange with a feeler gauge. The clearance should be between 0.002–0.005 in. If the clearance is excessive, the flange should be replaced.

   b. On 1647cc engines, make sure there is .012–.020 in. clearance between the chain and the tensioner pads.

   c. Use the proper seal installation tool to install a new camshaft oil seal.

   d. Install the camshaft from the timing chain end of the engine.

OHC Engines

1. Remove the rocker cover.

2. Remove the rocker shaft assembly.

3. Remove the camshaft thrust plate.

4. Remove the timing belt and camshaft sprocket as described earlier.

5. Remove the camshaft oil seal, taking great care to avoid scratching the seal bore.

6. Slide the camshaft from the head.

7. Installation is the reverse of removal. See

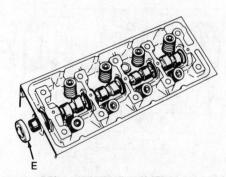

2.2L camshaft oil seal (E)

the procedures listed under Rocker Arm and Timing Belt for proper installation of components.

Pistons, Liners and Connecting Rods

REMOVAL

NOTE: *Special tools are required for this procedure.*

1. Remove the cylinder head.
2. Remove the oil pan.
3. Remove the oil pump.
4. Place the liner clamp, tool number Mot.521 in place on the block.
5. Mark the connecting rods and caps for reassembly. Note that number one cylinder is at the flywheel end.
6. Remove the connecting rod caps.
7. Remove the liner clamp and pull out the liner and piston assemblies.

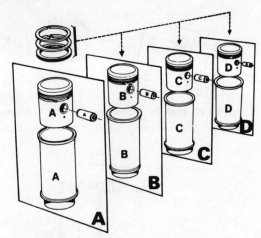

Pistons and liners are sold in matched sets, A-D. Keep them together

OVERHAULING

NOTE: *Special tools are required for this procedure.*

1. Clean the head and block mating surfaces using a commercially available gasket dissolver. Never scrape the mating surfaces.
2. Thoroughly clean the block bores, the liner seal locations and the crankshaft.

NOTE: *Liners, Pistons, Rings and Piston Pins are sold in matched sets. No honing of the liners is necessary. No adjustments to the rings are possible.*

3. Obtain a new, matched set of liner-piston assemblies. Mark each in order, one through four to assure easy installation.
4. All of the new parts are coated with an antirust film. Remove this film with a safe solvent.

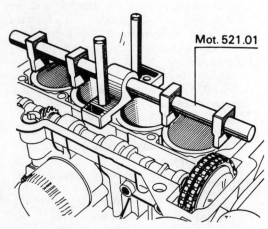

Liner retaining tool in place

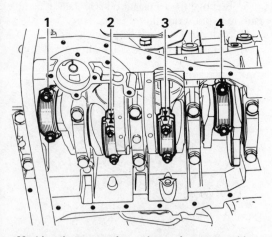

Marking the connecting rod caps for reassembly

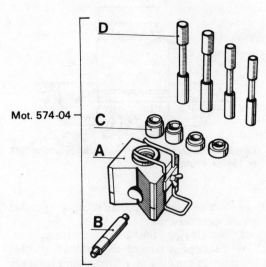

Piston pin removal and installation tool

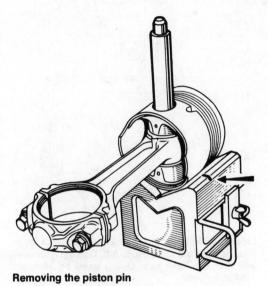

Removing the piston pin

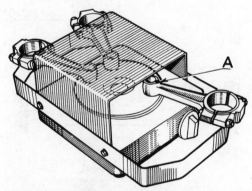

Heating the connecting rod ends in the special heater designed for that purpose

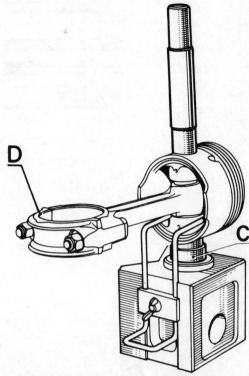

Inserting the piston pin. D is the marked side of the rod; C is the thrust collar

5. Drive the piston pins from the old piston and rod assemblies and assemble the new pistons to the rods using the new pins. If there is any difficulty inserting the new pins into the rods, the rods must be heated to 482°F (250°C). A special hot plate tool is available for this purpose. Since only the affected end of the rod should be heated to this degree, this tool, rather than an oven, is recommended. The tool number is Mot.574.

NOTE: *When assembling the piston and rod, make sure that the arrow on the piston top faces the flywheel end of the engine and the mark made on the connecting rod faces the side away from the camshaft. The piston and rod must be assembled quickly to avoid heat loss. A press and mandrel are essential for rapid assembly. If one cannot be obtained, this job is best left to a machine shop. The pin must not protrude beyond the piston skirt on either side.*

6. The piston rings are pregapped. There is no adjustment possible. Use a ring compressor/expander to install the rings. The rings gaps

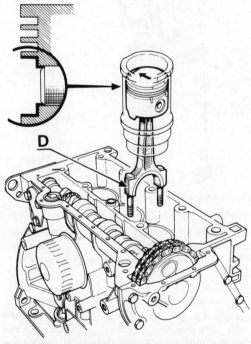

Proper pin installation should have the pin recess shown on the same side of the piston as the arrow denoting forward, which is stamped on top of the piston. D is the marked side of the rod

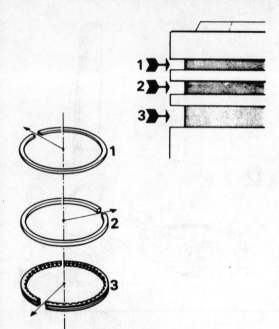

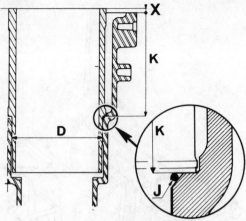

Liner installation. X is the liner protrusion; K is the liner height from shoulder to top; D is the liner width and J is the base seal O-ring used on 1565 and 1647cc engines

Proper piston ring installation

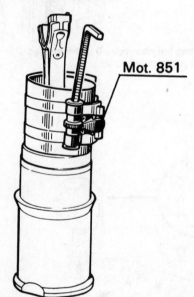

Installing the piston assembly into the liner

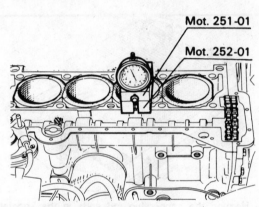

Measuring liner protrusion

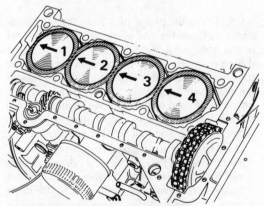

Piston and liner assemblies installed

should be staggered 90° apart, so that no two gaps line up. When installing the compression rings, make sure that the side stamped with an O faces up.

7. With the rings installed, lubricate the piston assembly with clean engine oil. Using a ring compressor, slide the piston/rod assembly into the liner. The machined sides of the connecting rod big end must be parallel with the flat edge on top of the liner.

8. Place the upper bearing half into the rod. NOTE: *When installing the liners, it is neces-*

sary to determine what thickness seals to use. To do this you must measure the liner protrusion above the block surface. Check the protrusion at two opposite points as shown and subtract the greater figure from .005". Choose a seal equal to or just above the result ob-

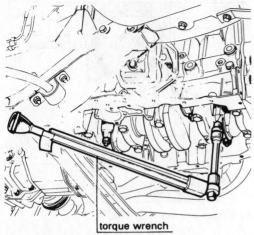

Torquing the connecting rod caps

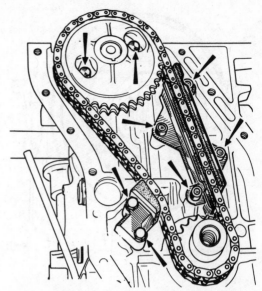

Bolts to be removed prior to timing chain removal on the 1565 and 1647cc engines

tained by subtraction. Seals are identified by a color spot to indicate thickness: Blue is .033", Red is .004", and Green is .005" thick. Place the new seals on the liners, insert the liners, press them down by hand, and recheck their protrusion According to the Piston and liner Chart. The difference between liners should not exceed .0016".

9. Slide the liner assemblies, in order, into the block. Don't forget that number one is at the flywheel end of the block. The arrows on the pistons must face the flywheel.

10. Position the liner clamp on the block.

11. Lubricate the crankshaft journals and pull each rod down into cnntact with the journals.

12. Lay a piece of Plastigage across each bearing cap on the bearing surface. Install each cap and torque it to the value shown on the Torque Specifications Chart. Remove the cap and check the width of the plastigage on the bearing, compare it to the bearing clearance shown in the Crankshaft Specifications Chart, and determine if you need new bearings.

13. Install the bearing caps and torque them.

14. Make sure that everything moves freely.

15. Assembly is the reverse of disassembly from here on.

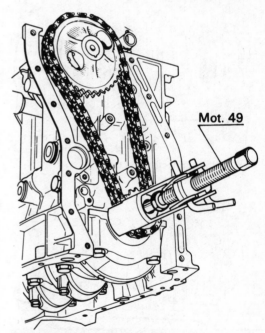

Mot. 49

Removing the crankshaft sprocket

Crankshaft

REMOVAL AND INSTALLATION

All Engines

1. Remove the engine. Remove the oil pan and pump.

2. Remove the crankshaft pulley.

3. Remove the flywheel.

4. Remove the bearing caps, keeping them in order.

5. Lift out the crankshaft. Take great care, if you are going to reuse the crankshaft, to keep it free from dirt and scratches.

CLEANING, INSPECTION AND REPAIR

1. Clean the crankshaft with a safe solvent and pass a length of soft copper wire through the oil passages to clean them out.

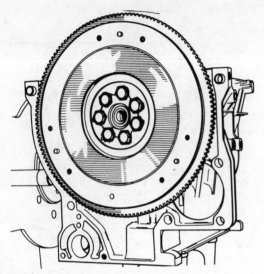

Flywheel

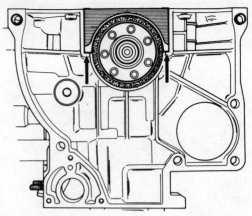

Rear main bearing

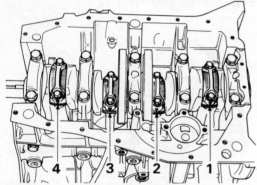

Marking the connecting rod caps

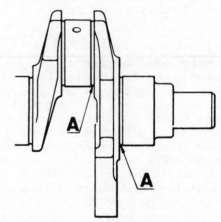

Checking bearing journal undercuts

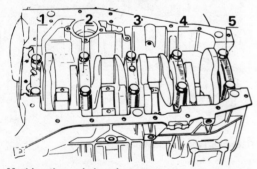

Marking the main bearing caps

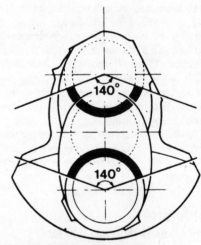

Crankshaft roll-hardened surfaces

2. Discard the old bearings from the caps and block.

3. Check the bearing caps for signs of obvious damage.

4. Check the crankshaft journals for scoring, heating, scratches and unusual wear. Using a micrometer, check the journal diameters against the values shown in the specifications chart. If the journals are worn beyond these values, the journals can be reground up to .0008″ on connecting rod journals and up to .0004″ on main bearing journals. This operation should be performed by

a qualified machine shop. Roll-hardening must be maintained over a 140° section facing the rotational centerline of the crankshaft.

INSTALLATION

1. Place new bearing upper halves in the rods and/or block.

NOTE: *On the 1289 and 1397cc engines, Nos. 1 and 3 main bearings have one oil hole each; Nos. 2 and 4 main bearings have two oil holes each.*

2. Coat the main bearing journals and rod journals with clean engine oil. Position the crankshaft in the block.

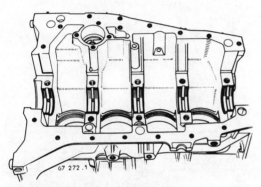

Main bearing upper half installation

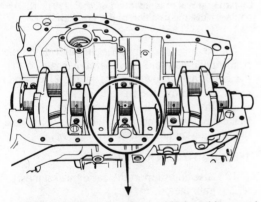

Installing the thrust washers with the white metal face toward the crankshaft

3. Install the thrust washers with the white metal face toward the crankshaft throws.

4. Install the main bearing and rod bearing lower halves in the caps.

5. Coat the bearing caps with clean engine oil and lay a strip of Plastigage across the bearing face. Make sure the caps are in order and install them in their original positions.

6. Torque the caps to the specification shown in the Torque Specifications Chart. Remove the caps and check the width of the Plastigage. The measurement should correspond with the bearing clearance shown in the Crankshaft Specifications Chart.

7. If the bearings are out of clearance specification, they may be replaced with oversized bearings. If the clearance is correct, replace the caps and torque them to specification.

8. Make sure the crankshaft turns freely.

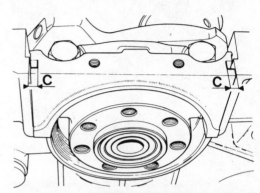

Measuring the distance, C, between the bottom of the block and main bearing seal housing on the 1647cc engine

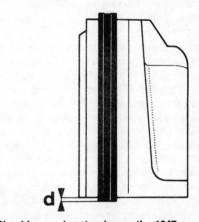

Checking seal protrusion on the 1647cc engine

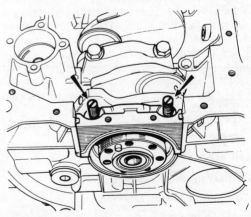

Installing the #1 main bearing cap using centering studs

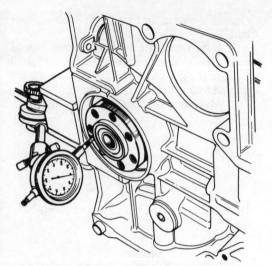

Checking crankshaft endplay with a dial indicator

9. Mount a dial indicator on the end of the crankshaft and push the shaft back and forth to check end play. End play should not exceed that shown in the Crankshaft Specifications Chart. If it does, change the thrust washers. Thrust washers come in four thicknesses ranging between 0.110–0.116 in.

10. Install a new main bearing oil seal. Be careful of the seal lip. It is very easily damaged. Lubricate the entire outer surface of the seal.

11. On 1565 and 1647cc engines, measure the distance between the bottom of the block and the main bearing seal housing, as shown. If the distance is less than 5mm (0.197 in.), select seals 5.1mm (0.201 in.) thick. If the distance is greater than 5mm, select seals 5.4mm (0.213 in.) thick.

12. Remove the cap and put the two new side seals in the cap. The seal groove should face upward. Seal protrusion should be $^{1}\!\!\;^{32}$ in. Coat the bearing cap and side seals with clean engine oil.

13. Screw two centering studs into the block adjacent to the seal as shown. Cover the seal with aluminum foil to prevent damage and slide the cap and seals into place. When the cap is about ¾ in., check seal protrusion to make sure they haven't moved. When the cap is seated, remove the foil and studs, then replace the cap bolts and torque them to specification.

14. Install the flywheel. The flywheel bolts are self-locking, therefore cannot be reused.

15. Install all other parts in reverse order of removal.

Oil Pan
REMOVAL AND INSTALLATION
1289cc and 1397cc Engines

1. Drain the oil.
2. Raise and support the car on jackstands.

3. Remove the front anti-Sway bar bushings.
4. Remove the lower transaxle shield.
5. Unbolt the gearshift control bracket from the transaxle.
6. Remove the right, lateral reinforcement piece.
7. Remove the clutch shield.
8. Place a floor jack under the nose of the transaxle and support it so that the front pad can be removed.
9. Raise the front of the transaxle as much as possible.

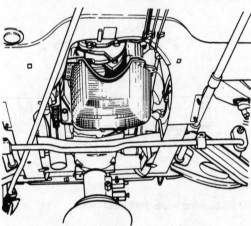

Oil pan removal or installation on the 1289 or 1397cc engine. Note the position of the crankshaft

10. Remove the oil pan bolts. Tilt down the front of the pan and turn the crankshaft so that the crankshaft throws do not interfere with pan removal. Remove the pan and gaskets.

11. Installation is the reverse of removal. Make sure that the mating surfaces are clean. Coat the new gasket and seals with sealer.

1565cc, 1647cc, 2167cc Engines

1. Raise and support the car on jackstands.
2. Drain the oil.
3. Remove the oil pan bolts and lower the pan.
4. Installation is the reverse of removal. Make sure that the mating surfaces are free of old gasket material and dirt. Never reuse a gasket. Coat the gasket surfaces with sealer, position the gasket and seals on the pan, install the pan and tighten the bolts to 5–7 ft. lb. (60–84 in. lb.).

Oil Pump
REMOVAL AND INSTALLATION
All Engines

1. Remove the oil pan.
2. Unbolt and remove the pump and pick-up.
3. Installation is the reverse of removal.

OVERHAUL

1289cc and 1397cc Engines

1. Remove the four pump cover bolts.

NOTE: *Don't let the ball seat, ball and pressure limiter valve jump out!*

2. Remove the driven gear, drive gear and drive gear shaft.

3. Clean all the parts in a safe solvent. Check

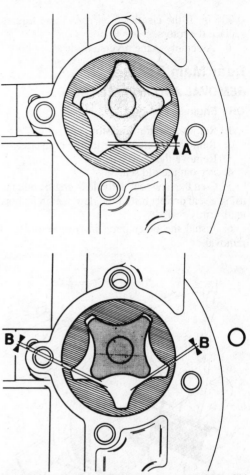

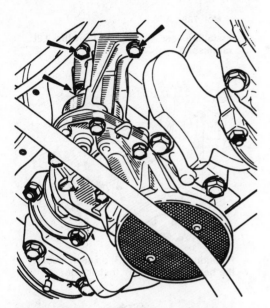

Oil pump for the 1289 or 1397cc engine

Checking oil pump rotor clearances. A=.002–.011 in.; B=.001–.006 in.

each part for signs of wear or damage. Replace parts as needed.

4. Check the pump seal surface. If the surface is at all marked, it must be polished or reground to remove the marks.

5. Check the clearance between the gears and pump body. Maximum clearance is 0.008 in. If the clearance exceeds that figure, the gears must be replaced.

6. Assembly is the reverse of disassembly.

1565cc, 1647cc, 2167cc Engines

1. Remove the pick-up tube bolts.

2. Remove the cotter pin from the pressure release valve and take out the spring cup, spring and piston.

3. Remove the rotors.

4. Clean all parts in a safe solvent and check them for wear or damage. Replace parts as necessary.

5. Check the rotor clearance as shown. In position 1, the clearance (A) should be 0.002–0.011 in. In position 2, clearance (B) should be 0.001–

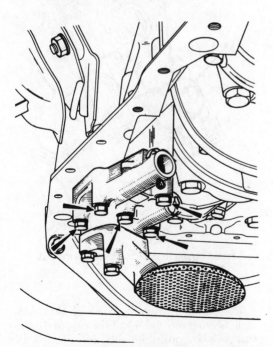

Oil pump on a 1565 or 1647cc engine

0.006 in. If the clearance exceeds these figures, replace the rotors.

6. Assembly is the reverse of disassembly.

Rear Main Seal

REMOVAL AND INSTALLATION

OHV Engines

1. Remove the transmission.
2. Remove the clutch, or torque converter.
3. Remove the flywheel.
4. Pry out the old seal.
5. Coat the new seal with clean engine oil and, using a seal driver, install the new seal in its bore until firmly seated.
6. Install the other parts in reverse order of removal.

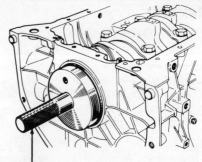

Mot. 788

Installing rear circular seal on the 2.2L crankshaft

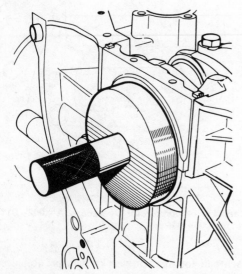

Rear main oil seal installation

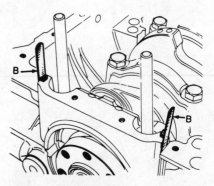

Position a strip of foil (B) on each side of the bearing cap before installation

OHC Engines

NOTE: *There are main seals at each end of the crankshaft. Each seal is replaced in the same manner. If the rear seal is replaced, the engine must be removed.*

1. Raise and support the car on jackstands.
2. Remove the oil pan.
3. Replacement seals are available in two sizes: 5.4mm and 5.1mm thick. Measure the distance between the bearing cap and the block (C in the illustration). If the distance is 5mm or less, use a 5.1mm seal. If the distance is greater, use the larger seal.
4. Remove the cap and pull out the old seal.
5. Insert the side seals in the cap with the groove facing outward. Each side seal should protrude about .2mm outward from the cap.
6. Lubricate the contact surfaces of the side seals with clean engine oil.

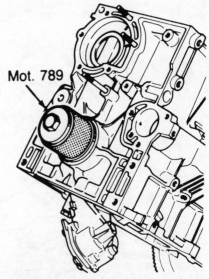

Mot. 789

Installing the front circular seal on the 2.2L crankshaft

7. Position a strip of foil on each side of the main bearing cap and install the cap. Make sure that each seal protrudes outwardly. Torque the cap bolts to 65–72 ft. lb.

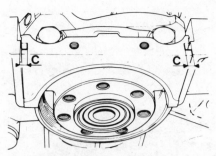

Measure the distance (C) between the bearing cap and the block on the 2.2L

8. Cut the seal ends so that a protrusion of .5–.7mm remains.

9. Install the front and rear circular seals with a seal driver as shown.

Flywheel and Ring Gear
REMOVAL AND INSTALLATION
All Engines

1. Remove the transmission.
2. Remove the clutch or torque converter.
3. Unbolt and remove the flywheel.
4. If the ring gear is being replaced, drill through the ring gear at any given point. Sometimes, this alone is enough to split the ring gear. If not, use a cold chisel at the drilled point, to split the ring gear. When the ring gear is split, slide it off of the flywheel.
5. Inspect the flywheel face for signs of cracking or heat scoring. If wear or damage is excessive, have the flywheel refaced. If refacing can't get rid of the cracks, or if the flywheel is warped beyond refacing, replace it.
6. To install a new ring gear, the ring gear must first be heated in an oven to 450–500°F. When this temperature is reached, quickly install the ring gear on the flywheel using heavy, heat shielding gloves. Allow it to cool.
7. Install the flywheel using new bolts. These bolts are of a self-locking thread design, so they can't be reused.
8. Install all other parts in reverse order of removal.

Water Pump
REMOVAL AND INSTALLATION
LeCar and Alliance

NOTE: *The water pump cannot be repaired. It is a sealed unit*

1. Disconnect the battery.
2. Drain the cooling system.
3. Loosen the alternator and move it out of the way.
4. Remove the water pump tensioner, the drive belt, the air pump, the water pump pulley and toothed belt and the temperature sending unit.
5. Unbolt and remove the pump. It may be necessary to tap the pump free with a wood mallet.
6. Clean the gasket mating surfaces thoroughly. Install the pump using a new gasket. Do not use sealer.

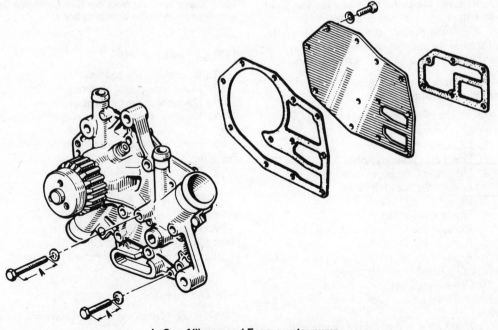

LeCar, Alliance and Encore water pump

R-12

NOTE: *The pump cannot be repaired, just replaced.*

1. Disconnect the battery.
2. Drain the cooling system.
3. Disconnect the hoses at the pump.
4. Remove the alternator and water pump drive bolts.

Water pump removal from the R-15, 17, Gordini, except 1975 Canadian Gordini Arrows show the attaching bolts

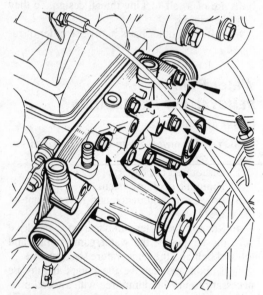

Removing the R-12 water pump. The arrows show the attaching bolts

5. Remove the water pump pulley.
6. Remove the camshaft pulley.
7. Remove the pump bolts and tap the pump loose with a wood or rubber mallet.
8. Clean the mating surfaces thoroughly. Installation is the reverse of removal. Always use a new gasket. Do not use sealer on the gasket!

R-15, R-17 and Gordini, except 1975 Canadian Gordini

NOTE: *The pump cannot be repaired, just replaced.*

1. Disconnect the battery.
2. Drain the cooling system.
3. Disconnect the hoses at the pump.
4. Loosen the pump drive belt.
5. Remove the fan shroud.
6. Remove the radiator.
7. Remove the fan and pump pulley.
8. Remove the pump belt.
9. Remove the pump bolts and tap the pump loose with a wood or rubber mallet.
10. Clean the gasket surfaces thoroughly. Always use a new gasket. Do not use sealer on the gasket.
11. Installation is the reverse of removal.

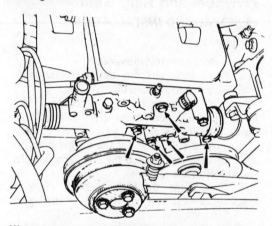

Water pump removal from the 1975 Canadian Gordini. Arrows show the attaching bolts

1975 Canadian Gordini

1. Disconnect the battery.
2. Drain the cooling system.
3. Disconnect the hoses at the pump.
4. Remove the pump and alternator drive belts.
5. Remove the alternator adjuster bolt from the pump.
6. Remove the pump pulley.
7. Remove the camshaft pulley.
8. Remove the water pump bolts and tap it loose with a wood or plastic mallet.
9. Remove the plate, discard the gasket and clean the gasket surfaces thoroughly.
10. Installation is the reverse of removal.

R-18 and Fuego

NOTE: *The pump cannot be repaired, just replaced.*

1. Disconnect the battery.
2. Drain the cooling system.
3. Disconnect the hoses at the pump.
4. Remove the upper grille crossmember.
5. Remove the grille.
6. Remove the radiator and fan.
7. Remove the pump drive belt.
8. Remove the pump bolts and tap the pump loose with a wood or rubber mallet.
9. Clean the gasket surfaces thoroughly. Always use a new gasket. Do not use sealer on the gasket. Installation is the reverse of removal.

Thermostat

REMOVAL AND INSTALLATION

All Engines

The thermostat is located in the water outlet hose at the pump. This is the large hose that runs from the pump to the top of the radiator. To replace the thermostat, simply disconnect the hose at the pump and remove the thermostat.

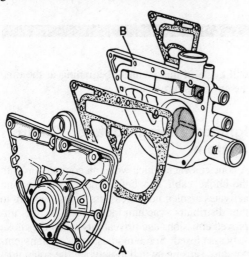

R-18 and Fuego water pump. A is the pump cover; B is the pump body

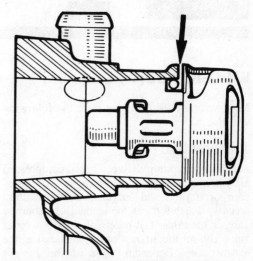

Alliance thermostat. Make sure that the ball check valve faces upward

Emission Controls and Fuel System

EMISSION CONTROLS

Most vehicles are equipped with the following systems:

Air Injection

A belt-driven pump delivers fresh, compressed air to the exhaust ports of the engine. The presence of oxygen will lengthen the combustion process, which reduces the amount of unburned gases in the exhaust. A relief valve and a diverter valve control the amount of air delivered to the exhaust ports. Depending upon whether the engine is accelerating/cruising or decelerating, the diverter valve either delivers the air to the exhaust ports, or closes off the air passage to the exhaust ports, respectively. A check valve is provided in the system which will prevent damage to the air injection pump should the engine backfire.

Accelerated Idle System

This system is intended to reduce the amount of hydrocarbon emissions during deceleration. The primary throttle plate is opened slightly during deceleration, between speeds of 15–20 miles per hour.

Evaporative Emission Control System

The main component is a canister containing charcoal and a filter. When the engine is off, gasoline vapor settles in the charcoal instead of being vented to the atmosphere. When the engine is started, intake manifold vacuum pulls fresh air in from beneath the charcoal (filtered) and carries the unburned gases to the intake manifold to be burned in the combustion chambers. The vacuum will continue to draw a small amount of vapor from the tank (through a calibrated orifice) even while the engine is running. The process

will cycle in this manner, beginning at the time the engine is turned off.

Ignition Timing Advance Control System

A contact switch which works in conjunction with the choke cable (on LeCar models) closes and activates a solenoid which admits full vacuum to the distributor vacuum advance unit for improved emissions and driveability when the choke valve is closed. Some models use a coolant temperature sensing switch to activate the solenoid.

Carburetor Air Intake Pre-Heating System

A thermostatically controlled air cleaner mixes heated and ambient incoming air to the carburetor, thereby improving fuel vaporization which assists in improving emissions and driveability during cold engine operation.

P.C.V. (Positive Crankcase Ventilation) System

Crankcase vapors are routed to the induction system to be burned in the combustion chambers instead of merely being vented to the atmosphere.

Catalytic Converter

The catalytic converter chemically alters the exhaust gases before the gases reach the atmosphere. A "two-way" catalyst uses either pellets or screens coated with platinum and palladium. The chemical content of the precious metals oxidizes (neutralizes) controlled amounts of carbon monoxide and hydrocarbons. A "three-way" catalyst uses platinum, palladium, and rhodium, which acts on oxides of nitrogen emissions. Some

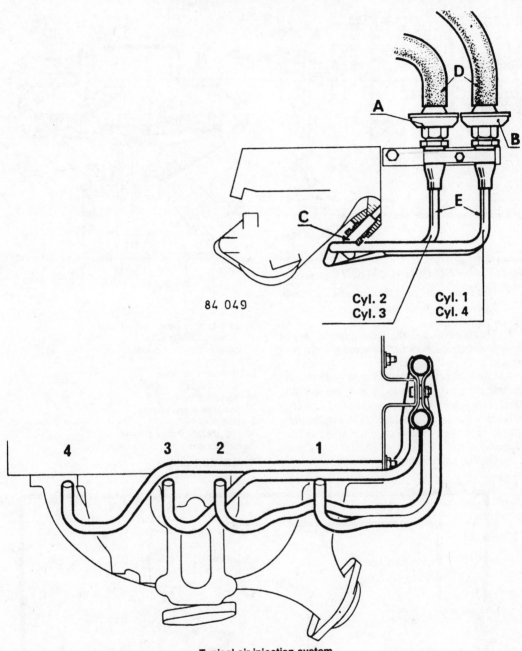

84 049

A

B

C

D

E

Cyl. 2
Cyl. 3

Cyl. 1
Cyl. 4

4   3   2   1

Typical air injection system

"three-way" converters also are ported to accept fresh air (from an injection pump) which further reduces oxides of nitrogen emissions.

E.G.R. (Exhaust Gas Recirculation) System

The E.G.R. valve admits varying amounts of exhaust gases into the combustion chambers, thereby diluting the incoming air/fuel mixture to reduce oxides of nitrogen. The introduction of "pre-burned" gases into the combustion cham-

bers also lowers combustion chamber temperature. If detonation is a problem, check the E.G.R. system for proper operation.

FUEL SYSTEM—CARBURETTED ENGINES

Fuel Pump

NOTE: *All carburetted engines use a mechanical fuel pump located on the engine block, on the distributor side.*

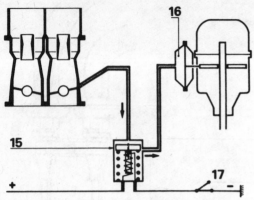

Ignition timing advance control system

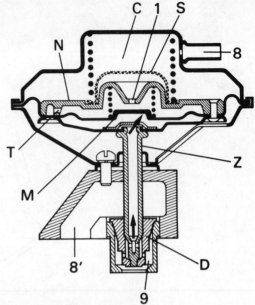

REMOVAL AND INSTALLATION

1. Disconnect and plug the hoses at the pump.
2. Remove the pump mounting bolts and lift off the pump.
3. Thoroughly clean the mounting surfaces of dirt and old gasket material. Discard the old gasket.
4. Using a new gasket, coated with sealer, position the pump on the block making sure that the drive surface of the pump actuating arm contacts the camshaft drive lobe. The engine may have to be rotated to ease installation. Install the mounting bolts.
5. Unplug and reconnect the hoses.

1. air chamber center bleed hole
8. vacuum take-off
8'. intake manifold outlet
9. piston chamber
C. vacuum chamber
D. valve guide
M. diaphragm
N. movable plate
S. strainer
T. peripheral air bleed holes
Z. Valve stem

Typical EGR valve

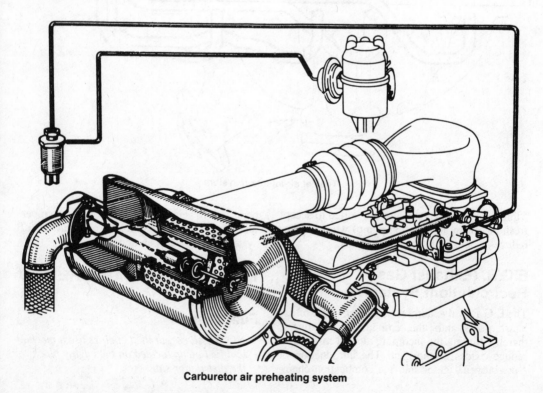

Carburetor air preheating system

TESTING

To test the pump, connect a pressure gauge in-line on the output side of the pump. The pressure should be equal to that listed in the Tune-Up chart in this book.

Carburetor

Carburetors used on Renault cars are as follows:

- LeCar 1976–77 Weber 32DIR46
- LeCar 1978
  - exc. Calif.   Weber 32DIR56
  - Calif.   Weber 32DIR53
- LeCar 1979
  - exc. Calif.   Weber 32DIR55
  - Calif.   Weber 32DIR53
- LeCar 1980
  - exc. Calif.   Weber 32DIR55
  - Calif.   Weber 32DIR80
- LeCar 1981–82
  - All   Weber 32DIR80
- R-12 1975
  - U.S. models   Weber 32DARA
  - Canada   Weber 32 DIR37C (MT)
  -                Weber 32DIR38 (AT)
- R-12 1976   Weber 32DARA10 (MT)
  - U.S. models   Weber 32DARA11 (AT)
- R-12 1977 49s   Weber 32DARA12 (MT)
  - and Canada   Weber 32DARA13 (AT)
  - Calif.   Weber 32DARA5201 (MT)
  -                Weber 32DARA5202 (AT)
- R-15 and R-17
  - 1975 U.S.
  - models   Weber 32DARA
  - Canada   Weber 32DIR37C (MT)
  -                Weber 32DIR38 (AT)
- R-15 and R-17
  - 1976 All   Weber 32DARA15 (MT)
  - models   Weber 32DARA16 (AT)
- R-17 1977 49s
  - and Canada   Weber 32DARA13
- R-18 Canada   Weber 32DARA27 (MT)
  -                Weber 32DARA28 (AT)

As you will note in the above chart, all the carburetors used are basically similar, being the Weber 32 model. This is the base model. All carburetors are variations on this base model. Adjustments and repair procedures for all models are, therefore, similar. Differences will be noted below.

REMOVAL AND INSTALLATION

1. Remove the air cleaner.
2. Disconnect the battery ground. Disconnect the carburetor linkage.
3. Disconnect and tag all wires and hoses attached to the carburetor. On those models with water heated choke, drain a little coolant from the radiator to avoid spillage.
4. Unbolt and remove the carburetor.
5. Install the carburetor using a new gasket. Do not reuse the old gasket. Do not use sealer on the gasket. Connect all wires and hoses. Connect the linkage.

THROTTLE LINKAGE ADJUSTMENT

1. Remove the carburetor.
2. Close the choke plate completely.
3. Check the gap between the throttle plate edge and the air horn wall. The gap should be as noted in the carburetor specifications chart later in this chapter. If not, turn the adjusting screw on the throttle linkage where it bears on the choke cam, until the proper gap is reached.
4. Install the carburetor.

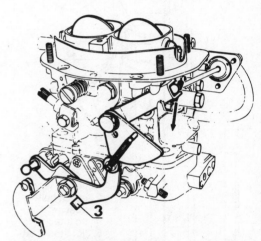

Throttle linkage adjustment points on the R-15 and 17. Bend tab 3 for adjustment

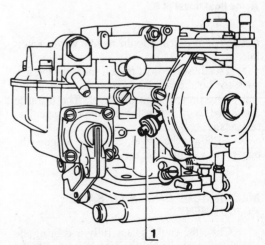

Throttle linkage adjustment on the R-18. Turn screw 1 to adjust

FLOAT ADJUSTMENT

1. Remove the top of the carburetor (float bowl cover).

2. Hold the top in a vertical position with the float end up, so that the weight of the float closes the needle valve without the check ball entering the valve.

3. Check the gap between the float chamber gasket and the float. The gap should be as noted in the carburetor specifications chart later in this chapter.

4. To adjust the gap, bend the float arm making sure that the tab resting on the needle valve

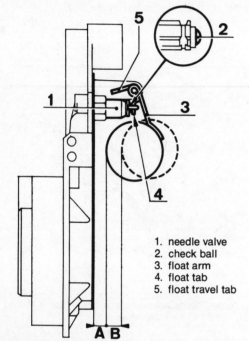

1. needle valve
2. check ball
3. float arm
4. float tab
5. float travel tab

Float adjustments. The float level is measured at A; the float travel at B

remains perpendicular to the needle valve center-line.

5. To adjust the float travel, measure the distance the float travels between the position above and its maximum point of travel. The distance should be as noted in the carburetor specifications chart.

6. To adjust the travel, bend the tongue (the bent portion of the float arm).

MECHANICAL CHOKE LINKAGE ADJUSTMENT

1. Close the choke plates fully and bring the sleeve on the choke linkage into contact with the cam by pushing on the choke plate.

2. Measure the choke plate initial opening,

between the bottom of the plate and the air horn wall. The gap should be as noted in the carburetor specifications chart later in this chapter.

3. If not, bend the choke cam link until it is.

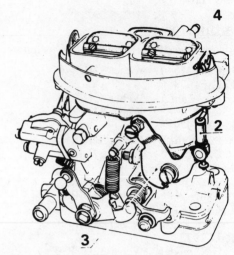

LeCar mechanical choke linkage adjustment. 2 is the sleeve, 3 is the cam and 4 is the link which is bent to make the adjustment

CHOKE VACUUM BREAK ADJUSTMENT

All except R-18

1. Push the vacuum break link in as far as possible, then close the choke plates using the choke cam link until the pull-down spring is slightly compressed.

2. Measure the choke plate initial opening between the bottom of the plates and the air horn wall. The gap should be as noted in the carburetor specifications chart later in this chapter.

3. To adjust the gap, remove the threaded plug from the vacuum break housing and turn the adjustment screw, located inside, until the gap is correct.

R-18

1. Push on the throttle plate linkage to close the choke plate.

2. Remove the choke thermostatic cover and push the vacuum break rod all the way into the vacuum break diaphragm.

3. Hold the lever, which engages the choke coil spring, against the vacuum break rod.

4. Measure the gap between the bottom of the choke plate and the air horn wall. The gap should be as noted in the specifications chart later in this chapter.

5. Adjust the gap using the adjusting screw inside the vacuum break housing cover.

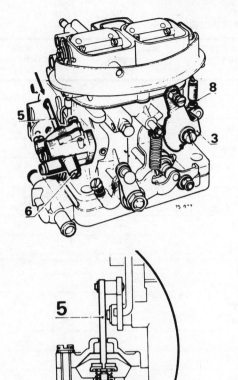

Choke vacuum break adjustment, typical of all except the R-18. 3 is the choke arm, 5 is the push link, 6 is the screw plug, 7 is the adjusting screw and 8 is the spring

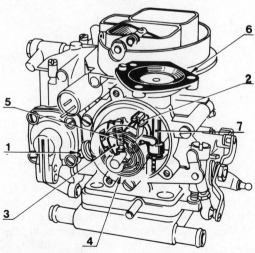

1. adjusting screw
2. lever
3. fast idle cam
4. thermostatic spring
5. spring
6. vacuum diaphragm
7. rod

R-18 Vacuum break adjustment

OVERHAUL

Efficient carburetion depends greatly on careful cleaning and inspection during overhaul, since dirt, gum, water, or varnish in or on the carburetor parts are often responsible for poor performance.

Overhaul your carburetor in a clean, dust-free area. Carefully disassemble the carburetor, referring often to the exploded views. Keep all similar and look-alike parts segregated during disassembly and cleaning to avoid accidental interchange during assembly. Make a note of all jet sizes.

When the carburetor is disassembled, wash all parts (except diaphragms, electric choke units, pump plunger, and any other plastic, leather, fiber, or rubber parts) in clean carburetor solvent. Do not leave parts in the solvent any longer than is necessary to sufficiently loosen the deposits. Excessive cleaning may remove the special finish from the float bowl and choke valve bodies, leaving these parts unfit for service. Rinse all parts in clean solvent and blow them dry with compressed air to allow them to air dry. Wipe clean all cork, plastic, leather, and fiber parts with a clean, lint-free cloth.

Blow out all passages and jets with compressed air and be sure that there are no restrictions or blockages. Never use wire or similar tools to clean jets. Clean valves separately to avoid accidental interchange.

Check all parts for wear or damage. If wear or damage is found, replace the defective parts. Especially check the following:

1. Check the float needle and seat for wear. If wear is found, replace the complete assembly.

2. Check the float hinge pin for wear and the float(s) for dents or distortion. Replace the float if fuel has leaked into it.

3. Check the throttle and choke shaft bores for wear on an out-of-round condition. Damage or wear to the throttle arm, shaft, or shaft bore will often require replacement of the throttle body. These parts require a close tolerance of fit; wear may allow air leakage, which could affect starting and idling.

NOTE: *Throttle shafts and bushings are not included in overhaul kits. They can be purchased separately.*

4. Inspect the idle mixture adjusting needles for burrs or grooves. Any such condition requires replacement of the needle, since you will not be able to obtain a satisfactory idle.

5. Test the accelerator pump check valves. They should pass air one way but not the other. Test for proper seating by blowing and sucking on the valve. Replace the valve if necessary. If the valve is satisfactory, wash the valve again to remove breath moisture.

6. Check the bowl cover for warped surfaces with a straightedge.

Carburetor Specifications

Year	Float Level (in.)	Float Travel (in.)	Throttle Plate Initial Opening (in.)	Mechanical Choke Adjustment (in.)	Choke Vacuum Break (in.)
Le Car					
1976–78	9/32	5/16	3/64	13/64	1/4
1979 Calif.	9/32	5/16	3/64	5/32	9/32
49s	9/32	5/16	3/64	3/16	17/64
1980 49s	9/32	5/16	3/64	3/16	17/64
Calif.	9/32	5/16	3/64	17/64	13/32
1981 Calif.	9/32	5/16	3/64	17/64	13/32
–82 49s	9/32	5/16	3/64	15/64	23/64
R-12					
1975 USA	9/32	5/16	3/64	9/32	13/64
Can.	9/32	5/16	3/64	15/64	15/64 ①
1976 USA	9/32	5/16	3/64	9/32	15/64
Can.	9/32	5/16	3/64	15/64	15/64
1977	9/32	5/16	3/64	15/64	9/32
R-15 & R-17					
1975 USA	9/32	5/16	3/64	9/32	15/64
Can.	9/32	5/16	3/64	15/64	15/64 ①
1976 USA	9/32	5/16	3/64	9/32	15/64
Can.	9/32	5/16	3/64	9/32	9/32
1977	9/32	5/16	3/64	9/32	15/64
R-18 Canada					
All	9/32	5/16	3/64	5/32	5/16

① with automatic transmission: 25/64

7. Closely inspect the valves and seats for wear and damage, replacing as necessary.

8. After the carburetor is assembled, check the choke valve for freedom of operation.

Carburetor overhaul kits are recommended for each overhaul. These kits contain all gaskets and new parts to replace those that deteriorate most rapidly. Failure to replace all parts supplied with the kit (especially gaskets) can result in poor performance later.

Some carburetor manufactures supply overhaul kits of three basic types: minor repair; major repair; and gasket kits. Basically, they contain the following:

Minor Repair Kits:
- All gaskets
- Float needle valve
- Volume control screw
- All diaphragms
- Spring for the pump diaphragm

Major Repair Kits:
- All jets and gaskets
- All diaphragms
- Float needle valve
- Volume control screw
- Pump ball valve
- Main jet carrier
- Float

Gasket Kits:
- All gaskets

After cleaning and checking all components, reassemble the carburetor, using new parts and referring to the exploded view. When reassembling, make sure that all screws and jets are tight in their seats, but do not overtighten as the tips will be distorted. Tighten all screws gradually in rotation. Do not tighten needle valves into their seats; uneven jetting will result. Always use new gaskets. Be sure to adjust the float level when reassembling.

FUEL SYSTEM—FUEL INJECTED ENGINES

All fuel injected engines are equipped with the Bosch L-Jetronic direct injection system, except for the Alliance and Encore models built for sale outside of California. These 49 state models use a Throttle Body Injection system (TBI) regulated by an Electronic Control Unit (ECU).

Fuel Pump

All injected engines use an electric fuel pump. On the Gordini, 18i and Fuego, the pump is located on the right rear frame member. On the Alliance and Encore, the pump is located in the fuel tank.

REMOVAL AND INSTALLATION

All except Alliance, LeCar and Encore

1. Disconnect the battery ground.
2. Disconnect and plug the fuel lines at the pump.
3. Remove the pump.
4. Installation is the reverse of removal.

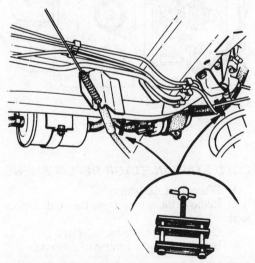

Typical fuel filter and pump location for all except Alliance. Clamp the hoses where shown for removal

Alliance, LeCar and Encore

1. Disconnect the battery. Drain the fuel tank.
2. Remove the fuel cap and remove the screws holding the filler neck pipe to the sheet metal.
3. Clean the areas surrounding the rubber connecting pipe between the filler neck and the tank. Unclamp and remove the pipe.

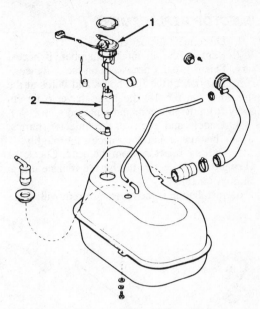

Alliance fuel pump removal and installation

4. Some tanks are secured directly to the floor by bolts; others are secured by straps. Place a floor jack under the tank to support it and remove the bolts and/or straps. Lower the tank slightly and disconnect the wiring and remaining hoses. Lower the tank completely and remove it from the car.

CAUTION: *When working around the gas tank, be extremely careful. Even if empty, the vapors in the tank are highly explosive. DO NOT SMOKE ANYWHERE NEAR THE FUEL TANK! DO NOT CAUSE ANY SPARKS WHEN WORKING ON THE FUEL TANK!*

5. The locking ring around the pump can be turned with a screwdriver. If it is stuck, tap it off using a hammer and brass drift. Do not use a hammer and steel or iron drift as sparks could occur. After removing the locking ring, check the rubber O-ring or gasket. Discard it if damaged or squashed.

6. Remove the fuel pump and sending unit.
7. Disconnect and tag the wires. One terminal is marked +, the other is marked −.
8. Unbolt the pump.
9. Installation is the reverse of removal. Use a new gasket or O-ring under the locking ring, if necessary.

Bosch L-Jetronic System

NOTE: *Never replace a component unless the ignition switch is off!*

FUEL FILTER REPLACEMENT

The filter is located on the right rear frame rail on all cars. It is an in-line type, replaced simply by unclamping and replacing.

INJECTOR REPLACEMENT

1. Disconnect the battery.
2. Remove the air intake chamber, if necessary. This is usually necessary on the Alliance.
3. Disconnect the fuel hoses and wires at the injectors. On the 18i the hoses have to be cut away from the injectors and replaced.
4. Unbolt and remove the injector ramps. Clean the area around the injector thoroughly.
5. Pull the injectors from the head. Check the O-ring on the injector. It's best to replace it if at all questionable.
6. Installation is the reverse of removal.

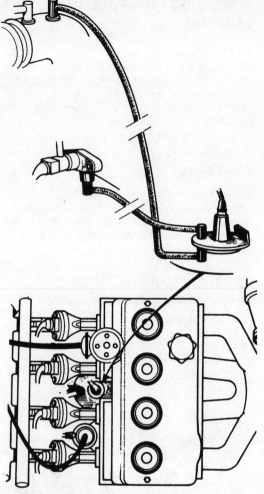

Auxiliary air regulator

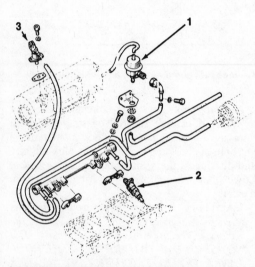

Injector replacement. 1 is the pressure regulator; 2 is the injector; 3 is the cold start injector

AUXILIARY AIR REGULATOR REPLACEMENT

1. Disconnect the battery.
2. Disconnect the wiring at the air regulator.
3. Disconnect the inlet and outlet air hoses.
4. Unbolt and remove the regulator. Replace the bolts immediately to prevent coolant leakage.
5. Installation is the reverse of removal.

COOLANT TEMPERATURE SENSOR REPLACEMENT

1. Disconnect the wiring at the sensor.
2. Unscrew the sensor and plug the hole to prevent coolant leakage.
3. Installation is the reverse of removal. Coat the threads with a light coat of sealer.

COLD START INJECTOR REPLACEMENT

1. Disconnect the battery.
2. Remove the wiring from the cold start injector.
3. Unbolt and remove the injector.
4. Installation is the reverse of removal.

OXYGEN SENSOR AND PERIODIC MAINTENANCE INDICATOR

The Alliance, 18i and Fuego have this equipment. An indicator, connected to the speedometer cable and attached to the air cleaner bracket, lights up between 29,686 and 30,106 miles. This system lights a warning lamp when the oxygen sensor needs replacement. The sensor is located in the exhaust pipe, just below the manifold. The sensor is replaced by simply unscrewing the old one and screwing in the new one. The threads of the new sensor must be coated with anti-seize

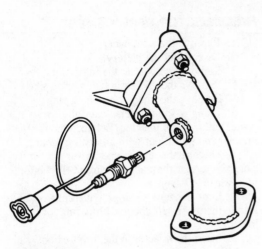

Oxygen sensor

compound prior to installation. To turn off the indicator lamp after the sensor has been replaced, remove the indicator switch cover. Turn the square head button one quarter turn counterclockwise, toward the stamped O. Replace the cover and wires.

LEAK-TESTING THE AIR INTAKE SYSTEM

1. Disconnect the hose that runs from the auxiliary air regulator to the right side of the cold start injector.
2. Plug the exhaust pipe outlet with a rag.
3. Apply 15 psi air pressure to the open fitting on the cold start injector. Open the throttle plate.
4. Apply a soapy water solution to all points on the system likely to leak, and watch for bubbles.

FUEL PRESSURE TEST

1. Disconnect the hose between the pressure regulator and the injector ramp. Tee-in a pressure gauge.
2. Disconnect the vacuum hose from the pressure regulator and connect it to a vacuum pump.

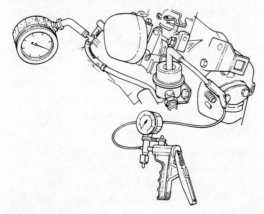

Fuel pressure test

3. Start the engine. A pressure of 33–39 psi should be noted.
4. Apply a vacuum of about 16 in.Hg. at the pressure regulator. The fuel pressure should drop by 7psi.

CHECKING THE FUEL PUMP OUTPUT

1. Disconnect the fuel return line at the pressure regulator and place the end in a 2 quart graduated beaker.
2. Turn on the ignition.
3. Open the sensor flap in the airflow meter through the input hole to start the pump, or, connect pins 36 and 39 in the airflow meter connector. Minumum pump output should be 1 liter (a little more than a quart) per minute.

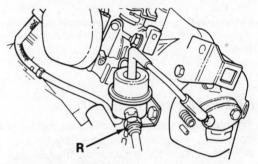

Fuel pump output test. R is the return hose

INJECTOR TEST

To test the injectors, simply unplug the electrical connector at each injector, in turn, with the engine running. A loss of engine rpm should be noted each time an injector is disconnected.

IDLE SPEED ADJUSTMENT

Gordini

1. Clamp the air injection hose below the relief valve.
2. Connect a tachometer to the engine.
3. Start the engine and allow it to reach normal operating temperature.
4. Turn the flowmeter bypass screw all the way shut.
5. Adjust the throttle plate housing screw to give an idle speed of 850 rpm (1975) or 900 rpm (1976 and later).
6. Turn the flowmeter bypass screw out to produce a 50 rpm drop in the idle speed.
7. Remove the clamp from the air injection tube idle speed should stabilize at 800–900 rpm for 1975 models, or 850–950 rpm for 1976 and later models. If not, turn the throttle plate housing screw until it is.

181, Fuego and Alliance

1. Start the engine and run it to normal operating temperature.

2. Connect a tachometer to diagnostic connectors D1-1 and D1-3.

3. Turn all accessories off.

4. Wait for the electric fan to cycle on, then off.

5. With the fan off, adjust the throttle bypass screw to establish the idle at 600–700 rpm with the transmission in neutral (MT) or Drive (AT).

Throttle Body Fuel Injection

All Alliance and Encore models, except those built for sale in California, use this system. The throttle body system injects fuel into a throttle body (visually resembling a carburetor). Fuel is metered through a throttle blade by an electronically controlled fuel injector. The Electronic Control Unit (ECU controls injectors through input sent by sensors that detect exhaust gas oxygen content, coolant temperature, manifold pressure, crankshaft position and throttle position.

FUEL FILTER REPLACEMENT

The filter is located in-line, under the right rear floorpan. It is replaced by unclamping from the rubber connectors and replacing the filter, clamps and rubber connecting hoses.

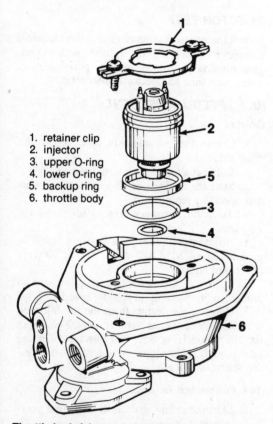

1. retainer clip
2. injector
3. upper O-ring
4. lower O-ring
5. backup ring
6. throttle body

Throttle body injector replacement

FUEL INJECTOR REPLACEMENT

1. Remove the air cleaner.

2. Disconnect the battery.

3. Remove the wire at the injector.

4. Remove the injector retaining ring screws.

5. Remove the injector retaining ring.

6. Using a small pliers, carefully grasp the center collar of the injector (Between the two terminals) and pull it out with a twisting motion.

7. Discard the upper and lower rubber O-rings. Note that the back-up ring at the bottom, fits over the O-ring.

8. Coat the new O-rings with light oil and install them. Install the back-up ring over the lower O-ring.

9. Insert the injector in the throttle body with a pushing twisting motion, making certain that it seats fully. Make sure that the wire terminals are parallel with the retaining ring screws.

10. Install the retaining ring and screws.

THROTTLE POSITION SENSOR REPLACEMENT

1. Disconnect the wire connector from the sensor.

2. Remove the Torx-head retaining screws.

3. Remove the throttle position sensor from the throttle shaft lever.

4. Installation is the reverse of removal.

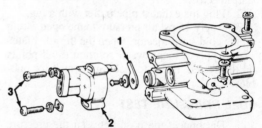

Throttle position sensor replacement. 1 is the throttle shaft lever; 2 is the TPS; 3 are the Torx-head screws

PRESSURE REGULATOR REPLACEMENT

1. Remove the three screws that hold the pressure regulator to the throttle body.

2. Note the location of the components for reassembly reference. Remove the pressure regulator.

3. Installation is the reverse of removal. Always use a new gasket. Check for leaks.

IDLE SPEED CONTROL SWITCH AND MOTOR

The switch and motor are integral.

1. Disconnect the throttle return spring.

2. Disconnect the wire from the motor.

3. Unbolt and remove the motor from the bracket.

4. Installation is the reverse of removal.

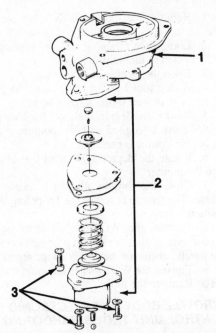

Pressure regulator replacement. 1 is the throttle body; 2 is the regulator and 3 are the screws

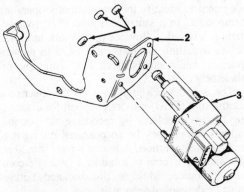

Idle speed control motor replacement. 1 are the nuts; 2 is the bracket; 3 is the ISC motor

THROTTLE BODY REPLACEMENT

1. Remove the throttle cable and return spring.
2. Disconnect the injector wiring.
3. Disconnect the wide open throttle switch wire.
4. Disconnect the Idle Speed Control motor wiring.
5. Disconnect the fuel pipe at the throttle body.
6. Disconnect the fuel return pipe at the throttle body.
7. Disconnect and tag the vacuum hoses at the throttle body.
8. Unbolt and remove the throttle body from the manifold.
9. Installation is the reverse of removal.

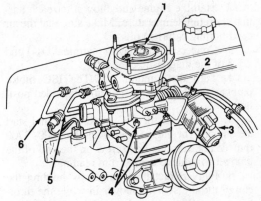

1. injector
2. Wide open throttle switch
3. ISC motor
4. nuts
5. fuel return pipe
6. fuel supply pipe

Throttle body replacement

FUEL BODY ASSEMBLY REPLACEMENT

1. Remove the throttle body.
2. Remove the three Torx screws retaining the fuel body from the throttle body.
3. Lift off the fuel body.
4. Installation is the reverse of removal.

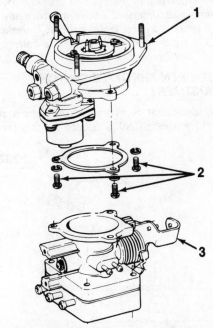

Fuel body replacement. 1 is the fuel body; 2 are the Torx-head screws; 3 is the throttle body

IDLE SPEED CONTROL MOTOR ADJUSTMENT

Adjustment is necessary only to establish the initial position of the plunger after the ISC motor has been replaced.

1. Remove the air cleaner.

2. Start the engine and allow it to reach normal operating temperature. Make sure that the air conditioning is turned off.

3. Connect a tachometer to terminal D1-1 and D1-3 of the diagnostic connector.

4. Turn the ignition off. The ISC motor plunger should move to the fully extended position.

5. Disconnect the ISC motor wire and start the engine. The engine idle should be 3300–3700 rpm. If not, turn the hex screw on the end of the plunger to achieve a 3500 rpm reading.

6. Fully retract the plunger by holding the closed throttle switch plunger in while the throttle is open. If the closed throttle switch plunger touches the throttle lever when the throttle is closed, check the throttle linkage for binding or damage and correct as required.

7. Connect the ISC motor wire.

8. Turn the ignition off for 10 seconds. The ISC plunger should fully extend.

9. Start the engine. The idle should be 3500 rpm for a short period, then gradually reduce to the specified idle speed.

10. Turn off the ignition and disconnect the tachometer.

NOTE: *Holding the closed throttle switch plunger as described above may activate an intermittant trouble code in the ECU memory. To erase the code, disconnect the battery for at least 10 seconds.*

WIDE OPEN THROTTLE SWITCH ADJUSTMENT

This adjustment is necessary only on a new switch. A special tool is needed for this procedure.

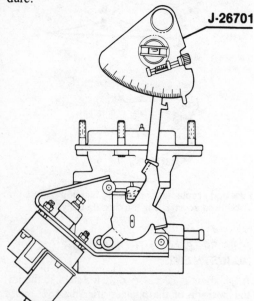

Wide open throttle switch adjustment

1. Remove the throttle body from the engine.

2. Loosen the retaining screws securing the WOT switch to the throttle body.

3. Open the throttle completely.

4. Attach tool J-26701, or its equivalent, to the top, flat surface of the throttle lever.

5. Rotate the degree scale on the tool until the 15° mark is aligned with the pointer. Adjust the bubble until it is centered.

6. Rotate the degree scale until 0 is aligned with the pointer.

7. Close the throttle slightly to center the bubble. The throttle is now at the 15° before WOT position.

8. Position the WOT switch lever on the throttle cam so that the switch plunger is closed, just barely, at the 15° before WOT position.

9. Tighten the WOT switch retaining screws.

10. Remove the tool.

THROTTLE BODY AND ELECTRONIC CONTROL UNIT TROUBLESHOOTING

In the following procedures, only complete (non-intermittent) failures are considered. In most instances, intermittent failures can be detected by using diagnostic codes as a guide along with your judgment to identify the intermittently operating component. In a situation where ECU replacement is advised, follow the precautions indicated before installing a replacement ECU to prevent external malfunctions from damaging the replacement unit.

The self-diagnostic failure of the electronic control unit (ECU) provides support for diagnosing system problems by recording six possible failures should they be encountered during normal engine operation. Additional tests should allow specific tracing of a failure to a single-component source. Multiple disassociated failures must be diagnosed separately.

It is possible that the test procedures can cause false interpretations of certain irregularities and consider them as ECU failures. It is therefore appropriate that all ECU's that are to be returned as failed units be screened by the dealer self-test equipment.

In the following procedures, no specialized service equipment is necessary. It is necessary however that you have available a volt-ohmmeter, a twelve volt test lamp and an assortment of jumper wires and probes. It is expected that you will successfully be able to test the system electrically following the procedures.

Trouble Code Test Lamp

Poor fuel economy, erratic idle speed, power surging and excessive engine stalling are typical symptoms that you will notice when the fuel system has a component failure. If the ECU is func-

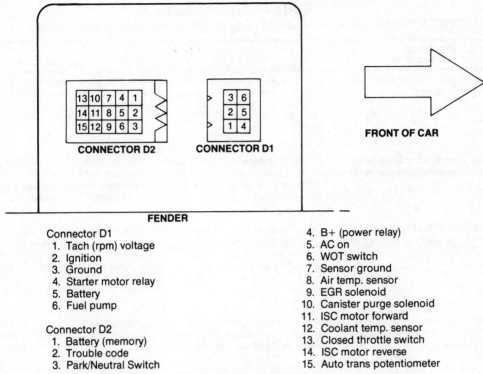

FRONT OF CAR

CONNECTOR D2   CONNECTOR D1

FENDER

Connector D1
1. Tach (rpm) voltage
2. Ignition
3. Ground
4. Starter motor relay
5. Battery
6. Fuel pump

Connector D2
1. Battery (memory)
2. Trouble code
3. Park/Neutral Switch

4. B+ (power relay)
5. AC on
6. WOT switch
7. Sensor ground
8. Air temp. sensor
9. EGR solenoid
10. Canister purge solenoid
11. ISC motor forward
12. Coolant temp. sensor
13. Closed throttle switch
14. ISC motor reverse
15. Auto trans potentiometer

TBI diagnostic connector

tional, service diagnostic codes can be obtained by connecting a No. 158 test bulb (or equivalent) to pins D2-2 and D2-4 of the large diagnostic connector.

With test bulb installed, push the WOT switch lever on the throttle body, and with the ISC motor plunger (closed throttle switch) also closed, have a helper turn on the ignition switch while observing the test bulb.

If the ECU is functioning normally, the test bulb should light for a moment then go out. This will always occur regardless of the failure condition, and serves as an indication that the ECU is functional.

After the initial illumination, the ECU will cycle through and flash a single digit code if any system malfunctions have been detected by the ECU during engine operation.

The ECU is capable of storing two different trouble codes in memory. The initial trouble detected will be flashed first and then, followed by a short pause, the second trouble detected will be flashed. There will somewhat longer pause between the second code and the repeat cycle of the first code again. This provides distinction between codes 3-6 and 6-3. While both codes indicate the same two failures, the first digit indicates the initial trouble while the last digit indicates the most recent failure.

The trouble codes are as listed:

1 Flash—Manifold Air/Fuel Temperature (MAT) Sensor Failure
2 Flashes—Coolant Temperature Sensor Failure
3 Flashes—Simultaneous WOT and Closed Throttle Switch Input
4 Flashes—Simultaneous Closed Throttle Switch and High Air Flow
5 Flashes—Simultaneous Closed Throttle Switch and High Air Flow
6 Flashes—Oxygen Sensor Failure

In a situation where further testing indicates no apparent cause for the failure indicated by the ECU self-diagnostic system, an intermittent failure should be suspected. This must be diagnosed the same way as a complete failure, except that marginal components must be more closely examined. If the trouble code is erased and quickly returns with no other symptoms, the ECU should be suspected. However, in the absence of other negative symptoms, replacement of the ECU is not advisable. In instances where no symptom problems are detected, the ECU can be suspected. Again, because of the cost involved and the relative reliability of the ECU, the ECU should never be replaced without testing with dealer test equipment. If the ECU is determined to be defective, it must be replaced. There are no dealer serviceable parts in the ECU. No repairs should be attempted.

Code Interpretation

The chart below contains a list of troubles, possible causes and suggested corrections

Trouble Code/Condition	Possible Cause	Correction
CODE 1 (poor low air temp. engine performance).	Manifold air/fuel temperature (MAT) sensor resistance is not less than 1000 ohms (HOT) or more than 100 kohms (VERY COLD).	Replace MAT sensor if not within specifications. Refer to MAT sensor test procedure.
CODE 2 (poor warm temp. engine performance-engine lacks power).	Coolant temperature sensor resistance is less than 300 ohms or more than 300 kohms (10 kohms at room temp.).	Replace coolant temperature sensor. Test MAT sensor. Refer to coolant temp. sensor test and MAT sensor test procedures.
CODE 3 (poor fuel economy, hard cold engine starting, stalling, and rough idle).	Defective wide open throttle (WOT) switch or closed (idle) throttle switch or both, and/or associated wire harness.	Test WOT switch operation and associated circuit. Refer to WOT switch test procedure. Test closed throttle switch operation and associated circuit. Refer to closed throttle switch test procedure.
CODE 4 (poor engine acceleration, sluggish performance, poor fuel economy).	Simultaneous closed throttle switch and manifold absolute pressure (MAP) sensor failure.	Test closed throttle switch and repair/replace as necessary. Refer to closed throttle switch test procedure. Test MAP sensor and associated hoses and wire harness. Repair or replace as necessary. Refer to MAP sensor test procedure.
CODE 5 (poor acceleration, sluggish performance).	Simultaneous WOT switch and manifold absolute pressure (MAP) sensor failure.	Test WOT switch and repair or replace as necessary. Refer to WOT switch test procedure. Test MAP sensor and associated hoses and wire harness. Repair or replace as necessary. Refer to MAP sensor test procedure.
CODE 6 (poor fuel economy, bad driveability, poor idle, black smoke from tailpipe).	Inoperative oxygen sensor.	Test oxygen sensor operation and replace if necessary. Test the fuel system for correct pressure. Test the EGR solenoid control. Test canister purge. Test secondary ignition circuit. Test PCV circuit. Refer to individual component test procedure.
No test bulb flash.	No battery voltage at ECU (J1-A with key on). No ground at ECU (J1-F).	Repair or replace wire harness, connectors or relays.
	Simultaneous WOT and CTS switch contact (Ground at both D2 Pin 6 and D2 Pin 13).	Repair or replace WOT switch, CTS switch, harness or connectors.
	No battery voltage at test bulb (D2 Pin 4).	Repair wire harness or connector.
	Defective test bulb.	Replace test bulb.
	Battery voltage low (less than 11.5V).	Charge or replace battery, repair vehicle wire harness.
		Check ECU with tester.

Trouble Code/Condition	Possible Cause	Correction
Fuel pump operates continuously.	Fuel pump relay shorted to ground.	Check J1-K for short to ground with key off and fuel pump relay disconnected.
		Repair wire harness short circuit.
		Disconnect ECU from wire harness.
		If pump stops, check ECU with tester.
		Disconnect fuel pump relay and check for short circuit.
		Replace relay.
		Test ECU with tester.
Fuel pump will not operate for one second with the ignition switch On.	Open circuit.	Connect jumper wire across fuel pump relay.
		If pump operates, check for battery voltage at relay. Check continuity between relay and Pin J1-K at the ECU. Repair wire harness as necessary. Replace fuel pump relay. Check ECU with tester.
		Check for continuity between fuel pump and relay contacts.
		Check pump ground circuit.
		Repair wire harness as necessary.
	Fuel pump ballast resistor defective.	Replace fuel pump ballast resistor.
		Note: The fuel pump ballast resistor can be bypassed using the pigtail wire connector located below the resistor.
Fuel pump will not operate when starter motor is engaged.	Fuel pump defective.	Replace fuel pump
	Open circuit.	Connect positive battery voltage to pump contact on starter motor relay.
		If pump operates, repair or replace starter motor relay.
		If pump does not operate, repair wire harness between starter motor relay and pump side of the ballast resistor.
		Check if pump runs one second with ignition switch On.

Code Interpretation (continued)

Trouble Code/Condition	Possible Cause	Correction
ISC (Idle Speed Control) motor does not extend on engine shutdown (symptom is slow, poor quality idle after cold start).	ECU, wire harness, or motor.	Connect test bulb between D2 Pin 14 and D2 Pin 11 with engine operating. Shut engine off. If bulb does not light momentarily on shutdown: test ECU with tester. If bulb lights at shutdown: check harness and connector at ISC motor. Repair as necessary. Check for motor jammed in the full retract position. Extend manually. Apply battery voltage to Pins C and D on ISC motor. **Note:** The motor must be disconnected from the wire harness for all tests. Replace ISC motor.
Idle speed erratic, low, or high consistently.	ISC motor inoperative,	Battery voltage supplied to motor, positive battery post connected to Pin D, and Pin C to ground should advance motor. Extending motor also verifies that motor is not jammed in retract position. All motor tests done with motor disconnected from harness. Replace ISC motor. Check closed throttle switch and associated wiring. Refer to test procedure.
	No ECU output.	Connect test lamp from J1-C to J1-D on ECU. Remove ISC motor from bracket and close CTS switch manually. With engine warmed-up at idle, manually open throttle to a speed well above normal idle. Light should flash. Close throttle so speed drops well below normal idle. Light should flash. **Note:** Improper handling of ISC motor outputs can result in system damage. Never connect to ground or battery. If light flashes on both over and under speed idle: Check wiring harness between ECU and ISC motor for open or short wire. Recheck ISC motor function. If light fails to flash on either over or underspeed: Check ECU with tester.

CHILTON'S
FUEL ECONOMY
& TUNE-UP TIPS

Tune-up • Spark Plug Diagnosis • Emission Controls

Fuel System • Cooling System • Tires and Wheels

General Maintenance

CHILTON'S FUEL ECONOMY & TUNE-UP TIPS

Fuel economy is important to everyone, no matter what kind of vehicle you drive. The maintenance-minded motorist can save both money and fuel using these tips and the periodic maintenance and tune-up procedures in this Repair and Tune-Up Guide.

There are more than 130,000,000 cars and trucks registered for private use in the United States. Each travels an average of 10-12,000 miles per year, and, and in total they consume close to 70 billion gallons of fuel each year. This represents nearly ⅔ of the oil imported by the United States each year. The Federal government's goal is to reduce consumption 10% by 1985. A variety of methods are either already in use or under serious consideration, and they all affect you driving and the cars you will drive. In addition to "down-sizing", the auto industry is using or investigating the use of electronic fuel delivery, electronic engine controls and alternative engines for use in smaller and lighter vehicles, among other alternatives to meet the federally mandated Corporate Average Fuel Economy (CAFE) of 27.5 mpg by 1985. The government, for its part, is considering rationing, mandatory driving curtailments and tax increases on motor vehicle fuel in an effort to reduce consumption. The government's goal of a 10% reduction could be realized — and further government regulation avoided — if every private vehicle could use just 1 less gallon of fuel per week.

How Much Can You Save?

Tests have proven that almost anyone can make at least a 10% reduction in fuel consumption through regular maintenance and tune-ups. When a major manufacturer of spark plugs sur-

TUNE-UP

1. Check the cylinder compression to be sure the engine will really benefit from a tune-up and that it is capable of producing good fuel economy. A tune-up will be wasted on an engine in poor mechanical condition.

2. Replace spark plugs regularly. New spark plugs alone can increase fuel economy 3%.

3. Be sure the spark plugs are the correct type (heat range) for your vehicle. See the Tune-Up Specifications.

Heat range refers to the spark plug's ability to conduct heat away from the firing end. It must conduct the heat away in an even pattern to avoid becoming a source of pre-ignition, yet it must also operate hot enough to burn off conductive deposits that could cause misfiring.

The heat range is usually indicated by a number on the spark plug, part of the manufacturer's designation for each individual spark plug. The numbers in bold-face indicate the heat range in each manufacturer's identification system.

Manufacturer	Typical Designation
AC	R **45** TS
Bosch (old)	WA **145** T30
Bosch (new)	HR **8** Y
Champion	RBL **15** Y
Fram/Autolite	**415**
Mopar	P-**62** PR
Motorcraft	BRF-**42**
NGK	BP **5** ES-15
Nippondenso	W **16** EP
Prestolite	14GR **5** 2A

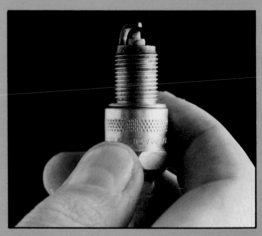

Periodically, check the spark plugs to be sure they are firing efficiently. They are excellent indicators of the internal condition of your engine.

On AC, Bosch (new), Champion, Fram/Autolite, Mopar, Motorcraft and Prestolite, a higher number indicates a hotter plug. On Bosch (old), NGK and Nippondenso, a higher number indicates a colder plug.

4. Make sure the spark plugs are properly gapped. See the Tune-Up Specifications in this book.

5. Be sure the spark plugs are firing efficiently. The illustrations on the next 2 pages show you how to "read" the firing end of the spark plug.

6. Check the ignition timing and set it to specifications. Tests show that almost all cars have incorrect ignition timing by more than 2°.

omy by tampering with emission controls is more likely to worsen fuel economy than improve it. Emission control changes on modern engines are not readily reversible.

16. Clean (or replace) the EGR valve and lines as recommended.

17. Be sure that all vacuum lines and hoses are reconnected properly after working under the hood. An unconnected or misrouted vacuum line can wreak havoc with engine performance.

23. Check for fuel leaks at the carburetor, fuel pump, fuel lines and fuel tank. Be sure all lines and connections are tight.

24. Periodically check the tightness of the carburetor and intake manifold attaching nuts and bolts. These are a common place for vacuum leaks to occur.

25. Clean the carburetor periodically and lubricate the linkage.

26. The condition of the tailpipe can be an excellent indicator of proper engine combustion. After a long drive at highway speeds, the inside of the tailpipe should be a light grey in color. Black or soot on the insides indicates an overly rich mixture.

27. Check the fuel pump pressure. The fuel pump may be supplying more fuel than the engine needs.

28. Use the proper grade of gasoline for your engine. Don't try to compensate for knocking or "pinging" by advancing the ignition timing. This practice will only increase plug temperature and the chances of detonation or pre-ignition with relatively little performance gain.

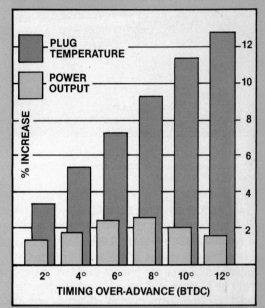

Increasing ignition timing past the specified setting results in a drastic increase in spark plug temperature with increased chance of detonation or preignition. Performance increase is considerably less. (Photo courtesy Champion Spark Plug Co.)

that form in the engine should be flushed out to allow the engine to operate at peak efficiency.

35. Clean the radiator of debris that can decrease cooling efficiency.

36. Install a flex-type or electric cooling fan, if you don't have a clutch type fan. Flex fans use curved plastic blades to push more air at low speeds when more cooling is needed; at high speeds the blades flatten out for less resistance. Electric fans only run when the engine temperature reaches a predetermined level.

37. Check the radiator cap for a worn or cracked gasket. If the cap does not seal properly, the cooling system will not function properly.

42. Be sure the front end is correctly aligned. A misaligned front end actually has wheels going in differed directions. The increased drag can reduce fuel economy by .3 mpg.

43. Correctly adjust the wheel bearings. Wheel bearings that are adjusted too tight increase rolling resistance.

Check tire pressures regularly with a reliable pocket type gauge. Be sure to check the pressure on a cold tire.

GENERAL MAINTENANCE

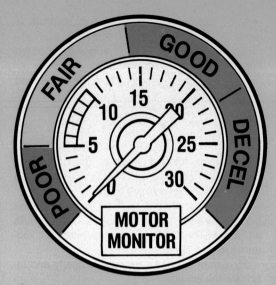

Check the fluid levels (particularly engine oil) on a regular basis. Be sure to check the oil for grit, water or other contamination.

A vacuum gauge is another excellent indicator of internal engine condition and can also be installed in the dash as a mileage indicator.

44. Periodically check the fluid levels in the engine, power steering pump, master cylinder, automatic transmission and drive axle.

45. Change the oil at the recommended interval and change the filter at every oil change. Dirty oil is thick and causes extra friction between moving parts, cutting efficiency and increasing wear. A worn engine requires more frequent tune-ups and gets progressively worse fuel economy. In general, use the lightest viscosity oil for the driving conditions you will encounter.

46. Use the recommended viscosity fluids in the transmission and axle.

47. Be sure the battery is fully charged for fast starts. A slow starting engine wastes fuel.

48. Be sure battery terminals are clean and tight.

49. Check the battery electrolyte level and add distilled water if necessary.

50. Check the exhaust system for crushed pipes, blockages and leaks.

51. Adjust the brakes. Dragging brakes or brakes that are not releasing create increased drag on the engine.

52. Install a vacuum gauge or miles-per-gallon gauge. These gauges visually indicate engine vacuum in the intake manifold. High vacuum = good mileage and low vacuum = poorer mileage. The gauge can also be an excellent indicator of internal engine conditions.

53. Be sure the clutch is properly adjusted. A slipping clutch wastes fuel.

54. Check and periodically lubricate the heat control valve in the exhaust manifold. A sticking or inoperative valve prevents engine warm-up and wastes gas.

55. Keep accurate records to check fuel economy over a period of time. A sudden drop in fuel economy may signal a need for tune-up or other maintenance.

Trouble Code/Condition	Possible Cause	Correction
ECU does not turn off after engine shut down (Symptom: battery loses charge with key off.)	Throttle position incorrect.	Check to ensure that throttle is resting on switch at normal idle. Connect voltmeter form D2 Pin 13 to D1 Pin 3. Should read ground at a normal idle.
		Check for vacuum leaks. Check closed throttle switch using test procedure.
	MAP sensor voltage supply. (ECU Pin J2-2) voltage should go from 5V to zero within 30 seconds after key off.	Check coolant temperature sensor. Refer to test procedure.
		Check starter motor relay for short circuit. With key off, check relay for battery voltage.
		Replace relay.
		Check ECU with tester.
		Check ignition switch and harness for short to battery voltage. Repair or replace as necessary.
EGR solenoid control is erratic. (Symptoms: poor idle quality, bad driveability, inactive oxygen sensor.)	Defective solenoid.	Check solenoid valve. Connect valve (out of harness) to 12V and determine if it opens and closes.
		Check for 12V to solenoid valve coil.
		Replace valve.
		Repair wiring harness.
		Check ECU with tester.
Canister purge is erratic (Symptoms: poor idle quality, driveability complaint, inactive oxygen sensor.)	Defective solenoid.	Follow procedure above (EGR) for canister purge valve.
Fuel pressure is low at test point on throttle body (14–15 psi at idle). (Symptoms: poor driveability, inactive oxygen sensor, hard cold starts.)	Fuel pump malfunction.	Check pump for proper voltage. (Nominally 7.5V)
		Check fuel filter. Replace filter.
		Replace fuel pump ballast resistor. Repair wiring harness.
		Check fuel pressure regulator for proper function. With engine idling, gently pinch off rubber fuel return line to fuel tank. Pressure should rise dramatically as line is restricted. Check fuel pressure out of pump. With gauge directly on fuel inlet line, (line dead headed at gauge), several cycles of key on should produce pressure well over 20 psi. Warning: This should only be done for a short time, as the fuel system is not rated for high pressures.
		Install fuel pressure regulator kit. Replace throttle body. Replace fuel pump.

Code Interpretation (continued)

Trouble Code/Condition	Possible Cause	Correction
Fuel pressure high at test point on throttle body (over 14–15 psi at idle). (Symptoms: poor driveability, hard starts, hot black smoke, inactive oxygen sensor.)	Fuel restriction.	Check fuel pressure with oversize temporary fuel return line. Line should replace the existing return line. It should be securely fastened at the throttle body and discharge gasoline into an approved closed container.
		If pressure drops, replace fuel return line. Inspect fuel tank fittings and replace if restricted. If pressure does not drop, install fuel pressure regulator kit.
Engine will not start.	Defective WOT switch.	Refer to WOT switch test procedure.
	Low battery.	Replace or charge battery.
	Fuel supply too low.	Replenish as necessary.
	Low fuel pressure.	Refer to fuel pressure test. Correct as necessary. Replace fuel filter.
	Fuel pump inoperative.	Repair or replace as necessary.
	Defective secondary ignition circuit.	Lay spark plug (with ignition wire) on engine block. Crank engine and observe spark.
		Repair or replace ignition module or wiring.
	Primary ignition input to ECU defective.	Connect voltmeter between D1 Pin 1 and ground. With key on (engine stopped) voltage should be close to battery voltage.
		Check harness and connectors between ECU and ignition module. Service ignition module as necessary.
	No battery voltage applied to injector. (12V from one pin to chassis ground.)	Check B+ relay. Check harness and connectors. Repair or replace as necessary.
	Injector resistance too high. (ohmmeter should read less than 10 ohms).	Replace injector.
	ECU is not switching injector.	Remove injector connector. Connect test lamp across connector. Crank engine. Lamp should pulse dimly.
		Check ECU with tester.
	Leaking injector.	Check to determine if injector is discharging fuel when engine is cranked.
		Install O-ring kit if leaking fuel. Replace injector if it either discharges no fuel with engine cranking or drips fuel with engine stopped.

Trouble Code/Condition	Possible Cause	Correction
Engine will not start.	No start signal voltage.	Check start signal (voltmeter from D1 Pin 4 to ground should show battery voltage in crank).
		Service starter relay or wire harness.
	ISC motor plunger is not extended.	Refer to ISC motor test procedure.
	Coolant temperature sensor inoperative.	Refer to coolant temperature sensor test procedure.
		Perform self-diagnostic test.
		Check to ensure that spark plugs are not fouled or wet.
		Replace as necessary.
Engine starts but will not idle.	Fuel pump inoperative.	Check fuel pump.
	Ignition system malfunction.	Check ignition system. Repair as necessary.
		Check start signal after crank. Voltmeter from D1 Pin 4 to D1 Pin 3 should indicate zero volts.
		Repair wire harness as necessary.
		Check MAP sensor. Repair as necessary.
		Test ECU with tester.
Driveability or fuel economy complaint.	High fuel pressure.	Perform self-diagnostic test. Refer to trouble codes.
		Check fuel pressure.
		Test ECU on tester.
		Replace ECU if necessary.
		Check to determine if the oxygen sensor is functioning.
		Replace if necessary.
	Injector defective.	Replace injector.
	WOT switch malfunction.	Check WOT switch.
		Adjust, repair or replace switch to ensure that WOT voltage (D2 Pin 6) is low during actual wide open throttle condition.
	Air filter restricted.	Check air filter.
		Replace as necessary

Code Interpretation (continued)

Trouble Code/Condition	Possible Cause	Correction
Driveability or fuel economy complaint.	EGR valve malfunction.	Check EGR valve and hoses. Repair or replace.
	Canister purge malfunction.	Check canister purge system. Repair.

It is important to note that the trouble memory is erased if the ECU power is interrupted by any one of the following:
disconnecting the wire harness from the ECU,
disconnecting either battery cable terminal,
and allowing the engine to remain unstarted in excess of five days.

It is equally important to erase the trouble memory when a defective component is replaced. This can be done by any one of the actions listed above.

Chassis Electrical

HEATER

Blower Motor

REMOVAL AND INSTALLATION

LeCar

1. Disconnect the battery.
2. Remove the heater case door control cable.
3. Disconnect the wiring from the fan motor.
4. Unclip the bleed screw hose and the accelerator cable at the case.
5. Unbolt and remove the air inlet chamber.
6. Remove the clips and separate the air duct case halves.
7. Unclip and remove the heater case door support panel.
8. Remove the three motor mount screws on the air inlet fan housing top case. Save the rubber antivibration washers.
9. Remove the locking sleeve and take out the blower fan.
10. Installation is the reverse of removal. Make sure that the case door control cable is properly adjusted.

Alliance

The blower is removed along with the heater core.

1. Remove the instrument panel.
2. Disconnect the wires and cables at the case.
3. Drain the cooling system. Disconnect the heater hoses at the core tubes.
4. Remove the 4 screws retaining the heater assembly and lift it out of the car.
5. Bend out the 4 tabs holding the core and remove the core from the case.
6. Remove the retaining clips from the motor and the case halve clips and open the case. Lift out the blower motor.
7. Installation is the reverse of removal.

LeCar blower motor

R-12

1. Carefully pull back the glove compartment cardboard tray.
2. Disconnect the blower motor wires.
3. Remove the motor housing retaining screws and remove the motor housing.
4. Remove the fan blade locknut, the fan and remove the motor-to-housing screws.
5. Installation is the reverse of removal.

R-15, R-17 and Gordini

1. Remove the heater assembly.
2. Unclip and remove the air entry shroud.
3. Remove the fan and motor from the case.
4. Installation is the reverse of removal.

R-18 and Fuego

The blower is removed along with the heater core.

1. Disconnect the battery.

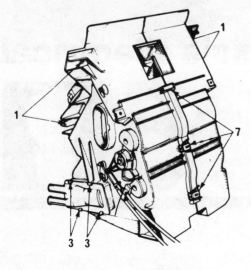

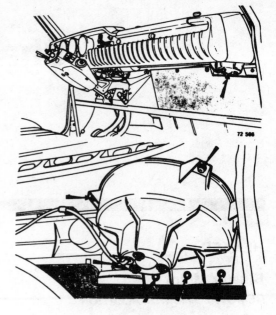

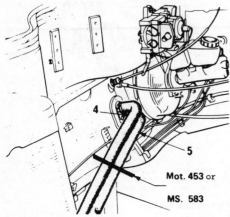

Mot. 453 or

MS. 583

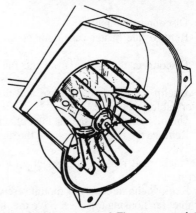

R-12 heater blower removal. The arrows point to the attaching screws

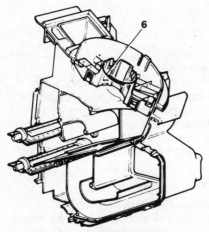

1. attaching screws
4. & 5 hoses
6. & 7 clips

Alliance blower motor and heater core removal.

2. Drain the cooling system.

3. Disconnect the heater hoses at the core tubes.

4. Disconnect the fan motor wiring and the windshield wiper motor wiring junction block.

5. Disconnect the air door cable.

6. Remove the three screws and two nuts securing the heater case and lift out the case.

7. Remove the heater case seal.

8. Unclip the case halves, separate the halves and lift out the blower motor.

9. Installation is the reverse of removal. Use RTV sealer on the housing seal and make sure that the blowers turn freely with equal play at each end.

Heater Core

REMOVAL AND INSTALLATION

Alliance, R-18 and Fuego

See the blower motor removal and installation procedure.

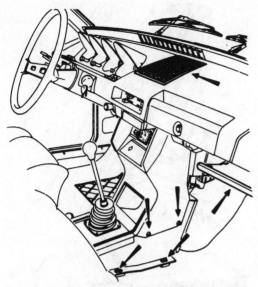

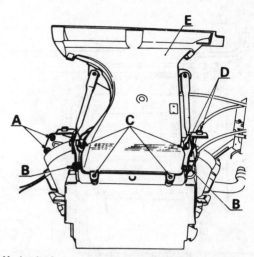

Heater removal from the passenger compartment side on R-15, 17 and Gordini

Underdash removal points for the R-15, 17 and Gordini heater. A are the scuttle nuts, B are the tie bar bolts, C are the top attaching bolts, D are the underdash attaching bolts, E is the top of the case

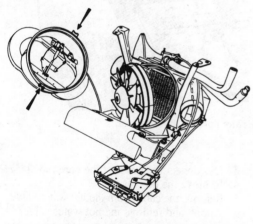

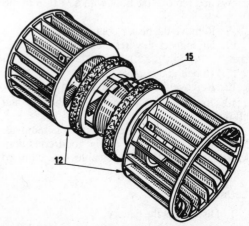

Heater case removed from the R-18 or Fuego. 11 are the clips; 14 is the seal

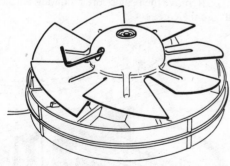

Removing the fan and motor from the R-15, 17 or Gordini

R-12

1. Remove the cowl vent grille panel.
2. Drain the cooling system.
3. Disconnect the heater hoses at the core tubes.

Heater blower from the R-18 or Fuego. 12 are the fans; 15 is the motor

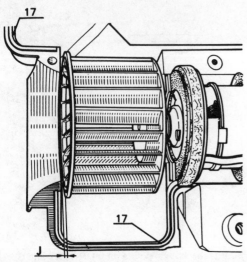

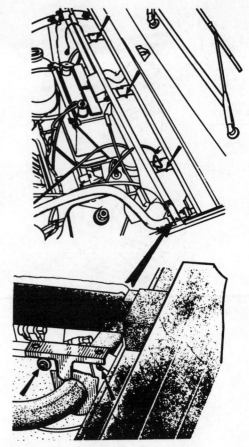

Installing the blower motor on the R-18 or Fuego. Smear the seal surface, 17, with RTV sealant and make sure that the blower endplay, J, is the same on both sides

4. Cut the core hook retaining wires and lift up on the hooks.

5. Unbolt the heater control valve from under the dashboard.

6. Pull the core out of the vent grille opening.

7. Installation is the reverse of removal.

Heater core on the R-12

R-15, R-17, and Gordini

1. Disconnect the battery.
2. Drain the cooling system.
3. Remove the radio speaker.
4. Remove the glove compartment.
5. Remove the radio.
6. Disconnect the wiper switch wires.
7. Remove the center console retaining bolts.
8. Remove the shift lever boot retaining screws and remove the boot with a ¼ turn to the left.
9. Remove the heater control cables.
10. Disconnect all wires attached to the heater case.
11. Unbolt and remove the case.
12. Remove the heater valve from the case.
13. Remove the core cover from the case and lift out the core.
14. Installation is the reverse of removal. Make sure that all seals are in good condition. Make sure that the control cables are adjusted properly.

LeCar

1. Disconnect the battery.
2. Drain the cooling system.

3. Disconnect the hoses at the core tube.s
4. Remove the blower fan.
5. Remove the cable from the hot water valve.
6. Unbolt and remove the hot water valve.
7. Remove the heater core mounting bolts and lift out the core.

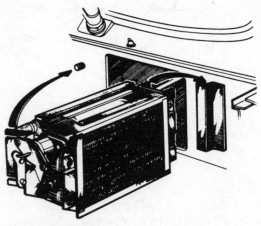

Heater core, LeCar

RADIO

Radios in Renault cars are dealer-installed items and vary according to availability. The removal and installation procedures, therefore, vary.

WINDSHIELD WIPERS

Motor and Linkage
REMOVAL AND INSTALLATION

LeCar

FRONT WIPER MOTOR

1. Remove the driving arm nut from the motor shaft.
2. Remove the motor mounting screws and lift out the motor. Disconnect the wiring connector.
3. Installation is the reverse of removal.

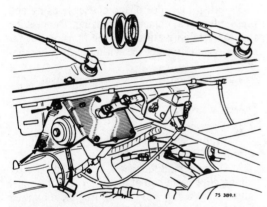

Wiper motor removal from LeCar

REAR WIPER MOTOR

1. Disconnect the wiring from the motor.
2. Remove the wiper arm.
3. Remove the outside nut and the inside bolts which hold the motor in place.
4. Installation is the reverse of removal.

Alliance

1. Disconnect the battery.
2. Remove the wiper arms.
3. Remove the wiper driveshaft nuts on the cowl.
4. Remove the linkage junction block.
5. On vehicles equipped with air conditioning, unbolt the evaporator core and move it out of the way, without disconnecting any refrigerant lines.
6. Remove the windshield wiper assembly.
7. Remove the linkage crank nut.

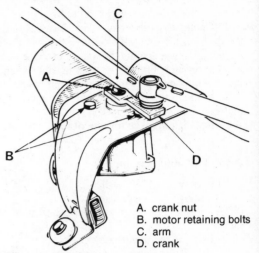

A. crank nut
B. motor retaining bolts
C. arm
D. crank

Alliance and Encore wiper linkage

8. Unbolt and remove the motor.
9. Installation is the reverse of removal.

R-12

1. Remove the wiper arms.
2. Remove the wiper arm driveshaft nuts on the cowl.

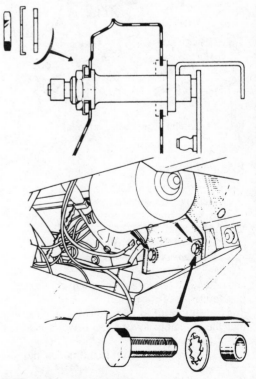

R-12 wiper motor removal

3. Remove the heater control unit.

4. Unclip the rubber air flap, located under the dash on the firewall. Remove the two plate retaining screws, and pull the plate out to the right of the steering column. The steering linkage and motor will come out with the retaining plate.

5. Remove the crank arm nut and unbolt the motor.

6. Installation is the reverse of removal.

R-15, R-17, and Gordini

1. Remove the cowl grille.

2. Remove the wiper arms.

3. Remove the wiper arm driveshaft nuts on the cowl.

4. Remove the junction block.

5. Unbolt the wiper assembly retaining plate and lift out the assembly.

6. Remove the crank arm nut and unbolt the motor.

7. Installation is the reverse of removal.

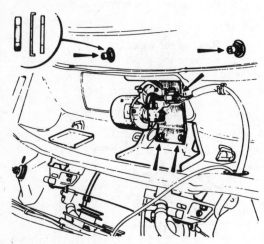

R-15, 17, Gordini wiper motor removal

R-18 and Fuego

1. Remove the wiper arms.

2. Remove the wiper arm driveshaft nuts on the cowl.

3. Remove the electrical junction block.

4. Disconnect the ground wire at the wiper mechanism plate.

5. Remove the wiper mechanism mounting plate bolt.

6. Push inward to free the two spindles, then pull the assembly toward the driver's side and out of the car.

7. Remove the crank nut and unbolt the motor.

8. Installation is the reverse of removal.

INSTRUMENT CLUSTER

REMOVAL AND INSTALLATION

LeCar

1. Disconnect the battery.

2. Unclip the speedometer cable in the engine compartment.

3. Unclip and remove the instrument cluster trim panel.

4. The cluster is secured by one clip on each side. Press inward on the side clips until they clear the support plate, then pull the cluster out.

5. Unscrew the speedometer cable.

6. For access to any gauge, remove the cluster cover glass.

7. Installation is the reverse of removal.

Alliance

1. Disconnect the battery.

2. Remove the cluster retaining bolts (2) at the bottom of the cluster housing.

3. Grasp the sides of the cluster housing and press inwards to detach the housing. Depress the two top retaining clips, pull the housing out far enough to disconnect the wiring and speedometer cable.

4. Installation is the reverse of removal.

R-12

1. Disconnect the battery.

2. From behind the cluster, disconnect the wiring and speedometer cable.

3. From behind the panel, depress the two retaining clips at the top of the panel. Tilt the panel outward at the top and lift it to free the mounting pegs at the bottom.

4. Installation is the reverse of removal. Make certain that the lower mounting pegs are engaged in their slots.

R-15, R-17 and Gordini

1. Disconnect the battery.

2. Unscrew the two knurled nuts on the fusebox bracket and tilt it.

3. Remove the four cluster retaining screws at the corners.

NOTE: *the speaker grille will have to be removed to get at the right side screws.*

4. Carefully pry up at the bottom of the cluster to free the bottom center retaining clip.

5. Pull down and out on the cluster to free the top retaining clips.

NOTE: *Take great care to avoid damage to the printed circuit board on the back of the cluster.*

6. Disconnect the wiring and speedometer cable.

7. Installation is the reverse of removal.

R-18 and Fuego
CUSTOM MODELS

1. Disconnect the battery.
2. Remove the upper and lower steering column covers.
3. Remove the two screws securing the instrument panel to the dash. The screws are at the bottom.
4. Reach behind the panel and disconnect the wiring and speedometer cable.
5. Tilt the panel forward, and using a small screwdriver, pry out on the top of the panel, while pushing the bottom in by hand.
6. Installation is the reverse of removal. Make sure that the panel hinges on the two pins when installing.

DELUXE MODELS

1. Disconnect the battery.
2. On either side of the panel there are three button or switch positions. On all models the bottom ones are blank. These are covers over the cluster retaining screws. Pry these covers off and remove the screws. Lift off the cluster bezel.
3. Disconnect the switches and remove the switch panel.
4. Squeeze the instrument panel retaining clips and pull the panel out far enough to disconnect the speedometer and wiring. Lift the panel out of the car.
5. Installation is the reverse of removal.

Speedometer Cable
REPLACEMENT

The cable is replaced by disconnecting the cable at both the speedometer and the transmission. Unless the speedometer drive gear is being replaced, retain it for use on the new cable. If the speedometer drive gear is being replaced, make sure that it has the same number of teeth as the original.

HEADLIGHTS

REMOVAL AND INSTALLATION

On each model, a trim plate or trim ring must be removed first. On R-15, 17, 12 and Gordini, the headlights are held in place by clips and hooks; all other models have the lights held by screws and a retaining ring.

CIRCUIT PROTECTION

Fuses

On all models, except the Alliance, the fuse panel is located on the left side, under the dash, next to the steering column. On the Alliance, the fuse panel is located under the glove compartment. To remove the fuse panel, on all except Alliance, remove the attaching screws and/or clips. To remove the Alliance fuse panel, first depress the clips and swing the fuse panel cover out of the way, then unscrew the fuse panel.

WIRING DIAGRAMS

Wiring diagrams have been left out of this book. The chief reason is the size and complexity of the wiring circuits on new cars, with their long lists of optional equipment, makes the reproduction of these circuits in a book of this size, impractical.

Clutch and Transaxle

![6]

MANUAL TRANSAXLE

REMOVAL AND INSTALLATION

LeCar

1. Disconnect the battery leads and the transaxle ground wire.
2. Disconnect the speedometer cable.
3. Remove the water pump drive belt.
4. Remove the camshaft pulley, the air pump filter, the air pump and the mounting bracket.
5. Remove the two upper bolts on the starter.

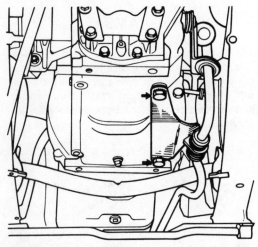

Support plate mounting bolts on LeCar transmission

6. Remove the clutch housing bolts which are on the engine.
7. Remove the wheels and the brake calipers without disconnecting the brake hoses.
8. Disconnect the steering arms at the steering rack end.
9. Disconnect the upper ball joints from the upper suspension.

10. Remove the drive shafts from the side gears by tilting the stub axle carriers downward.
CAUTION: *Do not damage the oil seal lips on the differential adjusting nuts while removing the drive shafts.*
11. Remove the two mounting bolts from the support on the transaxle.

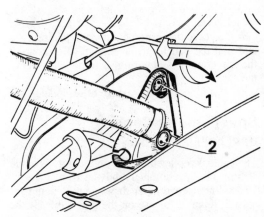

Remove the tubular crossmember in the direction of the arrow

12. Disconnect the clutch cable at the lever and push the sleeve retainer to free it from the supporting tab.
13. Remove the top bolt and then the tubular crossmember, in the direction of the arrow.
14. Replace the top bolt in the frame hole and then remove the bottom bolts from the crossmember.
15. Tap the crossmember towards the rear of the vehicle and remove it.
16. Replace the bottom bolt in the frame hole.
17. Support the front end of the transaxle with a jack and remove the front mounting pad with its bracket.
18. Remove the starter bottom bolt and then the starter.

19. Remove the side reinforcement mounting bolts and the clutch cover.

20. Special holding tools should be used to hold the engine while the transaxle is removed from the vehicle body. Remove the transaxle assembly.

21. The installation of the transaxle is the reverse of the removal procedure. The clutch free-play at the end of the clutch lever should be adjusted to within ⅛ to ⁵/₃₂ inch.

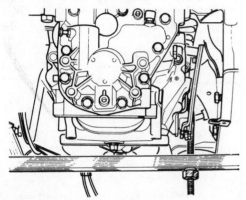

Special tool used to hold the engine while the transaxle is out

Alliance and Encore

NOTE: *This procedure covers both the JB-O 4-speed and the JB-1 5-speed transmissions.*

1. Place the vehicle on jack stands.

2. Remove the filler and drain plugs and drain the transaxle.

3. Remove the front wheels and disconnect the drive shafts.

4. Disconnect the gearshift lever linkage and the engine-transaxle support rod.

5. Remove the clutch shield and all mounting pad nuts.

6. Remove the air filter.

7. Disconnect the backup lamp switch wire connector and remove the TDC sensor.

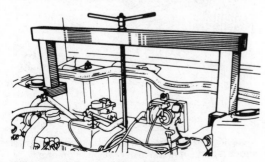

Alliance and Encore lifting device

8. Disconnect the clutch cable, speedometer cable and ground wire.

9. Remove the radiator and lay it on the engine without disconnecting the hoses.

10. Using a suitable lifting device, raise the engine slightly to free the rear mounts.

11. Attach a second lifting device to the clutch cable bracket and bolt on the transaxle.

12. Remove the starter motor mounting bolts.

13. Remove the transaxle retaining bolts, separate the transaxle from the engine and lift it free of the chassis.
NOTE: *For the JB 1 transaxle, slide the 5th speed casing between the sidemembers.*

14. Raise the engine and slide the transaxle into the clutch splines.

15. Install the transaxle retaining nuts and remove the lifting device from the transaxle.

16. Install the starter motor mounting bolts.

17. Lower the engine onto the mounting pads, install the nuts and tighten them to 40–50 ft. lb.

18. Install the radiator and the clutch shield.

19. Connect the clutch cable, the speedometer cable and the ground wire. Secure the speedometer cable with the clip.

20. Connect the backup lamp wire connector switch and install the TDC sensor.

21. Install the air filter.

22. Connect the gearshift lever linkage and the engine-transaxle support rod.

23. Connect the drive shafts.

24. Install the front wheels and tighten the nuts to the specified torque.

25. Refill the transaxle and install the filler plug.
NOTE: *Remove the breather plug before attempting to refill the transaxle to allow for air displacement.*

R-12, R-15, R-17, Gordini

Some special tools are required for this procedure.

1. Disconnect and remove the battery.

2. Remove the air cleaner.

3. Remove the starter.

4. Disconnect the clutch cable and remove its bracket.

5. On the R-12 and Canadian 1975 Gordini, remove the camshaft and water pump pulleys.

6. On the R-12 and Canadian 1975 Gordini, loosen the alternator, tilt it all the way in toward the engine and tighten it there.

7. Place tools T.Av.509 between the shock absorber lower mounts and the lower control arm hinge pins.

8. Raise and support the front of the car on jackstands.

9. Drain the transmission.

10. Using a drift, drive out the driveshaft roll

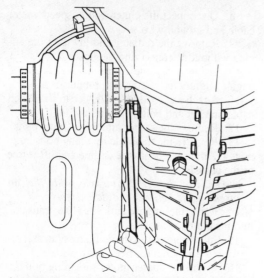

Installing tool T.Av509 on the R-12, 15, 17, Gordini

pins and disconnect the driveshafts from the transaxle.

11. Using a ball joint separator, disconnect the steering arm joint and the upper control arm ball joints.

12. Tilt the stub axle carrier, which will free the driveshafts from the transaxle.

13. Disconnect the speedometer cable, the shift linkage and the backup light switch control wires from the transaxle case.

14. Remove the engine crossmember.

15. Remove the exhaust pipe.

16. Place a jack under the transmission tailshaft and take up the weight of the case. Remove the transmission crossmember.

17. Lower the jack to gain access to the transmission-to-engine bolts. Remove the clutch housing cover and unbolt the transmission from the engine.

18. Carefully back the transaxle away from the engine and out from under the car.

19. Installation is the reverse of removal. Lightly grease the clutch plate splines and the driveshaft splines with chassis lube. Connect the linkage with the transaxle in fourth gear. Adjust the clutch to give a free play of $^7/_{64}-^9/_{64}$ inch at the release lever.

R-18, Fuego and Sport Wagon

NOTE: *It is not necessary to drain the lubrication from the transmission since the side gears are sealed.*

1. Disconnect the battery, the positive cable to the starter and the power lead to the solenoid.

2. Remove the three starter attaching bolts from the bell housing.

3. Remove the rear attaching bolt of the starter.

4. Loosen the bolt of the engine mount on the starter side and swing the rear fixing bracket into a horizontal position.

5. Pull the starter back the length of its nose. On the 352 model transmissions, turn the starter 90 degrees and remove the starter (both transmission models).

6. Disconnect the clutch cable at the fork lever.

7. Place the special transmission removal tool support plates between the lower shock absorber fixing pins and the lower suspension arm shafts, if using the tool.

8. Loosen the front wheel bolts.

9. Raise the vehicle on a hoist or by other means.

10. Remove the front wheels.

11. Remove the brake calipers from both front wheel assemblies.

12. Punch out the roll pins on the sides of the gear/axle shafts.

13. Remove the steering tie rod ball joint nut and loosen the tie rod ball joint.

14. Loosen the upper suspension ball joint stud after removing the retaining nut.

15. Tilt the stub axle carrier, disengaging the drive axle shaft from the side gear shaft. Remove the opposite axle shaft in the same manner.

16. Disconnect the speedometer cable and the wiring to the back-up lights and emission control switches.

17. Disconnect the gear shift linkage.

CAUTION: *Do not remove the gear shift linkage ball joints from their housings.*

18. Remove the clutch protective shield.

19. If using the transmission remover jack assembly, place it under the transmission and lift the transmission slightly. Remove the left and right transmission mounts.

20. Remove the transmission attaching bolts

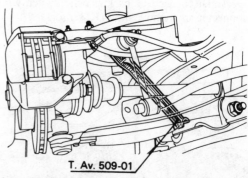

T. Av. 509-01

Installing the support arm tools between the lower shock mounts and the lower suspension arms

and pull the assembly to the rear, being careful not to damage the pressure plate. Lower the transmission to the floor.

To install:

1. Lightly lubricate the splines of the clutch shaft and raise the transmission in line with the engine/flywheel assembly.

2. Push the transmission assembly forward into the position with the engine, while engaging the clutch shaft into the clutch plate.

3. Install the left and right transmission supports and remove the installing jack.

4. Install the clutch protective cover and be sure the top dead center sensor is positioned 1.0 mm (0.039 inch) from the engine flywheel.

5. Reconnect the speedometer cable, the back-up light wires, the emission control switch wires and the gear shift linkage.

6. Lightly lubricate the splines of the differential side gears and position the drive axle shaft next to the side gear (either side).

7. Tilt the stub axle while engaging the drive axle shaft in the side gear. Line the holes in the drive shaft and stub axle and install the roll pin. Do the same procedure on the opposite side. Be sure the roll pin is installed.

8. Engage the stub axle carrier in the upper suspension ball joint and lock the cone. Tighten the nut to 48 ft. lb.

9. Engage the tie rod ball joints. Tighten the nuts to 48 ft. lbs.

10. Install the front calipers on the front suspension.

11. Install the front wheels and lower the vehicle. Tighten the wheel lugs.

12. Connect the clutch cable to the fork.

13. Place the starter in its housing, pull the support bracket into position and tighten the bracket bolt.

14. Tighten the starter attaching bolts.

15. Check the gear shift lever adjustment and the clutch cable adjustment.

NOTE: *The release bearing must be in constant contact with the pressure plate diaphragm.*

16. Complete the assembly of disconnected components.

17. Connect the battery and road test the vehicle.

SHIFT LINKAGE ADJUSTMENT

LeCar, R-12, R-15, R-17, Gordini

1. Remove the shift lever boot.

2. Place the transaxle in 3rd gear.

3. Press the lever over towards the 1st-2nd gear position.

4. Using the slots cut in the stop plate, visually check the clearance between the end of the lever and the stop plate. Clearance should be ⅛ inch for the LeCar, $^{13}/_{64}$–¼ inch for the R-12, 15, 17 and Gordini. Adjustment is made by placing washers between the stop plate and floor panel.

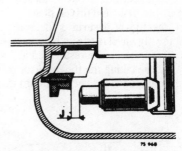

Lever-to-stop plate clearance adjustment. J is the gap to be measured on the LeCar, R-12, 15, 17 and Gordini

R-18, Fuego and Sport Wagon

1. Place the transaxle in neutral.

2. Unlock the shift linkage yoke nut so that the linkage can turn freely.

3. Place the case shift lever against the 3–4 shift point.

4. Place a shim (2mm for the 4-speed and 10mm for the 5-speed) between the endpiece of the linkage and the surface of the case. Tighten the yoke nut.

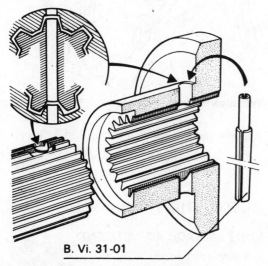

B. Vi. 31-01

Aligning the stub axle shaft roll pins

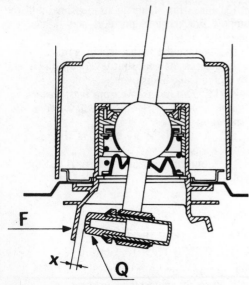

Shift linkage adjustment point on the R-18 and Fuego. The gap should be measured between the link, F, and the end piece, Q

CLUTCH

REMOVAL AND INSTALLATION

NOTE: *A clutch aligning tool is needed for this job.*

1. Remove the transaxle.

2. Remove the pressure plate bolts evenly and in a cross-wise pattern to avoid distortion. Remove the pressure plate and driven plate.

3. Check the flywheel surface for cracks or scoring. If the flywheel surface is excessively cracked or scored, it must be resurfaced at a machine shop. Before taking the flywheel for resurfacing, remove the dowels. The minimum thick-

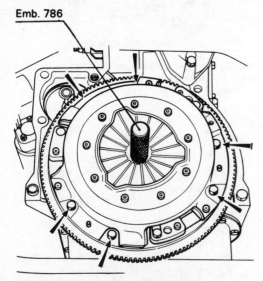

Clutch positioning with an aligning tool

ness for the flywheel for LeCar and Alliance, 1.531 inch for R-15, 17, Gordini, and R-12 is .894 inch. If resurfacing would take it below this figure, it must be replaced. When you get the resurfaced flywheel back, install the dowels making sure that they protrude .276 inch above the flywheel surface.

4. Make sure that the flywheel is free of grease and position the new driven plate against the flywheel with the protruding hub facing the engine.

5. Install the aligning tool and position the pressure plate against the flywheel. Tighten the bolts cross-wise to 20–30 ft. lb. Remove the aligning tool.

6. Install the transaxle.

7. Adjust the clutch.

ADJUSTMENT

All except Alliance and Encore

1. From under the car, unscrew the locknut on the clutch lever link.

2. Screw the adjusting nut in or out to obtain a clearance of $1/8$–$5/32$ inch for the LeCar, $7/64$–$9/64$ inch for the R-12, $5/64$–$1/8$ inch for the R-15, 17 and Gordini and $3/32$ inch for the R-18 and Fuego at the end of the lever.

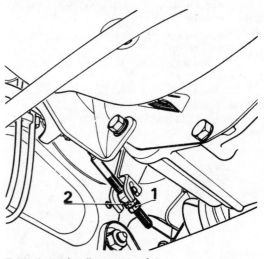

Typical clutch adjustment point

Alliance and Encore

An automatic adjuster is used with no manual adjustment possible.

AUTOMATIC TRANSAXLE

SHIFT LINKAGE ADJUSTMENT

Alliance and Encore

1. Place the selector in Park.

2. Raise and support the car on jackstands.

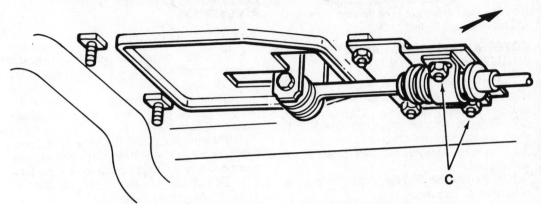

Alliance and Encore automatic transmission shift linkage adjustment

3. Loosen the adjustment yoke nuts and slide the yoke and cable forward to take up all slack.

4. Tighten the yoke nuts and lower the car.

R-12, R-15, R-17, Gordini

1. Place the selector level in Park. In this range it must be as truly vertical as possible.

2. To attain a vertical alignment in Park, loosen the two shift quadrant retaining bolts and slide the quadrant back and forth until the shifter is as vertical as possible. Tighten the bolts.

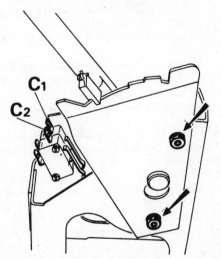

R-12, 15, 17, Gordini shift linkage control adjustment points

R-18, Fuego and Sport Wagon

1. Raise and support the car on jackstands.

2. Place the shifter in neutral.

3. Unbolt the shift linkage rod at the shifter end, make sure that the transmission case shift lever is in the neutral position.

4. Reconnect the linkage rod and torque the bolt to 13 ft. lb.

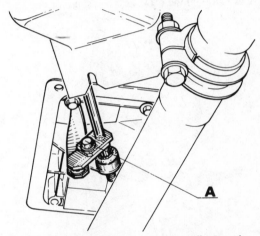

R-18 and Fuego shift control linkage adjustment

KICK-DOWN SWITCH ADJUSTMENT

This adjustment is closely related to the governor cable adjustment and should be made in conjunction with that adjustment. Kickdown adjustment is made at the accelerator pedal.

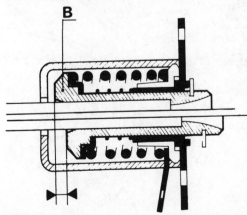

Kickdown switch adjustment. B is the gap measurement point

With the accelerator pedal completely depressed, make sure that the cable stop sleeve can still move about 1/16 inch.

GOVERNOR CONTROL CABLE ADJUSTMENT

1. Back off the locknut on the governor cable at the governor control lever. Remove the cable end from the control lever.
2. Turn the threaded cable end so that it is about one half way into the control lever.
3. Place the cable end ball into its slot in the control lever.
4. Make sure that the other end of the cable is in place at the carburetor.
5. Depress the accelerator all the way, and remove all play from the cable by adjusting the sleeve stop on the cable at the carburetor end.

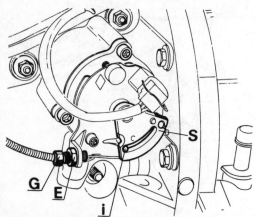

Governor cable adjustment location. G is the locknut, E is the adjusting nut, I is the cable end, and S is the quadrant

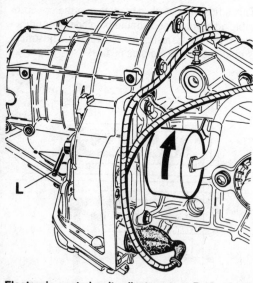

Electronic control unit adjustment on R-12, 15, 17 and Gordini. L is the lever

ELECTRONIC CONTROL UNIT ADJUSTMENT

R-12, 15, 17 and Gordini

1. Turn the control unit central shaft to the maximum position. This will correspond to 1st gear ''Hold''.
2. Set the lever, where it comes out of the case, to the 1st gear ''Hold'' position. Loosen the control unit screws.
3. Turn the lever, and the body of the electronic control unit, simultaneously, in toward the transmission case, until a turning resistance is felt.
4. Tighten the retaining screws carefully to avoid squashing the plastic shims.

TRANSMISSION REMOVAL AND INSTALLATION

Alliance and Encore

1. Disconnect the battery.
2. Drain the transaxle fluid.
3. Drain the engine oil.
4. Drain the cooling system.
5. Remove the air cleaner.
6. Remove the radiator.
7. Disconnect and tag all wires, hoses and cables from the engine and transaxle.
8. Disconnect the exhaust pipe at the manifold.
9. Disconnect the transaxle linkage.
10. Remove the front wheels.
11. Disconnect the tie rod ends using a ball joint separator.
12. Unbolt the brake calipers and hang them out of the way without disconnecting the brake hoses.
13. Disconnect the driveshafts at the transaxle.
14. Place a jack under the engine-transaxle unit and unbolt the mounts. Attach a lifting device to the engine and lift it from the car.
NOTE: *When separating the engine from the transaxle, first unbolt the torque converter. Take care not to drop the converter.*
15. Installation is the reverse of removal.
NOTE: *When attaching the exhaust pipe, tighten the bolts until each spring on each bolt is 1.71 in. (43.5mm) long. Tighten the torque converter bolts in alternating order to 20–25 ft. lb.*

R-12, R-15, R-17, Gordini

1. Disconnect the battery.
2. Remove the starter.
3. Disconnect the transmission vacuum line.
4. Remove the camshaft pulley.
5. Disconnect the transmission wiring harness and remove its bracket.
6. Drain the transmission fluid.

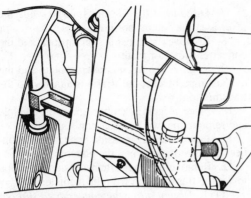

Installing tool T.Av.509

7. Insert spacers, Tool T.Av.509 or equivalent, between the shock absorber lower mount and the lower control arm hinge.

8. Raise and support the front end on jackstands.

9. Using a drift, punch out the driveshaft roll pins.

10. Using a ball joint separator, disconnect the steering arm ball joints and the upper control arm ball joints.

11. Tilt the driveshaft carriers, freeing the driveshafts from the transaxle.

12. Move the selector lever to 1st gear and disconnect the selector linkage and electronic control unit linkage.

13. Remove the dipstick tube and converter cover.

14. Remove the three torque converter-to-flywheel bolts.

15. Disconnect the exhaust pipe bracket at the case.

16. Place a floor jack at the rear of the transaxle and take up the transaxle weight.

17. Remove the rear crossmember.

18. Lower the jack slightly and disconnect the speedometer and governor cables.

19. Unbolt the engine from the transaxle and roll the transaxle from under the car. Take care to avoid dropping the torque converter.

20. Assembly is the reverse of disassembly. Note the following points:

   a. When bolting up the torque converter, note that one converter arm is marked with a dab of paint and has machined sharp angles. This arm is lined up with the timing hole in the flywheel.

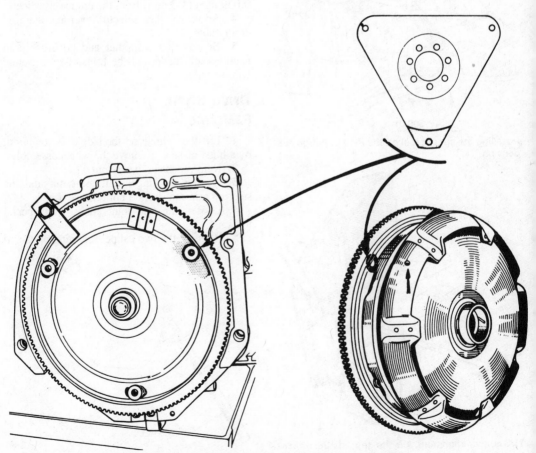

Proper converter alignment on the R-12, 15, 17 and Gordini

b. Grease the driveshaft splines with chassis lube prior to installation.

c. Adjust all linkage points as described earlier.

R-18, Fuego and Sport Wagon

1. Disconnect the battery and drain the transmission assembly.

2. Disconnect the vacuum control hose and the wiring connectors. Remove the support.

3. Special spacers should be placed between the lower shock absorber base and the lower suspension arm pivot shaft.

4. Place the vehicle on jack stands and drive out the roll pins from the drive shafts.

5. Separate the steering ball joints and the upper suspension ball joints.

6. Tilt the stub axle carriers to free the drive shafts from the side gears.

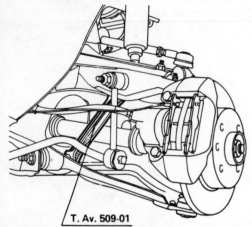

T. Av. 509-01

Installing the spacer tool on the R-18 or Fuego suspension

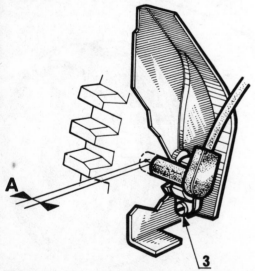

TDC sensor alignment. A is the gap; 3 is the attaching screw

7. Disconnect the selector linkage while the lever is in the neutral position.

8. Remove the transmission dipstick and the converter protector plate.

9. Remove the three converter bolts and the exhaust pipe bracket nut which is attached to the transmission.

10. Place a jack assembly under the vehicle and remove the two transmission supports.

11. Lower the transmission enough to disconnect the speedometer and the governor cables.

12. Remove the engine/transmission bolts and lower the transmission from the vehicle.

NOTE: *Do not allow the converter to slip out of bell housing.*

Installation is the reverse of the removal procedure. Note the following steps:

1. When installing the converter, place the boss that is located opposite the timing hole in line with the sharp cornered edge on the converter drive plate, which is marked by a dab of paint.

2. Lightly lubricate the side gear splines and position the drive shafts in line with the side gears.

3. If the vehicle is equipped with a TDC sensor, the sensor must be positioned approximately 0.039 inch (1.0 mm) from the engine flywheel.

4. Adjust the gear selector lever and the governor cable.

5. Be sure the computer and governor connections are made and the transmission ground wire is connected.

Drive Shaft
REMOVAL

1. Lift the vehicle on the side to be repaired, by a hoist or jack. Remove the wheel assembly.

2. Remove the stub axle nut.

3. Loosen the upper ball joint nut and the steering arm nut, but do not remove them.

4. Loosen the ball joint cones with special tools.

5. Remove the two caliper retaining bolts and

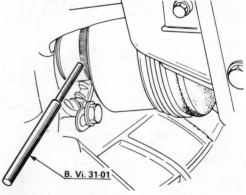

B. Vi. 31-01

Driving out the roll pins

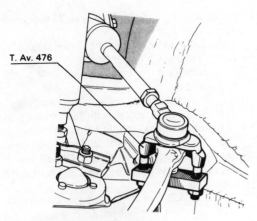

T. Av. 476

Disconnecting the ball joints

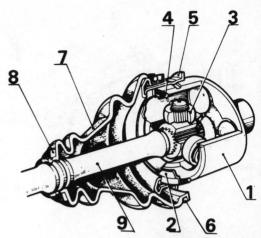

1. Yoke
2. Locking Plate
3. Spider
4. Seal
5. Metal Cover
6. Retaining Spring
7. Rubber Boot
8. Retaining Collar
9. Drive Shaft

Rubber boot replacement

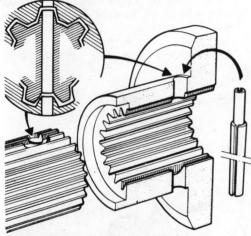

Roll pin alignment and installation

lift the caliper assembly from the rotor. Do not disconnect the brake hose.

6. Drive the roll pins from the drive shaft coupling on the gear box side of the driveshaft.

7. Remove the ball joint and steering arm nuts and tilt the stub axle carrier in order to disengage the driveshaft.

8. Remove the driveshaft.

9. Installation is the reverse of removal.

BOOT REPLACEMENT

1. Remove the collar from the stub axle.

2. Remove as much grease as possible from the assembly.

3. Remove the bell-shaped stub axle from the driveshaft by raising the arms of the retaining starplate, one by one.

CAUTION: *Do not twist the arms of the star-plate.*

4. Remove the boot. Save the thrust ball and the spring.

NOTE: *A special boot replacing tool should be used to install the boot to avoid damage.*

5. Place the driveshaft in a vise with the shaft yoke up. Fully engage the installing tool on the shaft yoke.

6. Lubricate the inside of the boot with clean engine oil.

7. Pull the boot over the end of the special tool with the small end first.

8. Bring the boot as close as possible to the cylindrical part of the tool and let it return half-way back. Do this several times in order to soften the rubber of the boot. Relubricate the arms of the tool and the boot as required during the installation.

9. Place the spring and the thrust ball joint in the spider.

10. Move the roller cages towards the center and position the retaining star plate. Each arm should be the bisector of the angles formed by the spider.

11. Install the collar and secure.

AXLE U-JOINT OR YOKE REPLACEMENT

1. Place a piece of adhesive tape or a protective end piece on the seal surface of the differential adjuster nuts.

2. Cut the retaining collar and the boot along their whole length. Remove as much of the grease as possible.

3. Remove the three tabs of the locking plate and remove the yoke.

NOTE: *Do not remove the rollers from their respective journals. The roller cages and needle bearings are matched and must never be separated. To prevent the separating of the unit during this operation, mount the plastic collar that is furnished with new spiders. Tape*

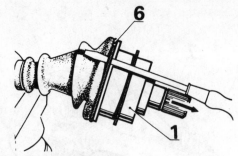

Retaining spring removal

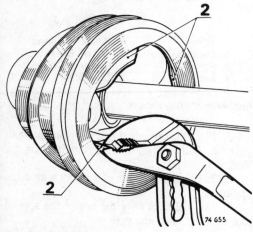

Lock plate, 2, removal

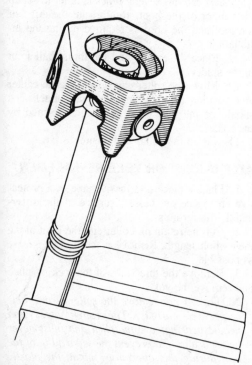

Plastic collar removal

the collar as a safeguard to prevent the collar from coming off.

4. Using a press, remove the spider assembly.

5. To replace the spider or a boot:

  a. Lubricate the driveshaft and slide on the new retaining collar and boot.

  b. Push the spider back on the splined shaft.

  c. Make three crimps with 120° spacing by stamping the metal splines on the driveshaft.

  d. Take off the plastic collar and/or tape. Engage the spider in the yoke and insert a shim (special tool) between the locking plate and the yoke.

  e. Carefully put the locking tabs of the plate back into their original positions and then remove the special tool shim.

  f. Put approximately 5¼ oz. of grease into the boot and yoke. Position the lips of the boot in the grooves of the drive shaft and on the metal housing.

  g. Install the retaining spring on the boot. Insert a smooth round-ended rod between the

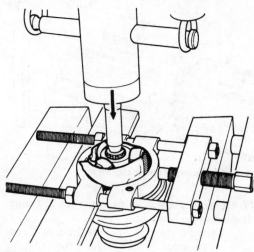

Pressing out the spider

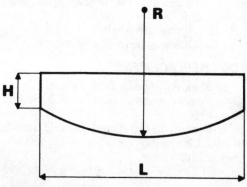

Fabricating the shim:
  L=40mm
  H=6mm
  R=45mm
  Shim thickness=2.5mm

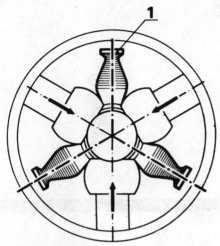

Starplate positioning

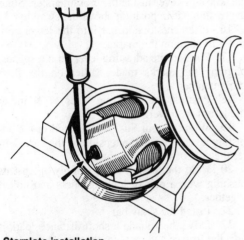

Starplate installation

1.0 mm) is obtained between the end of the boot and the largest diameter machined face of the yoke. When the joint has been adjusted correctly, remove the air release rod.

i. Place the retaining spring on the boot with a flexible wire.

CAUTION: *The spring must not be stretched and the coils must be still touching after assembly.*

6. If the yoke must be replaced:

a. Lubricate the drive shaft and slide on the retaining collar and the new boot.

b. Engage the yoke's metal housing on the shaft and the spider on the splines of the shaft.

c. Make three crimps with 120° spacing by stamping the metal splines on the drive shaft.

d. Fit the two bosses of the metal housing facing a perforation on the yoke, supplied with its new "O" ring and fit the parts one inside the other.

e. The crimping of the housing is on the yoke and is done on a press, by a hammer and a crimping tool.

INSTALLATION

1. Coat the splines of the shaft with lubricant and engage the drive shaft into the side gear. Check the positioning of the drive shaft retaining pin holes.

2. Install the retaining roll pins.

3. Engage the drive shaft into the hub. Install the washer and stub axle nut on the axle.

4. Reconnect the upper ball joint and steering arm joint and install the nuts. Tighten as required.

5. Torque the stub axle nut to 185 ft. lbs.

6. Reinstall the brake caliper and the wheel assembly. Operate the brakes several times to reseat the disc pads to the rotor.

boot and the yoke to relieve the air trapped in the boot.

h. Lengthen or shorten the joint until a measurement of 6.378 ± 0.039 inch ($162.0 \pm$

Suspension and Steering

FRONT SUSPENSION

Torsion Bars
REMOVAL AND INSTALLATION
LeCar

The following procedure requires the use of a special tool.

1. Tilt the front seat forward.
2. There are four bolts on the front face of the seat well. The largest of these is the torsion bar cam bolt. Loosen, but do not remove, the bolt and turn the cam left all the way to zero it.
3. Raise the front end and place jackstands under the frame so that the wheels hang freely.
4. Remove the torsion bar adjusting lever cover.
5. Insert tool Sus.545 in the adjusting lever.
6. In the front seat well, remove the three other bolts mentioned in step 2. These are the adjusting lever housing attaching bolts.
7. Remove the housing cover cam assembly and gradually ease the pressure on the tool.
8. Mark the position of the adjusting lever on the floor pan.
9. Mark the position of the torsion bar on the lower arm anchor sleeve.
10. Remove the sway bar bushings.
11. Remove the torsion bar from the control arm and check that the marks made previously are lined up with the punch mark on the end of the bar. If not, count and record the number of splines the marks are off.
12. Remove the torsion bar.
13. Apply chassis lube to the ends of the torsion bar.
14. Install the protective cover seal, the housing cover cam assembly and the adjusting lever on the torsion bar.
15. Pass the housing cover cam assembly and the adjusting lever inside the crossmember. Slide the torsion bar in position above the sway bar.
16. Insert the torsion bar into the lower control arm aligning the marks.
17. Position the adjusting lever on the splines, aligning the marks made earlier on the floor crossmember.
18. Position the adjusting lever ⅜–¾ in. to the left of its travel.
19. With the tool Sus.545 inserted in the adjusting lever, take up the tension on the bar. Center the cover by resetting the cam.
20. Hold the torsion bar assembly against its bushing with a pair of locking pliers and bolt it together.
21. Install the sway bar.
22. Drive the vehicle a short distance, park it on a flat surface and measure the ride height. Ride height is determined by calculating the difference between the distance from the wheel center to the ground and the distance from the underbody frame side member to the ground. The difference should be 1⅛–2⅝ in. To adjust the ride height, loosen the cam adjusting bolt in the seat well and turn the cam to obtain the proper ride height.

Shock Absorber
REMOVAL AND INSTALLATION
LeCar

1. Raise and support the car on jackstands.
2. Raise the lower control arm with a floor jack.
3. Disconnect the upper end of the shock.
4. Remove the sway bar.
5. Disconnect the lower end of the shock.
6. Install the shock absorber and sway bar, and tighten the bolts finger tight.
7. Let the lower control arm hang, then raise if 1¾ in., or, about half its travel. Tighten all fasteners.

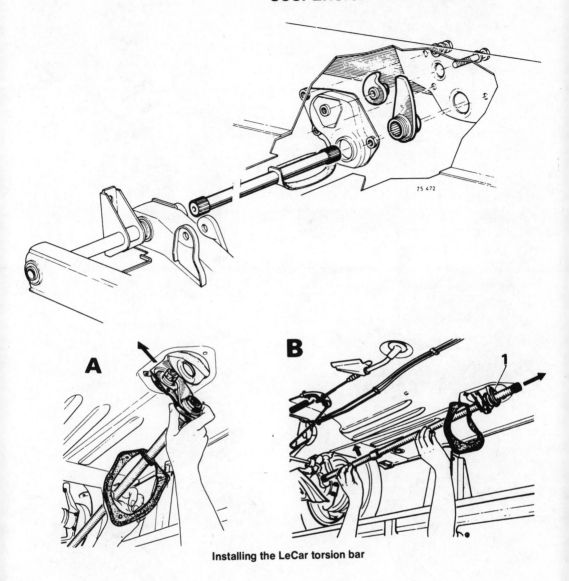

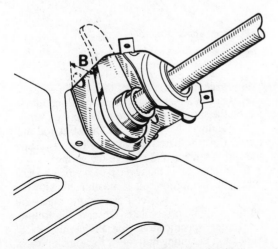

Installing the LeCar torsion bar

Positioning the LeCar torsion bar adjusting lever

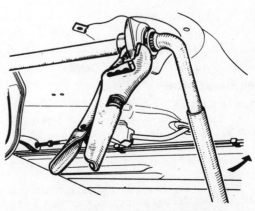

Gripping the torsion bar with a vise grip pliers

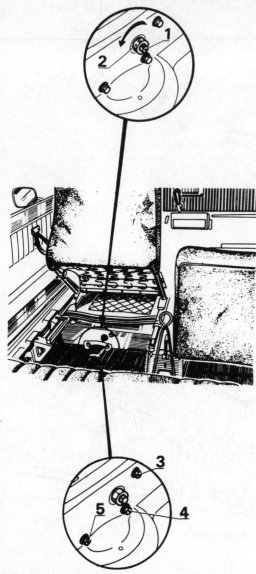

Torsion bar mounting and adjusting bolts on the LeCar

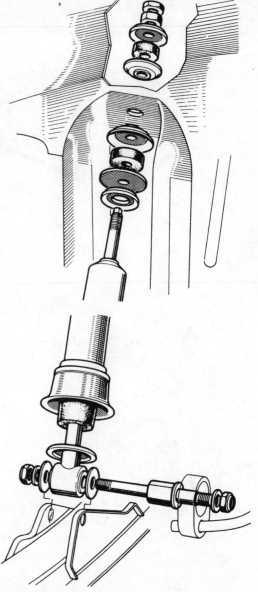

LeCar front shock absorber

Struts and Springs
REMOVAL AND INSTALLATION

All except LeCar

Special tools are needed for this job.

1. Raise and support the car on jackstands placed under the frame. Remove the wheel.

NOTE: *On all but the Alliance, a spring compressor must be used at this point to aid strut removal.*

2. Unbolt the strut at the top and bottom. Pull the strut out. It may be necessary to press down on the lower control arm.

3. Place the lower end of the strut in a vise.

4. On the Alliance, install a spring compressor on the spring and compress the spring evenly.

5. Remove the top nut on the strut rod and remove all the parts beneath it. Slowly release the spring tension and remove the spring.

6. Installation is the reverse of removal. Make sure that the spring coil is positioned with the open end of the lower coil against the raise stop on the bottom spring plate. Observe the following torque specifications for all but the R-18: Shock top mounting nut, 44 ft. lb.; shock bottom mounting nut, 55 ft. lb.; Shock top mounting pad

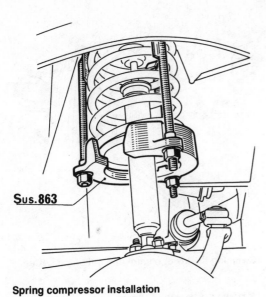

Sus. 863

Spring compressor installation

nuts, 17 ft. lb.; Piston rod retaining nut, 44 ft. lb. Observe the following specifications for the R-18: Shock upper mounting nut, 11 ft. lb.; shock lower mounting nut, 30 ft. lb.; shock piston rod nut, 59 ft. lb.

Ball Joints
REMOVAL AND INSTALLATION
All Models

NOTE: *The Alliance and Encore have no upper ball joint or control arm.*

1. Raise and support the car on jackstands.
2. Remove the ball joint nut. Using a ball joint separator, disconnect the ball joint.
3. Drill out the rivets securing the ball joint to the upper arm and remove the ball joint.

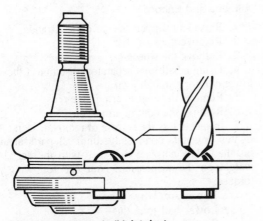

Drilling out a lower ball joint rivet

4. The new ball joint kit will come with bolts and nuts to replace the rivets and the upper ball joint has a shim which should go on top of the control arm. Install the ball joint and shim. The bolt heads go on the dust cover side. Torque the ball joint large nut to 49 ft. lb.

Upper Control Arm

NOTE: *The Alliance and Encore have no upper control arm.*

REMOVAL AND INSTALLATION
LeCar

1. Remove the coolant expansion bottle.
2. Remove the ignition coil.
3. Raise and support the front end on jackstands. Disconnect the ball joint.
4. Screw a nut, to be used as a locknut, on the front end of the control arm hinge pin.
5. Hold the locknut and remove the nut from the opposite end of the hinge pin.
6. Drive the hinge pin forward and out of the control arm.

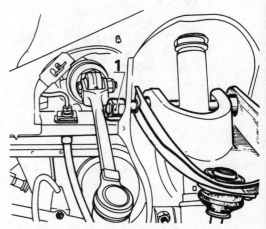

Installing a locknut on the arm bolt

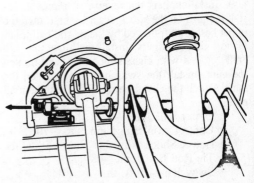

Driving out the upper arm hinge pin on LeCar

7. Remove the arm.

8. Installation is the reverse of removal. Tighten the hinge nuts to 70 ft. lb.

R-12, R-15, R-17, Gordini, R-18, Fuego and Sport Wagon

1. Raise and support the car on jackstands.
2. Disconnect the castor tie rod.
3. Remove the sway bar.
4. Using a ball joint separator, disconnect the ball joint.
5. Disconnect the tie-rod ball joint.
6. Unbolt and remove the upper arm hinge pin.
7. Disconnect the shock absorber lower end.

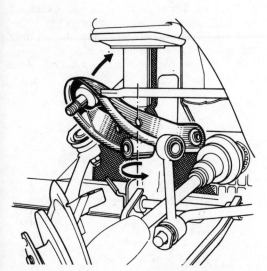

Removing or installing the upper arm on all but LeCar

8. Tilt the arm upward to free the ball joint and free the other end from the shock absorber.

9. Installation is the reverse of removal. Install the arm on the shock absorber first, then the upper ball joint followed by the tie rod ball joint. Hand tighten the nuts. Install the hinge pin, liberally coated with chassis lube and hand tighten the nuts. Install the sway bar; hand tighten the nuts. Attach the castor tie rod. NOW, tighten all nuts:

- Upper Ball Joint—47 ft. lb.
- Control Arm Hinge Pin Nuts—70 ft. lb.
- Lower Shock Absorber Nuts—55 ft. lb.
- Tie Rod Ball Joint—48 ft. lb.
- Sway Bar—20 ft. lb.
- Cater Link Nut—60 ft. lb.

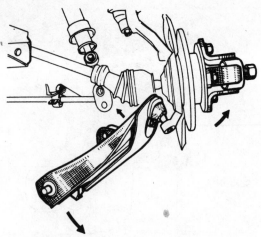

Swinging the lower control arm out of the LeCar

Lower Control Arm
REMOVAL AND INSTALLATION
LeCar

1. Remove the torsion bar.
2. Remove the driveshaft.
3. Remove the sway bar.
4. Disconnect the shock absorber lower end and remove the bolt.
5. Disconnect the steering arm ball joint and lower control arm ball joint with a ball joint separator.
6. Unbolt and remove the lower control arm hinge pin.
7. Install a hub puller on the hub end and tighten the puller until ball joint pulls free of the axle shaft carrier.
8. Installation is the reverse of removal. Observe the following torques:
- Lower control arm hinge pin nuts—75 ft. lb.
- Lower shock absorber nut—25 ft. lb.
- Lower ball joint nut—40 ft. lb.

Alliance and Encore

1. Raise and support the car on jackstands.
2. Remove the sway bar.
3. Remove the wheels.
4. Using a ball joint separator, disconnect the lower control arm ball joint.
5. Remove the control arm hinge pins.
6. Remove the control arm.
7. Installation is the reverse of removal. Don't tighten any nuts completely, until all parts are installed. The nuts are tightened with the car's weight on the suspension. Note the following torques:
- Lower arm hinge pins—55 ft. lb.
- Lower ball joint nut—40 ft. lb.
- Sway bar bolts—16 ft. lb.

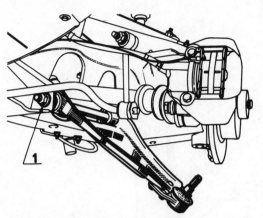

Lower ball joint disconnected on the R-12, 15, 17, 18, Fuego or Gordini

R-12, R-15, R-17, Gordini, R-18, Fuego and Sport Wagon

1. Raise and support the car on jackstands.
2. Using a ball joint separator, disconnect the lower ball joint.
3. Unbolt and remove the control arm hinge pin.
4. Free the lower ball joint from the spindle and remove the arm from the car.
5. Installation is the reverse of removal. Do not tighten any fasteners until all parts are installed. The fasteners must be tightened with the weight of the car on the suspension. Observe the following torques:

- Lower control arm hinge pin—80 ft. lb. (except 18 and Fuego) 67 ft. lb. (18 and Fuego)
- Ball joint nut—35 ft. lb.

REAR SUSPENSION

Torsion Bars

REMOVAL AND INSTALLATION

LeCar

A special tool, which can be made at home, will aid in the removal of the torsion bar.

1. Raise and support the car on jackstands.
2. Loosen the cam locking nut and zero the cam.
3. Remove the shock absorber.
4. Assemble the torsion bar tool in place of the shock absorber.
5. Tighten nut A until the adjusting lever lifts off of cam D.
6. Remove the torsion bar.
7. Move the adjusting lever until it touches the cam.
8. Apply chassis lube to the torsion bar splines and insert it into the lever and arm.

NOTE: *Adjust nut A on the torsion bar remover 23¼ inches for the right arm, or 23⅝*

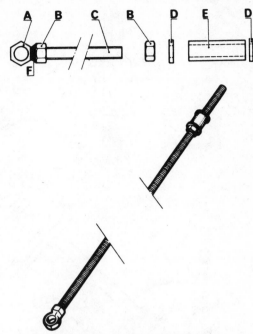

Home made rear torsion bar removal tool

inches for the left arm, prior to torsion bar installation.

9. Tighten the cam locknut. Remove the tool.
10. Install the shock absorber.
11. Lower the vehicle and check the ride height. Ride height is the difference between the distance measured from the wheel center to the ground, and the distance measured from the frame to the ground. The difference should be ¹/₁₆–¹³/₁₆ in. Turn the cam adjuster to obtain this hieght.

Alliance and Encore

1. Raise and support the car on jackstands.
2. Remove the sway bar.
3. Remove the shock absorber.

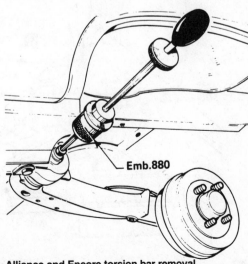

Emb.880

Alliance and Encore torsion bar removal

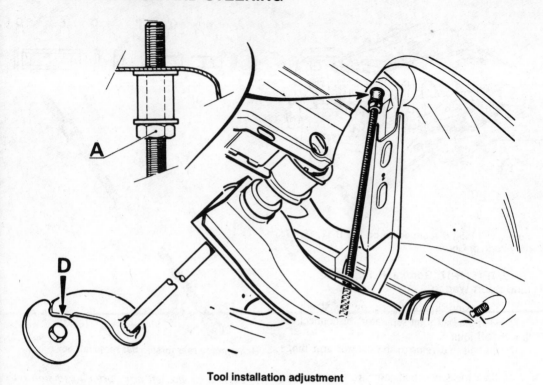

A

D

Tool installation adjustment

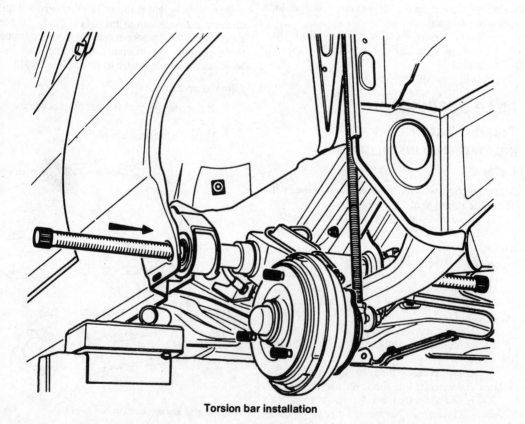

Torsion bar installation

4. Remove the torsion bar with a slide hammer.

5. For installation, make a tool identical to that described in the LeCar procedure, above. Install this tool in place of the shock absorber. Turn the nut to obtain a tool length of 24.04 inches for either side.

6. Coat the torsion bar splines with chassis lube and install it. Search around until the easiest point of entry, at each end, is found.

7. Remove the tool. Install the shock and sway bar.

8. Check and adjust the ride height, if necessary. To adjust the ride height, see the LeCar section above. Ride height should be 2.048 in.

Springs

REMOVAL AND INSTALLATION

R-12, R-15, R-17, Gordini, R-18, Fuego, and Sport Wagon

1. Raise and support the car on jackstands placed under the frame.

2. Disconnect the shock absorber lower end.

3. Compress the shock as far as it will go.

4. On the 18 and Fuego, remove the brake hose clips from the rear axle.

5. Jack up the rear of the car to allow the axle to drop and the spring to be pulled out and down.

6. Installation is the reverse of removal. Make certain that the lower open coil end is against the stop on the spring pad.

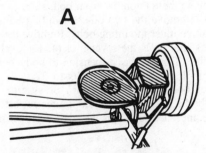

When installing the spring, make sure that the spring end is against the stop, A, on the pad

Shock Absorbers

REMOVAL AND INSTALLATION

LeCar, Alliance and Encore

1. Working through the trunk, remove the upper nut.

2. Raise and support the car on jackstands.

3. Remove the lower nut and remove the shock absorber.

4. Installation is the reverse of removal. It's best to attach the upper end first. Torque the upper nut to 18 ft. lb.; the bottom nut to 60 ft. lb.

R-12, R-15, R-17, Gordini

1. Remove the spring.

2. Disconnect the shock top nut and remove the shock.

3. Installation is the reverse of removal.

R-18, Fuego and Sport Wagon

1. Open tne trunk and remove the gas tank protection shield.

2. Remove the upper fastener (nut).

3. Raise the vehicle and remove the wheel(s).

4. Remove the lower fastening nut and compress the shock absorber by hand.

5. Remove the retaining clips of the brake hoses from the rear axle.

6. Push the axle assembly downward and remove the shock absorber with the spring. Remove the spacers and the rubber bushings.

Before installing a new shock absorber, pump it up and down manually several times while in an upright position.

1. Place the rubber insulators on the shock absorbers as required on both the top and bottom.

2. Push down on the rear axle assembly and engage the shock absorber with the spring, positioning the spring so that its lower end is placed in the stop of the lower cup.

3. Attach the upper half of the shock absorber with the retaining nut. Be sure to replace the bushings and cups as they were removed.

4. Extend the shock absorber and install its lower retaining nut. Again, be sure to replace the bushings and cups as they were removed.

5. Install the retaining clips of the brake hose to the rear axle.

6. Install the wheels and lower the vehicle to the ground.

Rear Axle Assembly

REMOVAL AND INSTALLATION

All except LeCar, Alliance and Encore

1. Position the vehicle on a hoist or on jack stands.

2. Remove the wheels and the lower mountings on the shock absorbers. Push the shock absorbers upward as far as possible.

3. Remove the flexible brake lines from the limiter.

4. Pull downward on the rear axle to remove the springs.

5. Remove the two side arm nuts on the chassis side and remove the two bolts.

6. Disconnect the parking brake cables at the adjusters, and remove them from the retaining bracket.

7. Place a jack under the rear axle assembly.

8. Disconnect the brake limiter valve.

9. Remove the two center arm bolts and remove the rear axle assembly.

The installation is the reverse of the removal procedure. With the components in place and tightened correctly, place the vehicle back on its wheels.

1. Check the brake limiter valve adjustment.
2. Bleed the brake system.
3. Adjust the parking brake.
4. With the weight of the vehicle on the rear suspension, retighten all bolts as required. Torque the center arm bolts to 59 ft. lb. and the side arm bolts to 25–30 ft. lb.

Center Arm

REMOVAL AND INSTALLATION

All except LeCar, Alliance and Encore

1. Place the vehicle on a lift and disconnect the brake limiter control rod.
2. Remove the nuts from the front and rear attaching bolts.
3. Remove the clamp and the center arm retaining bolts.
4. Remove the center arm. The bushings must be pressed in and out of the arm.

Installation is in the reverse of the removal procedure. Torque the bolts as required and check the adjustment of the limiter valve. Torque the rubber bushing bolt to 30 ft. lb.; the clamp nuts to 10 ft. lb.; the left and right bolts to 60 ft. lb.

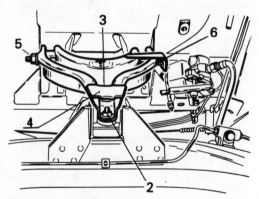

Center arm attaching points

Side Arms/Stabilizer Assembly

REMOVAL AND INSTALLATION

All except LeCar, Alliance and Encore

1. Place the vehicle on a lift and disconnect the two parking brake cables.
2. Remove the arm retaining nuts front and rear.
3. Drive the bolts from the arms and remove the arm stabilizer assembly. The bushings must be pressed from and into the arm.

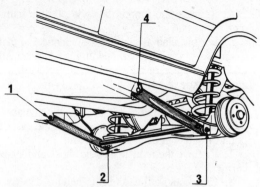

Side arm attaching bolts. The bolts must be removed and installed in the order shown

The installation is the reverse of the removal procedure. Torque the bolts to 30 ft. lb.

LeCar, Alliance and Encore

The rear suspension of the Le Car model is an individual torque arm type unit and each side is removed and replaced separately.

1. Support the rear of the vehicle with jack stands.
2. Remove the sway bar and the shock absorber.
3. Disconnect the flexible brake line and set the torsion bars to zero position by their adjusting cams.
4. Assemble the special torsion bar removal tool in place of the shock absorber and tighten the tool until the adjusting lever lifts off the cam. Remove the torsion bar from both sides.
5. Remove the two other mounting bolts and the three inner mounting bolts. Remove the arm.

Installation is the reverse of the removal procedure. Torque the suspension-to-body bolts to 55 ft. lb.; the sway bar bolts to 37 ft. lb.; the shock bottom nut to 60 ft. lb. Be sure to bleed the brake system, check the limiter cut-off pressure and check the rear wheels for proper tracking.

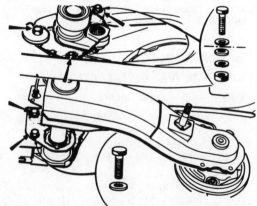

Alliance, Encore and LeCar side arm attaching points

Rear Axle Bearings

REMOVAL AND INSTALLATION

All except LeCar, Alliance and Encore

NOTE: *Several special tools are required for this procedure.*

1. Raise the rear of the vehicle and remove the rear wheels.

2. Remove the rear brake drum or caliper:

    a. Release the parking brake.

    b. Slacken the secondary cables of the parking brake so that the lever may be pulled back.

    c. Remove the dust plug in the backing plate so that the automatic adjusting system may be disengaged.

    d. Insert a screwdriver type tool (tool No. Rou 370-02) into the hole in the backing plate, through a companion hole in the brake shoe, to the parking brake lever.

    e. Push in with the tool to disengage the catch from the brake shoe. Push the lever to the rear with the tool.

    f. Remove the dust cover, the retaining lock nut/cotter pin, the stub axle nut and washer.

    g. Remove the drum, the outer bearing and seal as an assembly.

3. With the use of special pulling tools (No.

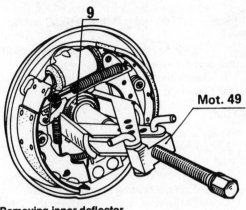

Removing inner deflector

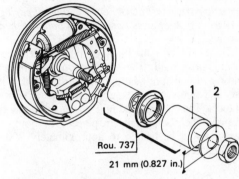

Installing the inner deflector

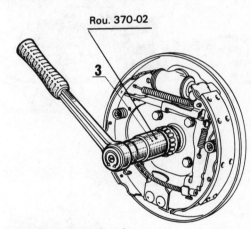

Installing the inner bearing

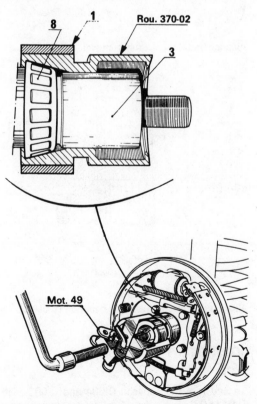

Inner bearing removal from all but LeCar, Alliance and Encore

Rou 15-01 and B. Vi. 28-01) the inner bearing is removed from the stub axle, along with the deflector.

4. Install the inner deflector, making sure it is mounted correctly.

5. Install the inner bearing on the stub axle by carefully driving it to its seat.

6. Install any of the bearing cups as required. Add lubricant to the bearings and cups.

7. Install the drum assembly in the reverse of its removal procedure.

8. Check the bearing end play, which should be between 0.000 and 0.001 inch (0.00 and 0.03 mm).

9. Adjust the foot brake by repeatedly pushing down on the brake pedal.

10. Adjust the parking brake. Install the plug in the rear of the backing plate.

LeCar

1. Raise the vehicle and support safely.

2. Remove the rear wheel(s) and the brake drum.

3. Remove the outer bearing and the oil seal.

4. Remove the bearing races as required.

5. With a special puller, remove the inner bearing from the rear axle spindle.

NOTE: *Some inner bearings will have a thrust washer that must be removed with the bearing assembly. A different type bearing puller is then used.*

There are two methods of bearing replacement, hot or cold. The hot method is preferred and consists of pre-heating the washer so that it can be assembled to the stub axle without the use of tools. The cold method utilizes the special tools to press the components in place. The components should be heated to approximately 200–250 degrees F.

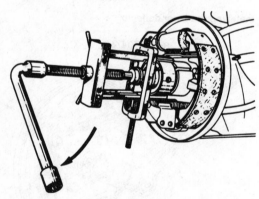

LeCar rear axle bearing removal

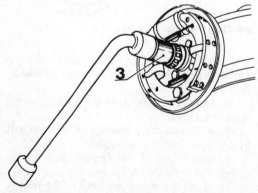

Cold method of installing the LeCar rear axle bearing

CAUTION: *Do not use an open flame to pre-heat the components.*

Alliance and Encore

NOTE: *This procedure requires the use of special tools.*

1. Raise and support the car on jackstands.

2. Remove the wheel.

3. Loosen the handbrake cable.

4. Remove the grease cap from the end of the axle shaft. Remove the shaft end nut and washer.

5. Remove the brake drum. It may be necessary to back off on the brake shoe adjustment to free the drum. If the drum still won't slide off, it will be necessary to mount a combination slide hammer/hub puller and remove the drum.

6. From the drum, remove the bearing retaining clip and drive the bearing out with a length of 49mm diameter pipe.

7. Installation is the reverse of removal. Drive the new bearing in with a length of 51mm pipe. Torque the shaft end nut to 118 ft. lb. Adjust the handbrake. Pump the brake pedal several times to adjust the brakes.

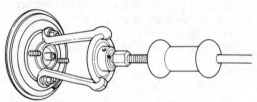

Alliance and Encore drum removal

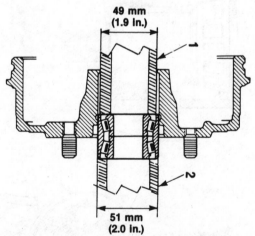

Alliance and Encore rear axle bearing installation

ADJUSTMENT

LeCar

An end play of between 0.004 and 0.002 inch (0.01 to 0.05 mm) should exist between the brake drum and the stub axle. Rotate the stub axle nut in or out to obtain this required adjustment. In-

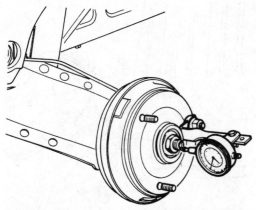

Adjusting the LeCar rear axle bearing, the adjustment by dial indicator for other models is similar

stall the lockplate, nut and cotter pin. Add ⅓ oz. of grease in the dust cover and install.

Alliance and Encore

No adjustment is necessary.

R-12, R-15, R-17, Gordini

NOTE: *A special tool is needed for this procedure.*

1. Raise and support the car on jackstands.
2. Back off the shaft nut, then, while rotating the drum by hand, tighten the shaft nut to 25 ft. lb.
3. Back off the nut ¼ turn. Tighten the nut until all bearing play is just removed. Mount a dial indicator under a lug nut and position the pointer on the end of the shaft.
4. Check the endplay by pushing and pulling on the drum. Endplay should be between .001–.004 in. Adjust using the shaft nut to obtain this figure.
5. Reassemble all parts.

R-18, Fuego and Sport Wagon

NOTE: *A special tool is needed for this procedure.*

1. Raise and support the car on jackstands.
2. Remove the wheel.
3. While turning the drum by hand, tighten the axle shaft nut to 22 ft. lb.
4. Tap the drum lightly to make sure the bearing is seated.
5. Back off the shaft nut about ¼ turn.
6. Attach a dial indicator under one of the lug nuts and mount the pointer on the end of the axle shaft.
7. Push and pull on the drum and check the endplay on the indicator. Endplay should be 0–.001 in. Use the shaft end nut to obtain this figure.
8. Assemble all remaining parts.

STEERING

Steering Wheel
REMOVAL AND INSTALLATION

Remove the snap cap and the steering wheel retaining nut from the steering shaft. Use a protective puller and remove the steering wheel from the steering shaft.

NOTE: *Depending upon the type puller used, the steering column top and bottom bezel may have to be removed to gain access.*

Combination Lighting— Directional Signal Switch
REMOVAL AND INSTALLATION
LeCar

1. Disconnect the battery.
2. Remove the instrument panel housing screws.

Wheel Alignment Specifications

Model	Toe-out Range in.	Preferred in.	Camber Range (deg)	Preferred (deg)	Caster Range (deg)	Preferred (deg)	Kingpin Inclination (deg)
1976–78 LeCar	³⁄₁₆ to ³⁄₆₄	⅛	0 to 1P	½P	12P to 13P	12½P	13.4
1979–83 LeCar	0 to ³⁄₆₄	¹⁄₆₄	0 to 1P	½P	3P to 6P	4½P	13.4
R-12	³⁄₆₄ to ⁵⁄₃₂	⁶⁄₆₄	1P to 2P	1½P	3½P to 4½P	4P	14.0
R-15/ R-17	³⁄₆₄ to ⁵⁄₃₂	⁶⁄₆₄	1P to 2P	1½P	3½P to 4½P	4P	14.0
R-18i	0 to ³⁄₆₄	¹⁄₆₄	½N to ½P	0	①	②	13.0
Alliance, Encore	¹⁄₆₄ to ³⁄₆₄	¹⁄₃₂	¹⁄₁₆N to ³⁄₁₆N	⅛N	1P to 1°52′P	1°26′P	—
Fuego	0 to ³⁄₆₄	¹⁄₆₄	½N to ½P	0	①	②	13.0

① Pwr. Str.: 1½P to 3½P   ② Pwr. Str.: 2½P
Non-Pwr. Str.: ½P to 2½P   Non-Pwr. Str.: 1½P

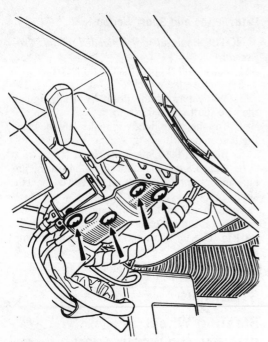

Combination switch removal on LeCar

3. Remove the switch bottom shell.

4. Remove the switch screws and disconnect the junction blocks.

5. Remove the switch.

Installation is the reverse of removal.

All except LeCar

1. Disconnect the battery.

2. Remove the steering wheel and the two half housings.

3. Remove the retaining bolt and the retaining screw. Remove the junction block.

4. Remove the switch assembly by pulling it upward.

Installation is the reverse of removal.

Ignition Switch

REMOVAL AND INSTALLATION

LeCar, R-15, R-17, and Gordini

1. Disconnect the battery and remove the combination switch shell assembly.

2. Disconnect the ignition switch connector.

3. Turn the key to the ''garage'' position and remove the key.

4. Remove the retaining screw from the side of the switch housing.

5. Press the retaining catch with the top of a scriber and push the switch out from behind to withdraw it.

To install the switch, reverse the removal procedure, using a new switch assembly.

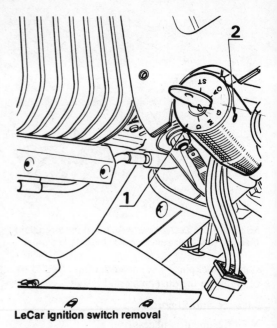

LeCar ignition switch removal

18i, Alliance Fuego, Encore, Sport Wagon

1. Disconnect the battery.

2. Remove the steering wheel and the two half housings around the steering column.

3. Disconnect the ignition switch connector.

4. Place the key in the park (off position for Alliance) position and remove the key.

5. Remove the retaining screw and push in on the retaining pin and push behind the switch to remove it from the housing.

Installation is the reverse of removal.

R-12, 15, 17, Gordini

1. Disconnect the battery.

2. Remove the steering wheel.

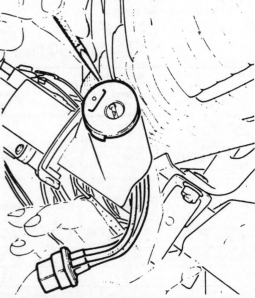

R-12 ignition switch removal

3. Remove the steering column upper and lower covers.

4. Disconnect the wiring.

5. Turn the key to a position halfway between ACC and ON. Pull out the key.

6. Remove the switch retaining screw, press down on the retaining notch with a small punch and push the switch out from behind.

7. Installation is the reverse of removal.

Steering Gear
REMOVAL AND INSTALLATION
Alliance and Encore

NOTE: *This procedure requires the use of special tools.*

1. Raise and support the front of the car on jackstands.

2. Remove the steering arm ball joint nuts.

3. Using a ball joint separator, disconnect the ball joints.

4. Remove the steering shaft universal bolt.

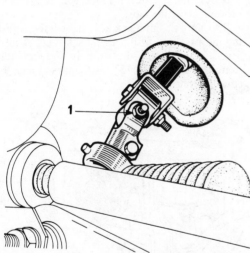

Alliance and Encore steering shaft U-joint bolt removal

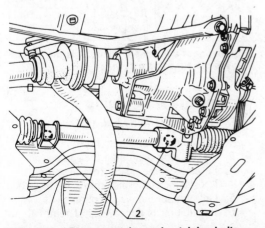

Alliance and Encore steering rack retaining bolts

5. Mark the position of the steering shaft, steering wheel, universal joint and steering rack and pinion in relation to one another.

6. Remove the two steering rack and pinion mounting bolts. On models with power steering, disconnect the hoses.

7. Lift out the rack and pinion, along with the steering arms.

NOTE: *The steering rack axial ball joints must NEVER be removed unless they are being replaced. When replaced, new lockwashers must be used.*

8. Installation is the reverse of removal. The steering arm ball joint nuts are torqued to 26 ft. lb.; the rack and pinion mounting bolts are torqued to 40 ft. lb.

LeCar

1. Disconnect the battery.

2. Remove the spare tire.

3. Remove the air cleaner.

4. Remove, but do not disconnect the cooling fan motor relay.

5. Disconnect the governor, connector and valve.

6. Disconnect the outlet pipe from the air pump.

7. Disconnect and place aside, the air pump and air pump filter.

8. Disconnect the steering shaft flexible coupling, but retain the rubber spacer.

9. Remove the rack and pinion attaching bolts.

10. Take note of the number and position of the adjusting shims and lift out the steering gear assembly.

11. Installation is the reverse of removal. Torque the steering shaft flexible coupling nuts to 10 ft. lb.; the rack and pinion mounting nuts to 25 ft. lb.

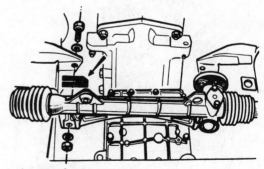

LeCar steering gear

R-12, R-15, R-17, Gordini

1. Remove the battery and its holddown.

2. Unbolt the steering shaft flexible coupling.

3. Disconnect the steering arms at the ends of the rack.

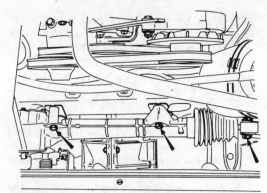

R-12, 15, 17 and Gordini steering rack mounting points

4. Remove the four attaching bolts holding the rack and pinion assembly and remove it from the car.

NOTE: *If the rack and pinion assembly is being reused, do not disturb the eccentric locking tabs folded over the crossmember. Disturbing these tabs will affect the initial steering gear height setting.*

5. Installation is the reverse of removal. Coat the steering arm pins with chassis lube. Torque the flexible coupling bolts to 10 ft. lb. and the other bolts to 25 ft. lb.

R-18, Fuego and Sport Wagon

NOTE: *This procedure requires the use of special tools.*

1. Raise and support the front end on jackstands.

2. Remove the tie rod end nuts.

3. Using a tool such as Renault no. T.Av. 476, remove the stub axle carrier ball joint cones.

4. Remove the steering shaft U-joint key bolt.

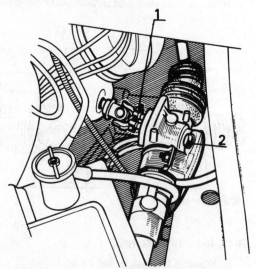

R-18 and Fuego steering U-joint. 1 is the key bolt; 2 is one of the four rack attaching bolts

Mark the position of the U-joint with respect to the shaft splines, and disconnect the U-joint.

5. Remove the four rack housing-to-crossmember bolts. On cars with power steering, clamp the hoses at the reservoir. Disconnect the pipes at the reservoir and the pump.

6. Remove the rack assembly through the hole on the cowl side.

NOTE: *Never unscrew the axial ball joints on the rack unless they are to be replaced. If they are being replaced, new lockwashers must be used.*

7. Installation is the reverse of removal. Torque the tie rod end nuts to 25 ft. lb.; the ball joint nut to 30 ft. lb.

RACK AND PINION ADJUSTMENTS

All Models

1. Raise and support the front end under the frame with jackstands, so that the steering is free to move.

2. Remove the front wheels.

3. Unlock the steering rack adjusting nut by bending away the tabs.

4. Using a 10mm hex key, tighten the adjusting nut to 7½–8 ft. lb., then back it off ¼ turn. The steering should move freely and smoothly from lock to lock. Bend back the tabs to lock the adjusting nut.

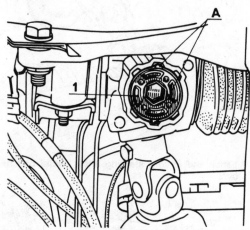

Steering gear adjustment points. A is the lock collar; 1 is the adjusting nut

Power Steering Pump
REMOVAL AND INSTALLATION

1. Clamp the pump input hose.
2. Place a drip pan under the car.
3. Disconnect the hoses from the pump.
4. Loosen the pump and remove the drive belt.
5. Unbolt and remove the pump.
6. Installation is the reverse of removal. Ad-

just the drive belt so that it has a ½ in. deflection when pressed at the mid-point of its longest straight run. Bleed the system.

BLEEDING THE POWER STEERING SYSTEM

NOTE: *System capacity is 1.33 qts.*

1. Completely fill the reservoir.

2. Start the engine and slowly turn the steering wheel from lock to lock and back to the mid-point.

3. Fill the reservoir to the FULL HOT mark.

4. Turn the steering wheel from lock to lock again.

5. Add fluid as necessary.

Brakes

BRAKE SYSTEM OPERATION

Adjustments

Disc brakes require no adjustments. The rear drum brakes on all models except LeCar are self-adjusting and require only an initial adjustment when new shoes are installed. The LeCar rear brakes require periodic adjustment.

LeCar

NOTE: *Always start with the leading shoe. The brakes are adjusted by means of eccentric cams which bear against the shoes. These cams are turned by rotating the lugs on the back of the backing plate. Turn each lug toward the outside of the drum until the shoe contacts the drum. With the shoe against the drum, the drum should not be hand-turnable. Back off on the shoe until the drum can just be turned by hand. Perform this for each shoe.*

R-12, R-15, R-17, Gordini

This adjustment is for new brake shoes. No periodic adjustments are necessary.

1. Remove the plug in the backing plate.
2. Insert a long, thin screwdriver or punch through the hole and push the handbrake operating lever in to free its peg from the brake shoe. The shoe is drilled to permit passage of the screwdriver. Once the peg is free, push the lever to the rear.

R-18, Fuego and Sport Wagon

1. Raise and support the rear of the car on jackstands.
2. Remove the wheels.
3. Remove the brake drums.
4. Look at the front shoe. The brake shoe cross link has a hooked end which enters the shoe webbing. Measure the gap (H in the illustration) be-

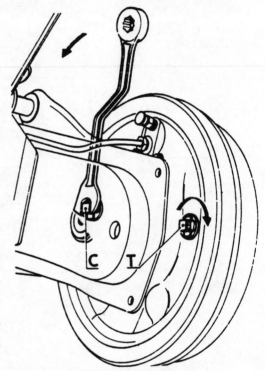

Adjusting the LeCar rear brakes

tween the inner face of the hooked end and the shoe webbing. The gap should be 1mm (.039 in.). This measurement should be taken with all tension released from the parking brake. If this dimension is not correct, it will be necessary to replace cross link tension spring as well as the two brake shoe holddown springs.

5. Install the brake drum and adjust the bearing end play.
6. Press down on the brake pedal several times.
7. Adjust the parking brake.

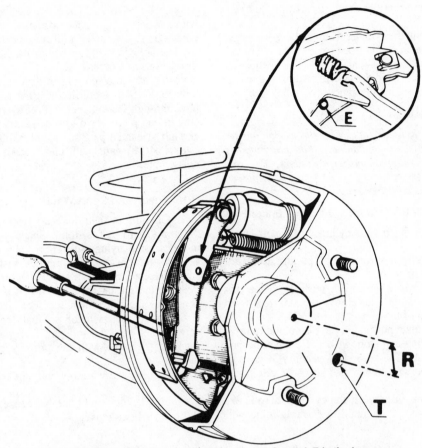

Rear brake adjustment on the R-12, 15, 17 and Gordini. E is the lever peg

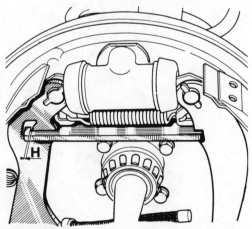

R-18 and Fuego rear brake shoe adjustment. Measurement should be made at H

Master Cylinder

REMOVAL AND INSTALLATION

LeCar

NOTE: *Renault states that the LeCar master cylinder is not rebuildable.*

1. Drain the fluid with a syringe such as a turkey baster, or with a sponge.

CAUTION: *Brake fluid is a fabulous paint remover. Take great care to avoid its contact with the car's sheet metal.*

2. Disconnect the brake lines from the master cylinder.

3. Disconnect the wiring from the master cylinder.

4. Unhook the pushrod from the brake pedal and pull it out of the master cylinder.

5. Unbolt and remove the master cylinder.

6. Installation is the reverse of removal. Coat the mating surface of the cylinder with RTV sealant. Check, and if necessary, adjust the pedal travel. Bleed the brake system.

Alliance, R-12, R-15, R-17, Gordini, R-18, Fuego, Encore, Sport Wagon

1. Drain the fluid from the master cylinder with a syringe such as a turkey baster or a sponge.

CAUTION: *Brake fluid is a fabulous paint remover. Take great care to avoid its contact with the car's sheet metal.*

2. Disconnect the brake lines from the cylinder.

3. Unbolt the cylinder from the power booster.

4. Installation is the reverse of removal. Torque the mounting nuts to 15 ft. lb. Adjust the pedal travel. Bleed the system. Adjust the master cylinder operating clearance.

OVERHAUL

NOTE: *Renault states that the LeCar master cylinder is not rebuildable. All the other models have rebuildable master cylinders. The primary and secondary pistons must be replaced as units and are not repairable.*

R-12, R-15, R-17, Gordini, Alliance, Encore

1. Place the master cylinder in a soft-jawed vise.

2. Remove the reservoir by pulling it upward and wiggling it off.

3. Using a wood dowel, push in on the pistons about 5mm and remove the setscrew from the bottom of the cylinder.

4. Continue pushing in the piston and remove the snap ring and stop washer. Remove the primary piston. The secondary piston will have to be removed with compressed air. A bicycle pump will do.

5. Check all parts. If the cylinder bore is excessively scored or pitted, the whole thing will have to be replaced. The bore can be repaired with a brake cylinder hone, available in most auto parts stores. The hone is drill-mounted. Follow the instructions that come with the hone. If no instructions accompany the hone, insert the hone, chucked into an electric hand drill, into the cylinder bore. Start the drill and push and pull the hone through the cylinder. NEVER let the hone stay in one place. Two to four passes should be enough. Clean all parts in clean brake fluid.

6. Coat all parts with clean brake fluid and reassemble.

R-18, Fuego and Sport Wagon

1. Obtain a ¼ inch diameter steel rod, about 385mm (15.16 inches) long. Shape it as shown in the accompanying illustration.

2. Using this tool, compress the pistons.

3. Place a 3.5mm (.138 in.) drill bit in a vise. Position the master cylinder so that the drill bit penetrates the roll pin of the secondary piston.

4. Rotate the cylinder so that the drill bit screws itself into the roll pin, then pull out the pin. Do the same with the primary piston roll pin.

5. Remove the wire tool and take out the pistons.

6. For cleaning and honing, see step 5 of the R-12 procedure, above.

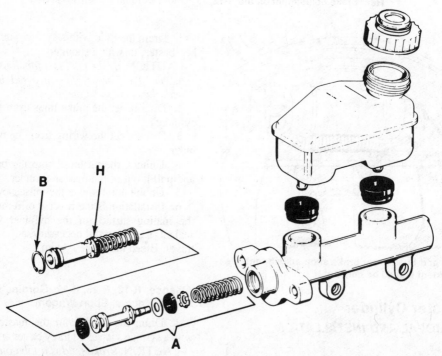

Master cylinder on all but R-18 and Fuego. A is the secondary piston assembly; B is the snap ring and H is the primary piston assembly

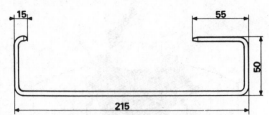

Home made tool for the R-18 and Fuego master cylinder

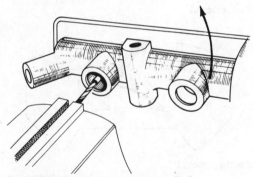

Installing the home made tool

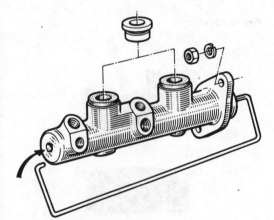

Removing the secondary piston roll pin

7. Installation is the reverse of removal. Install new roll pins.

MASTER CYLINDER OPERATING CLEARANCE ADJUSTMENT

All except LeCar

Operating clearance is determined by the length of the booster pushrod that protrudes past the face of the booster. Protrusion should be 9mm (.354 in. or 23/64 in.). Adjustment is made at the pushrod clevis, in at the brake pedal. Loosen the clevis locknut and turn the clevis until the proper protrusion is reached.

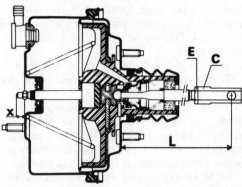

Adjusting master cylinder operating clearance. X is the pushrod protrusion; E is the locknut; C is the clevis and L is the link length (4.961 in.)

LeCar

1. Loosen the master cylinder pushrod locknut.

2. Turn the pushrod until pedal free travel, at the pedal surface is $13/64$ in.

3. Tighten the locknut.

Power Brake Booster
REMOVAL AND INSTALLATION
All Models

1. Disconnect the power booster pushrod at the pedal.

2. Disconnect the vacuum hose from the booster.

3. Unbolt the master cylinder from the booster and carefully move it forward without disconnecting the brake lines.

4. Unbolt and remove the booster.

5. Installation is the reverse of removal. Torque the booster-to-firewall nuts to 18 ft. lb. and the master cylinder-to-booster nuts to 15 ft. lb.

Combination Valve
REMOVAL AND INSTALLATION

These valves are not repairable or adjustable. They are generally located in the engine compartment below the master cylinder and serve to evenly distribute braking pressure through the system. They are retained by one bolt.

Brake System Bleeding

Whenever the brake hydraulic system is opened, air is allowed in. This air must be expelled. Unless you have a one person bleeder, which is available at some auto parts stores, a helper will be needed. The two person system is the one described here.

1. Have your assistant sit in the driver's seat.

2. You procede to the right rear wheel and remove the tire.

3. Attach a length of hose to the bleeder screw nipple and submerge the other end in a jar half full of clean brake fulid. The bleeder screw protrudes from the backing plate and is actually part of the wheel cylinder. It is located at the top.

4. Make sure that the master cylinder is full.

5. Place a wrench on the bleeder screw. Do not open it yet. Have you helper pump the brake pedal five or six times and hold it down as far as possible. At this point, open the bleeder screw and observe the jar. A rush of fluid will enter the jar. If air bubbles are present, you just expelled air from the system. Close the bleeder screw. THEN, tell your assistant to let up on the pedal. NEVER ALLOW THE PEDAL UP WHILE THE BLEEDER SCREW IS OPEN. Do this a couple more times, or until no bubbles are observed entering the jar. Check the master cylinder level frequently.

6. Do, in turn, the left front, left rear and right front. If you did a good job, the pedal action should be firm, not spongy. If a good bleeding job does not result in a firm pedal, then you've got problems. Check all components in the system for leaks.

FRONT DISC BRAKES

Disc Brake Pads

NOTE: *Brake pads must be replaced in "axle sets". That is, never replace just one side of the car. Both left and right brakes must be renewed at the same time.*

REMOVAL AND INSTALLATION

LeCar, R-12, R-15, R-17, Gordini

NOTE: *Replacement sets should have pads marked EXT. These pads are installed on the outboard sides.*

1. Raise and support the car on jackstands.

2. Remove the wheels.

3. Remove the four spring clips from the caliper.

4. Use a pin punch to tap out the keys.

5. Pull the caliper from the rotor.

6. Remove the pads.

7. Remove the springs from under the pads.

8. Remove about ½ of the fluid from the master cylinder reservoir.

9. Using a large C-clamp, push the piston completely into its bore.

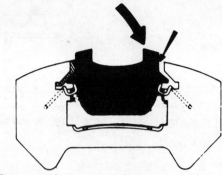

Key removal

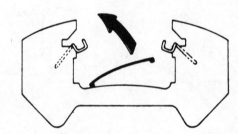

Pad removal

Spring removal

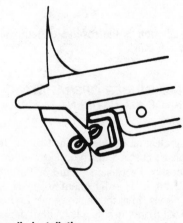

Spring clip installation

10. Install the springs into the caliper and install the new pads. The pads must slide easily.

11. Installation is the reverse of removal. Use new spring clips to retain the keys. Press the pedal several times to properly adjust the pad position.

Alliance and Encore

1. Remove about ⅔ of the fluid from the reservoir.

2. Raise and support the front end on jackstands.

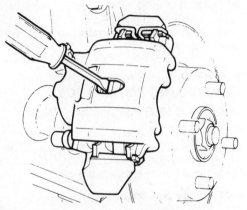

Prying back on the pads to push in the piston

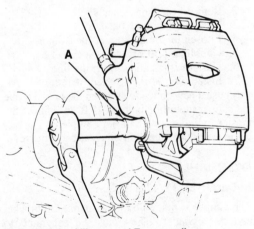

Unbolting the Alliance and Encore caliper

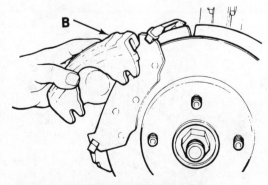

Removing the Alliance and Encore caliper

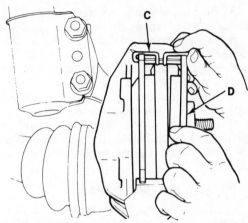

Holding the anti-rattle clip, C, against the anchor to remove the outer shoe D

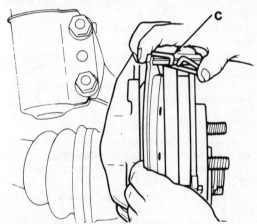

Removing the anti-rattle clip C

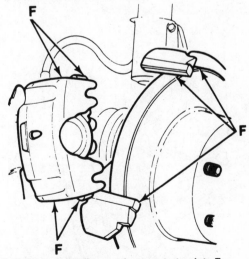

Lubricate the caliper and support at points F

3. Remove the front wheels.

4. Unscrew the caliper pins and lift off the caliper. If the caliper is difficult to remove, use a screwdriver to push the caliper piston back into its bore.

5. Hold the anti-rattle clip against the caliper anchor plate and remove the outboard brake shoe.

6. Remove the inboard brake shoe and the anti-rattle clip.

7. If the caliper shows signs of leakage, overhaul it as described later in this chapter.

8. Lightly lubricate the sliding surfaces of the caliper anchor with lithium grease.

9. Installation is the reverse of removal. The split end of the anti-rattle clip faces away from the shoes. Torque the caliper mounting bolts to 26 ft. lb.

R-18, Fuego and Sport Wagon

1. Raise and support the front end on jackstands.

2. Remove the front wheels.

3. Remove about ½ the fluid in the reservoir.

4. Disconnect the pad wear warning light wires.

5. Take out the anti-rattle clip and remove the pad retaining key.

6. With a screwdriver, gently pry on the outer pad between the rotor and pad to seat the caliper piston.

7. Pull out the pads.

8. If there is any sign of leakage in the caliper, remove and overhaul it at this time.

9. Using a large C-clamp, completely seat the piston in the caliper.

10. New pads should come with anti-squeal pins. If not, keep the old ones.

11. Position the new pads in the caliper.

12. It will be helpful, at this time, to file a

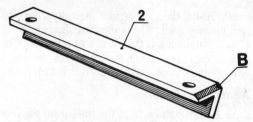

Filing a chamfer B on the key 2, prior to installation

chamfer on the leading edge of the key. This will aid installation. Install the key.

13. Install the clip and wire.

14. Push the pedal several times to properly position the pads.

Calipers

REMOVAL AND INSTALLATION

All except R-18, Fuego and Sport Wagon

See the brake pad removal and installation procedure. Unscrew the caliper from the brake line. Always use a new copper gasket on the line. Bleed the caliper that was removed.

R-18, Fuego and Sport Wagon

1. Raise and support the front end on jackstands.

2. Remove the front wheels.

3. Remove the brake pads.

4. Loosen the brake hose at the caliper.

5. Unbolt and lift off the caliper.

6. Unscrew the caliper from the line.

7. Installation is the reverse of removal. Always use a new copper washer on the line. Torque the caliper mounting bolts to 45 ft. lb. Unless the master cylinder level ran out completely, it will be necessary to bleed only the caliper removed.

OVERHAUL

LeCar, R-12, 15, 17 and Gordini

The caliper is made up of two parts, the bracket and the cylinder. They must be separated to change the cylinder.

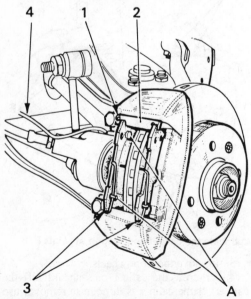

R-18 and Fuego front brake: A is the inner pad; 1 is the retaining clip; 2 is the key; 3 are the anti-squeal clips; 4 is the warning light wire

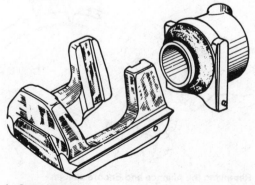

LeCar caliper

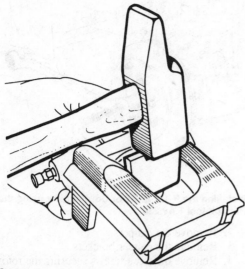

Separating the legs of the LeCar caliper with a wedge

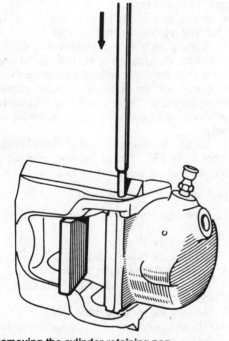

Removing the cylinder retaining peg

1. Separate the two legs of the bracket slightly by driving a wedge between them.

2. Use a pin punch to depress the cylinder retaining pin and slide the cylinder out of the bracket.

3. Installation is the reverse of removal. The cylinder is not repairable, but is replaced as a unit.

Alliance, R-18, Fuego, Encore, Sport Wagon

1. Remove the dust cover from the piston.

2. Place a thick rag or a thin block of wood in the caliper where the pads normally go.

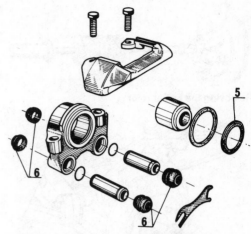

Caliper components on all except LeCar

3. Apply compressed air with the air chuck in the brake hose hole. Keep your fingers away from in front of the piston, as it can pop out with considerable force.

4. Remove the caliper seal from its groove in the bore.

5. Clean all parts in methyl alcohol. If the bore is pitted or scored, it can be honed by a machine shop. If damage is excessive, replace it.

6. Assemble all parts in reverse order of disassembly. Coat the piston and seal with clean brake fluid prior to assembly. Torque the caliper mounting bolts to 50 ft. lb. on the R-12, 15, 17 and Gordini; 44 ft. lb. on the R-18 and Fuego and 26 ft. lb. on the Alliance.

Rotor (Brake Disc)
REMOVAL AND INSTALLATION
Alliance and Encore

1. Raise and support the front end on jackstands.

2. Remove the caliper and suspend it out of the way. Do not disconnect the brake line.

3. Remove the stub axle nut and washer, and slide the rotor from the stub axle spindle.

4. Installation is the reverse of removal. Torque the stub axle nut to 90 ft. lb.

LeCar

NOTE: *Special tools are required for this procedure.*

1. Raise and support the front end on jackstands.

2. Remove the caliper and suspend it out of the way. Do not disconnect the brake lines.

3. Remove the caliper bracket.

4. Attach a slide hammer with hub puller adapter, under the lug nuts. Remove the stub shaft nut and washer.

5. Using the slide hammer, pull the hub and rotor.

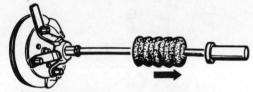

Removing the LeCar rotor

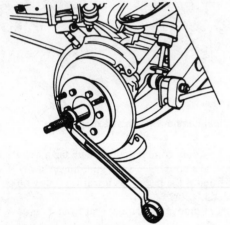

Installing the LeCar rotor

6. Install the rotor/hub assembly using Renault special tool number T.Av.409-01, or its equivalent. Torque the stub axle nut to 90 ft. lb.; the caliper bracket bolts to 50 ft. lb.

R-12, R-15, R-17, Gordini

NOTE: *Special tools are required for this procedure.*

1. Raise and support the front end on jackstands.

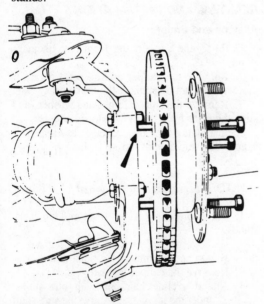

Removing the R-12, 15, 17 or Gordini rotor. The arrow shows the bolt installed at the front under-nut for the bearing closure plate

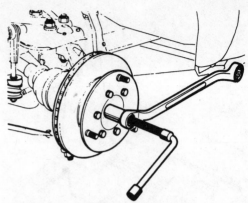

Installing the R-12, 15, 17 or Gordini rotor using the Renault tool T.Av.236

2. Remove the calipers.
3. Remove the caliper brackets.
4. Remove the three screws securing the rotor to the hub.
5. Clear the threads in the holes with an 8mm x 125 pitch tap.
6. Install Renault tool number Rou.436-01 on the hub and remove the stub shaft nut.
7. Screw three bolts tool number Rou.482-01 into the hub. Position one of the bolts at the front under the nut for the bearing closure plate fixing bolt. Check that the bolts are in direct contact with the stub axle. Tighten each bolt alternately, a little at a time, and remove the hub/rotor assembly.
8. Install the assembly using Renault tool number T.Av.236. Torque the stub axle nut to 115 ft. lb.; caliper bracket bolts to 50 ft. lb.

R-18, Fuego and Sport Wagon

1. Raise and support the front end on jackstands.
2. Remove the wheels.
3. Remove the brake pads.
4. Unbolt and remove the calipers.
5. Remove the rotor attaching bolts from the hub face.
6. Remove the rotor from the hub.
NOTE: *In some cases, it will be necessary to slightly loosen the stub axle end nut in order to free the bearing cup, so that the disc (rotor) can be removed.*
7. Installation is the reverse of removal. Torque the caliper bolts to 44 ft. lb.; the stub axle nut to 185 ft. lb.

Front Hub Bearings
REMOVAL AND INSTALLATION

NOTE: *Special tools are required for this procedure.*

Alliance and Encore

1. Raise and support the front end on jackstands.

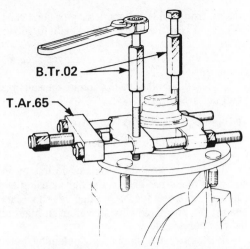

B.Tr.02

T.Ar.65

Removing the inner bushing from the Alliance and Encore front hub

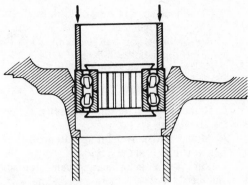

Pressing in the outer track ring

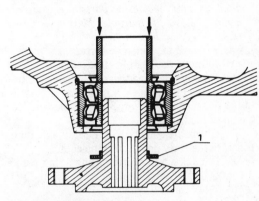

1

Pressing in the thrust washer

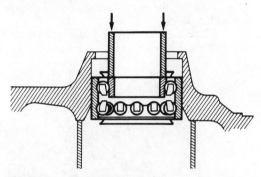

Pressing out the outer track ring

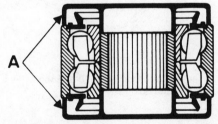

A

Removing the protective covers at each end of the new bearing

2. Remove the wheels.

3. Remove the caliper and suspend it out of the way, without disconnecting the brake hose.

4. Remove the rotor as described above.

5. Place the hub in a vise. Using Renault tool number T.Ar.65 and the bolts from Renault tool number B.Tr.02, or equivalent tools, remove the inner bushing from the hub.

6. Remove the thrust washer.

7. Using a ball joint separator, disconnect the steering arm from the stub axle carrier.

8. Remove the shock absorber lower bolt and remove the lower ball joint and nut.

9. Remove the snap ring from inside the hub.

10. Press out the outer track ring using one of the two original inner track rings. Leave the ball cage and seals in position.

11. The new bearing should have covers protecting the seals. Remove these.

12. Press in the complete bearing assembly, with the plastic sleeve holding the two inner track rings using a piece of tubing having an outside diameter of 63mm and an inside diameter of 59mm.

13. Place the assembly in a press with the press load on the outer track ring.

NOTE: *Bearings must always be replaced as a complete assembly. Once a bearing is removed, for any reason, it is damaged and must not be reused.*

14. Remove the plastic sleeve after the bearing is installed.

15. Install the snap ring against the face of the bearing outer track ring.

16. Coat the seal lips with chassis lube.

17. Slip the thrust washer onto the hub and press into position using a piece of tubing with an outside diameter of 45mm and an inner diameter of 39mm. Apply the press load to the inner bearing track ring.

18. Install all other parts. Observe the following torques:

- Shock absorber lower end: 40 ft. lb.
- Lower ball joint key nut: 40 ft. lb.
- Steering arm ball joint nut: 25 ft. lb.
- Caliper bolts: 26 ft. lb.
- Stub axle shaft nut: 157 ft. lb.

LeCar, R-12, R-15, R-17, Gordini

1. Remove the rotor/hub assembly as described above.

2. Mount protective fitting, Renault tool number Rou.15-01 on the hub.

3. Remove the outer bearing using Renault tool number B.V.28-01, or its equivalent.

NOTE: *If only the outer bearing is being installed, press it in at this time using a 1⅜ in. diameter pipe. Install the parts in reverse order of removal. If the inner bearing is being replaced, go on to step 4.*

4. Remove the stub axle carrier.

5. Remove the bearing closure plate.

6. Press out the inner bearing. Make sure that the press load is taken by a ring with a $2^9/_{16}$ in. inside diameter for LeCar; $3^5/_{32}$ in. diameter for the other models.

7. Check the condition of the stub axle bore. If it is excessively damaged, replace it.

8. Press in a new bearing using a ring with a 2⅜ in. outside diameter for LeCar; $2^{11}/_{16}$ in. O.D. for the other cars.

9. Pack the stub axle carrier center section with about 1 ounce of chassis lube or wheel bearing grease having a lithium base.

10. Mount the deflector and install the attaching bolts.

11. Press in the stub axle carrier/hub/rotor assembly using a 1⅜ in. diameter pipe for LeCar; $1^7/_{16}$ O.D. for the other cars. Don't forget the spacer.

12. Apply RTV sealer on the cover plate and install it.

13. Install all other parts. Torque the stub axle shaft nut to 90 ft. lb.

R-18, Fuego and Sport Wagon

1. Remove the rotor as described previously.

2. Remove the stub axle nut.

3. Remove the hub. You can do this by inserting a metal bar behind the hub housing and running two wheel lugs in through their holes and against the bar. Gradually tighten each lug until the hub comes off.

4. Remove the six bearing retaining bolts. They are Torx-head type.

5. Remove the bearing and inner race.

6. Remove the outer bearing race from the hub with a puller.

7. Place the inner bearing race on the stub axle and install the bearing.

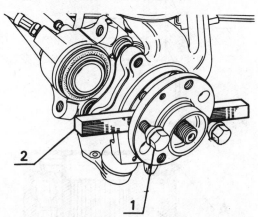

Removing the hub from an R-18 or Fuego. 1 is a lug nut; 2 is a metal bar

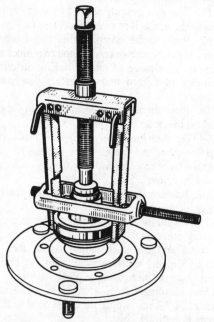

Removing the outer bearing from LeCar, R-12, 15, 17 or Gordini

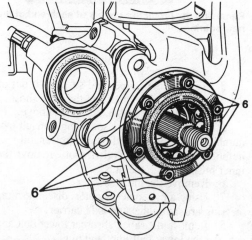

Removing the bearing retaining bolts

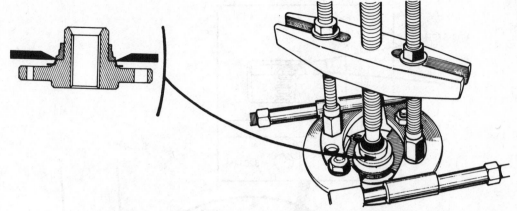

Removing the inner bearing race from the hub on the R-18 or Fuego

8. Drive the outer bearing race in the hub using a 40mm ID pipe.

9. Pack the bearing and races with multi-purpose chassis lube.

10. Place the hub on the stub axle. It may be necessary to drive it into position with a mallet, until the stub axle nut can be threaded on. Don't forget the positioning cup behind the nut.

11. Drive the hub all the way on with the shaft nut and torque the nut to 185 ft. lb.

12. Install all other parts as previously described. Torque the bearing retaining bolts to 11 ft. lb.; the caliper bolts to 74 ft. lb.

REAR DRUM BRAKES

Brake Drums

REMOVAL AND INSTALLATION

LeCar

NOTE: *A three jawed hub puller and a dial indicator are necessary for this procedure.*

1. Raise and support the rear end on jackstands.

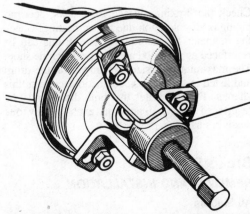

Removing the LeCar rear brake drum. R-12, 15 and 17 are similar

2. Remove the wheels.

3. Remove the grease cap.

4. Remove the cotter pin, shaft nut, lock plate and washer.

5. Back off the brake shoe adjustment.

6. Remove the drum with a three-jawed hub puller.

7. Install the drum by smearing the bore with chassis lube and driving it on using the shaft nut.

8. Adjust the rear axle bearings as described in Chapter 7.

Alliance and Encore

1. Raise and support the rear end on jackstands.

2. Remove the wheels.

3. Loosen the parking brake adjustment. Remove the grease cap and stub axle nut and washer.

4. Pull the drums off. If the drums are difficult to remove, it may be necessary to retract the brake shoes by removing the plug from the backing plate and backing off the adjusting starwheel with a screwdriver or brake adjusting tool. If the drum still won't come off, it will be necessary to remove it with a slide hammer with hub puller adapter.

5. Installation is the reverse of removal. Torque the stub axle nut to 118 ft. lb.

R-12, R-15, R-17

1. Raise and support the rear of the car on jackstands.

2. Remove the wheels.

3. Follow the adjustment procedure at the be-

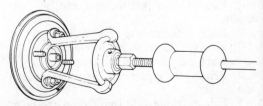

Removing the Alliance rear brake drum

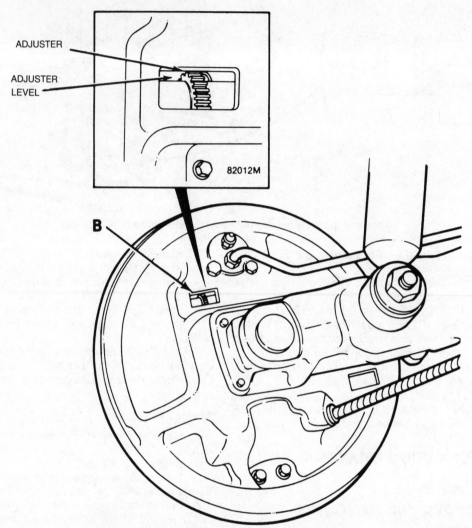

ADJUSTER

ADJUSTER LEVEL

82012M

B

Backing off the Alliance and Encore brake adjuster

ginning of this chapter to zero the shoe adjustment.

4. Remove the grease cap.

5. Remove the cotter pin, shaft nut and washer.

6. Using a hub puller, remove the drum.

7. Installation is the reverse of removal. Lightly grease the hub bore with chassis lube and drive the drum into place with the shaft nut. Adjust the bearings as described in chapter 7.

R-18, Fuego and Sport Wagon

1. Raise and support the rear end on jackstands.

2. Back off the parking brake adjustment.

3. Zero the self-adjusting mechanism as described at the beginning of this chapter.

4. Remove the grease cap, the cotter pin, nut and washer.

5. Pull the drum off. Don't drop the outer bearing.

6. Installation is the reverse of removal. Adjust the wheel bearings as described in chapter 7.

INSPECTION

Check the braking surface for cracks, scoring, pitting or discoloration due to overheating. Check the diameter for roundness. The drums can be resurfaced at any good automotive machine shop. The maximum oversize is stamped on the drum and listed in the brake specifications chart in this chapter. Renault states that both drums must be resurfaced an equal amount, even if only one needs resurfacing.

Brake Shoes
REMOVAL AND INSTALLATION
All Models

NOTE: *Special tools are helpful in this procedure.*

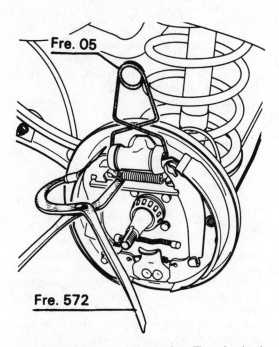

Fre. 05

Fre. 572

Removing the upper return spring. The wheel cylinder piston tool is in place

1. Raise and support the rear end on jackstands.

2. Remove the brake drums.

3. Install a wheel cylinder piston retainer on the wheel cylinder.

4. Remove the brake shoe holddown springs by pressing down on the springs bottoms with a tool designed for that purpose, or with a punch. Unhook the springs from the retainers.

5. Remove the brake shoe upper return spring with a pliers or brake spring tool.

6. Remove the brake shoes. Unless the parking brake cable or arm is being replaced, leave the cable attached to the arm.

7. Clean the backing plate and wheel cylinder. Check the wheel cylinder for signs of leakage. If leakage is noted, repair or replace the cylinder.

CAUTION: *The dust in and on the brake assembly and surrounding surfaces contains asbestos. Asbestos causes cancer! Never clean the brake surfaces with compressed air. Carefully clean the surfaces with a safe solvent. Avoid raising dust.*

NOTE: *Never change brakes on one side of*

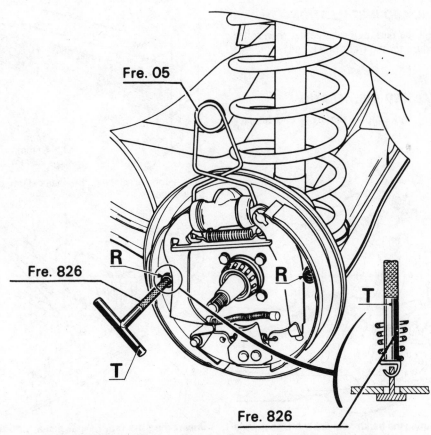

Fre. 05

Fre. 826   R   R

T   T

Fre. 826

Removing the holddown springs, R-18 shown; the others are similar

the car only. Both sides must be explained at the same time.

8. Installation is the reverse of removal. Apply a light coat of high temperature grease on the pads upon which the shoes rest. The shoe with the longer lining is the front shoe. Install the drum. Adjust the bearings as described in chapter 7. Adjust the brakes as described at the beginning of this chapter.

Wheel Cylinders

REMOVAL AND INSTALLATION

All Models

1. Raise and support the car on jackstands.
2. Remove the wheels, brake drums and brake shoes as described previously in this chapter.
3. Disconnect the brake pipe from the wheel cylinder.
4. Unbolt and remove the wheel cylinder.
5. Installation is the reverse of removal. Torque the wheel cylinder bolts to 10–13 ft. lb.

REAR DISC BRAKES

Brake Pads

REMOVAL AND INSTALLATION

Disconnect the parking brake cable, then follow the procedure for the front brake pads.

Calipers

REMOVAL AND INSTALLATION

1. Raise and support the front end on jackstands.

2. Disconnect the handbrake cable.
3. Disconnect the brake line from the caliper.
4. Unbolt and remove the caliper.
5. Installation is the reverse of removal. Torque the caliper bolts to 50 ft. lb.

OVERHAUL

NOTE: *Special tools are required for this procedure.*

1. Remove the caliper.
2. Place the caliper in a soft-jawed vise.
3. Remove the dust cover.
4. A tool can be made to unscrew the piston. Follow the accompanying illustration in making this tool.
5. Install the tool and unscrew the piston. When it turns freely, remove the tool and apply compressed air at the brake line port. Put a soft cloth in front of the piston. Never try catching the piston with your fingers. Crunched fingers would result.
6. Check the piston and bore. If any damage to either is noted, replace the unit.
7. Remove the piston seal. Discard it.
8. Clean all parts in methyl alcohol.

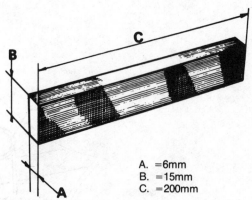

A. =6mm
B. =15mm
C. =200mm

Dimension for making the rear caliper piston remover tool

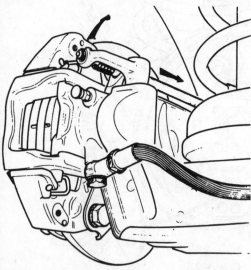

Disconnecting the handbrake cable on the rear caliper

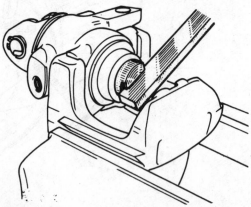

Unscrewing the rear caliper piston with the home made tool

9. Installation is the reverse of removal. Coat all parts with clean brake fluid prior to installation. Use your homemade tool to finish installing the piston. Always use a new piston seal and dust cover.

Rotors (Brake Discs)
REMOVAL AND INSTALLATION

1. Remove the caliper as described above.
2. Remove the caliper bracket.
3. Remove the grease cap.
4. Remove the cotter pin, nut lockplate, nut and washer.
5. Using a three-jawed puller, remove the hub/disc assembly. Be careful to catch the outer bearing as the hub comes off the spindle.
6. Unbolt the disc from the hub.
7. Installation is the reverse of removal. Bearing adjustment is the same as that for cars with drum brakes, given in chapter 7.

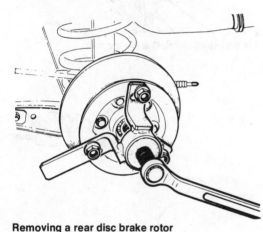

Removing a rear disc brake rotor

PARKING BRAKE

Cable
ADJUSTMENT
LeCar

NOTE: *The brake shoes must be properly adjusted before adjusting the handbrake.*
1. Release the handbrake completely.
2. Raise and support the car on jackstands.
3. Loosen the locknut on the handbrake rod.
4. The wheels should be turning freely by hand with no drag.
5. Turn the adjusting nut until a *slight* drag is felt at each rear wheel.
6. Lift the handbrake noting the number of notches in the complete travel. Six notches should be felt or heard.
7. Tighten the locknut.

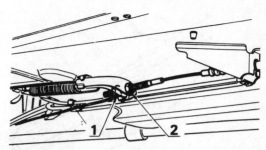

LeCar parking brake adjusting point

Alliance and Encore

NOTE: *The only time that the handbrake should be adjusted is when replacing the brake shoes, parking brake cables or lever.*
1. Release the handbrake completely.
2. Raise and support the rear end on jackstands.
3. Loosen the locknut on the handbrake rod.
4. Turn the adjusting nut until the brake shoes make light contact with the drums. Back off the adjusting nut until all drag is released.
5. Check the lever travel. 7 to 8 notches is the correct travel. If not, readjust the cable travel with the adjusting nut. When the adjustment is complete, tighten the locknut.

R-12, R-15, R-17, R-18, Sport Wagon, Fuego and Gordini with Drum Brakes

NOTE: *The only time that the parking brake is adjusted should be when the brake shoes, cable or lever is replaced. During adjustment, the car should be resting on its wheels.*
1. Fully release the lever.
2. Loosen the locknut at the adjusting clevis.
3. Turn the adjusting nut until all slack is removed from the cables, but the cables are not pulled taut.

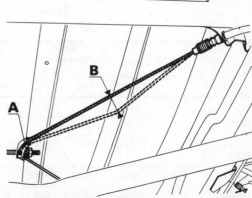

Parking brake cable adjustment on the R-12, 15, 17, 18, Fuego and Gordini. A is the adjusting nut; B is the deflection measurement

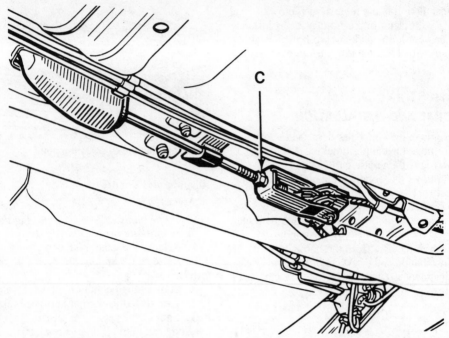

Alliance and Encore parking brake cable adjusting point. C is the locknut

4. Measure the distance from the mid-point of each cable to the floor pan. The distance should be $^{25}/_{32}$ in. for the 12, 17 and Gordini, and ¾ in. for the 18 and Fuego. If not, turn the adjusting nut until it is. Lever travel should be 12 or 13 notches total.

Cars with Rear Disc Brakes

1. Raise and support the rear end on jackstands.
2. Completely release the handbrake lever.
3. Loosen the locknut on the adjusting clevis.
4. Tighten the adjusting nut until the pads just touch the disc. Check the lever travel. Total travel should be 6 notches.

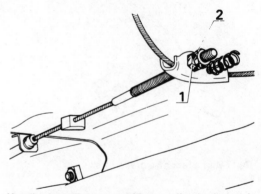

Handbrake adjustment with rear disc brakes. 1 is the adjusting nut; 2 is the locknut

Brake Specifications
(All measurements are given in inches)

Model	Master Cylinder Bore (in.)	Wheel Cylinder or Caliper Bore		Brake rotor or Drum Diameter		Minimum Lining Thickness	Brake Disc		Brake Drum Max. Diam.
		Front	Rear	Front	Rear		Minimum Thickness	Maximum Run-out	
LeCar	.811	1.772	.866	9.000	7.096	$^9/_{32}$	.354	.004	7.136
R-12	.748	1.890	.867	9.000	7.087	$^9/_{32}$	.355	.004	7.136
R-15/ R-17	.812	2.126	1.417	9.000	9.000	$^9/_{32}$	.355	.004	9.040
Gordini	.812	2.126	1.417	9.000	9.000	$^9/_{32}$	.433	.004	9.040
Fuego/ R-18i	.748	1.890	.866	9.370	9.000	$^9/_{32}$	.354	.004	9.040
Alliance, Encore	.811	1.772	.866	9.000	8.000	$^9/_{32}$	.433	.003	8.060

REMOVAL AND INSTALLATION

LeCar

Primary Cable

1. Release the handbrake.
2. Uncouple the primary and secondary cable at the junction under the floor.
3. Remove the cotter pin from the lever fork.
4. Remove the rod and cable.
5. Installation is the reverse of removal.

Secondary Cable

1. Release the handbrake.
2. Uncouple the primary and secondary cable at the junction under the floor.
3. Open the cable stop sector and remove the cable from the sleeve stop.
4. Remove the brake drum(s).

5. Using a pliers, pull back on the cable sheath spring and remove the cable from the actuating lever.
6. Installation is the reverse of removal.

All except LeCar

1. Raise and support the car on jackstands.
2. Remove the pin from the adjusting clevis.
3. Open the clevis and free the cable.
4. Remove the cable sleeve.
5. On cars with drum brakes, remove the brake drum(s) and disconnect the cable end(s) from the actuating lever using a pliers.

NOTE: *On the 18 and Fuego, it will be necessary to release the upper return spring first.* On cars with disc brakes, disconnect the cable from the caliper.

6. Installation is the reverse of removal.

Troubleshooting

10

This section is designed to aid in the quick, accurate diagnosis of automotive problems. While automotive repairs can be made by many people, accurate troubleshooting is a rare skill for the amateur and professional alike.

In its simplest state, troubleshooting is an exercise in logic. It is essential to realize that an automobile is really composed of a series of systems. Some of these systems are interrelated; others are not. Automobiles operate within a framework of logical rules and physical laws, and the key to troubleshooting is a good understanding of all the automotive systems.

This section breaks the car or truck down into its component systems, allowing the problem to be isolated. The charts and diagnostic road maps list the most common problems and the most probable causes of trouble. Obviously it would be impossible to list every possible problem that could happen along with every possible cause, but it will locate MOST problems and eliminate a lot of unnecessary guesswork. The systematic format will locate problems within a given system, but, because many automotive systems are interrelated, the solution to your particular problem may be found in a number of systems on the car or truck.

USING THE TROUBLESHOOTING CHARTS

This book contains all of the specific information that the average do-it-yourself mechanic needs to repair and maintain his or her car or truck. The troubleshooting charts are designed to be used in conjunction with the specific procedures and information in the text. For instance, troubleshooting a point-type ignition system is fairly standard for all models, but you may be directed to the text to find procedures for troubleshooting an individual type of electronic ignition. You will also have to refer to the specification charts throughout the book for specifications applicable to your car or truck.

TOOLS AND EQUIPMENT

The tools illustrated in Chapter 1 (plus two more diagnostic pieces) will be adequate to troubleshoot most problems. The two other tools needed are a voltmeter and an ohmmeter. These can be purchased separately or in combination, known as a VOM meter.

In the event that other tools are required, they will be noted in the procedures.

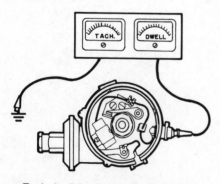

Tach-dwell hooked-up to distributor

Troubleshooting Engine Problems

See Chapters 2, 3, 4 for more information and service procedures.

Index to Systems

System	To Test	Group
Battery	Engine need not be running	1
Starting system	Engine need not be running	2
Primary electrical system	Engine need not be running	3
Secondary electrical system	Engine need not be running	4
Fuel system	Engine need not be running	5
Engine compression	Engine need not be running	6
Engine vacuum	Engine must be running	7
Secondary electrical system	Engine must be running	8
Valve train	Engine must be running	9
Exhaust system	Engine must be running	10
Cooling system	Engine must be running	11
Engine lubrication	Engine must be running	12

Index to Problems

Problem: Symptom	Begin at Specific Diagnosis, Number ___
Engine Won't Start:	
Starter doesn't turn	1.1, 2.1
Starter turns, engine doesn't	2.1
Starter turns engine very slowly	1.1, 2.4
Starter turns engine normally	3.1, 4.1
Starter turns engine very quickly	6.1
Engine fires intermittently	4.1
Engine fires consistently	5.1, 6.1
Engine Runs Poorly:	
Hard starting	3.1, 4.1, 5.1, 8.1
Rough idle	4.1, 5.1, 8.1
Stalling	3.1, 4.1, 5.1, 8.1
Engine dies at high speeds	4.1, 5.1
Hesitation (on acceleration from standing stop)	5.1, 8.1
Poor pickup	4.1, 5.1, 8.1
Lack of power	3.1, 4.1, 5.1, 8.1
Backfire through the carburetor	4.1, 8.1, 9.1
Backfire through the exhaust	4.1, 8.1, 9.1
Blue exhaust gases	6.1, 7.1
Black exhaust gases	5.1
Running on (after the ignition is shut off)	3.1, 8.1
Susceptible to moisture	4.1
Engine misfires under load	4.1, 7.1, 8.4, 9.1
Engine misfires at speed	4.1, 8.4
Engine misfires at idle	3.1, 4.1, 5.1, 7.1, 8.4

Sample Section

Test and Procedure	Results and Indications	Proceed to
4.1—Check for spark: Hold each spark plug wire approximately ¼″ from ground with gloves or a heavy, dry rag. Crank the engine and observe the spark.	If no spark is evident:	4.2
	If spark is good in some cases:	4.3
	If spark is good in all cases:	4.6

Specific Diagnosis

This section is arranged so that following each test, instructions are given to proceed to another, until a problem is diagnosed.

Section 1—Battery

Test and Procedure	Results and Indications	Proceed to
1.1—Inspect the battery visually for case condition (corrosion, cracks) and water level.	If case is cracked, replace battery:	**1.4**
	If the case is intact, remove corrosion with a solution of baking soda and water (**CAU-TION:** *do not get the solution into the battery*), and fill with water:	**1.2**

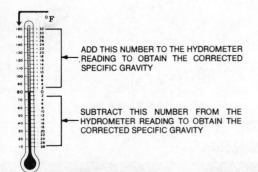

DIRT ON TOP OF BATTERY
PLUGGED VENT
CORROSION
LOOSE CABLE OR POSTS
CRACKS
LOW WATER LEVEL

Inspect the battery case

1.2—Check the battery cable connections: Insert a screwdriver between the battery post and the cable clamp. Turn the headlights on high beam, and observe them as the screwdriver is gently twisted to ensure good metal to metal contact.	If the lights brighten, remove and clean the clamp and post; coat the post with petroleum jelly, install and tighten the clamp:	**1.4**
	If no improvement is noted:	**1.3**

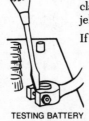

TESTING BATTERY CABLE CONNECTIONS USING A SCREWDRIVER

1.3—Test the state of charge of the battery using an individual cell tester or hydrometer.	If indicated, charge the battery. **NOTE:** *If no obvious reason exists for the low state of charge (i.e., battery age, prolonged storage), proceed to:*	**1.4**

°F
ADD THIS NUMBER TO THE HYDROMETER READING TO OBTAIN THE CORRECTED SPECIFIC GRAVITY

SUBTRACT THIS NUMBER FROM THE HYDROMETER READING TO OBTAIN THE CORRECTED SPECIFIC GRAVITY

Specific Gravity (@ 80° F.)

Minimum	Battery Charge
1.260	100% Charged
1.230	75% Charged
1.200	50% Charged
1.170	25% Charged
1.140	Very Little Power Left
1.110	Completely Discharged

The effects of temperature on battery specific gravity (left) and amount of battery charge in relation to specific gravity (right)

1.4—Visually inspect battery cables for cracking, bad connection to ground, or bad connection to starter.	If necessary, tighten connections or replace the cables:	**2.1**

Section 2—Starting System
See Chapter 3 for service procedures

Test and Procedure	Results and Indications	Proceed to
Note: Tests in Group 2 are performed with coil high tension lead disconnected to prevent accidental starting.		
2.1—Test the starter motor and solenoid: Connect a jumper from the battery post of the solenoid (or relay) to the starter post of the solenoid (or relay).	If starter turns the engine normally:	2.2
	If the starter buzzes, or turns the engine very slowly:	2.4
	If no response, replace the solenoid (or relay).	3.1
	If the starter turns, but the engine doesn't, ensure that the flywheel ring gear is intact. If the gear is undamaged, replace the starter drive.	3.1
2.2—Determine whether ignition override switches are functioning properly (clutch start switch, neutral safety switch), by connecting a jumper across the switch(es), and turning the ignition switch to "start".	If starter operates, adjust or replace switch:	3.1
	If the starter doesn't operate:	2.3
2.3—Check the ignition switch "start" position: Connect a 12V test lamp or voltmeter between the starter post of the solenoid (or relay) and ground. Turn the ignition switch to the "start" position, and jiggle the key.	If the lamp doesn't light or the meter needle doesn't move when the switch is turned, check the ignition switch for loose connections, cracked insulation, or broken wires. Repair or replace as necessary:	3.1
	If the lamp flickers or needle moves when the key is jiggled, replace the ignition switch.	3.3

Checking the ignition switch "start" position

STARTER RELAY
(IF EQUIPPED)

Test and Procedure	Results and Indications	Proceed to
2.4—Remove and bench test the starter, according to specifications in the engine electrical section.	If the starter does not meet specifications, repair or replace as needed:	3.1
	If the starter is operating properly:	2.5
2.5—Determine whether the engine can turn freely: Remove the spark plugs, and check for water in the cylinders. Check for water on the dipstick, or oil in the radiator. Attempt to turn the engine using an 18″ flex drive and socket on the crankshaft pulley nut or bolt.	If the engine will turn freely only with the spark plugs out, and hydrostatic lock (water in the cylinders) is ruled out, check valve timing:	9.2
	If engine will not turn freely, and it is known that the clutch and transmission are free, the engine must be disassembled for further evaluation:	Chapter 3

Section 3—Primary Electrical System

Test and Procedure	Results and Indications	Proceed to
3.1—Check the ignition switch "on" position: Connect a jumper wire between the distributor side of the coil and ground, and a 12V test lamp between the switch side of the coil and ground. Remove the high tension lead from the coil. Turn the ignition switch on and jiggle the key.	If the lamp lights:	**3.2**
	If the lamp flickers when the key is jiggled, replace the ignition switch:	**3.3**
	If the lamp doesn't light, check for loose or open connections. If none are found, remove the ignition switch and check for continuity. If the switch is faulty, replace it:	**3.3**

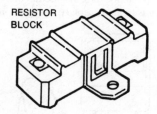

Checking the ignition switch "on" position

3.2—Check the ballast resistor or resistance wire for an open circuit, using an ohmmeter. See Chapter 3 for specific tests.	Replace the resistor or resistance wire if the resistance is zero. **NOTE:** *Some ignition systems have no ballast resistor.*	**3.3**

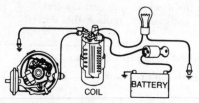

RESISTOR
BLOCK

CALIBRATED
RESISTANCE
LEAD

Two types of resistors

3.3—On point-type ignition systems, visually inspect the breaker points for burning, pitting or excessive wear. Gray coloring of the point contact surfaces is normal. Rotate the crankshaft until the contact heel rests on a high point of the distributor cam and adjust the point gap to specifications. On electronic ignition models, remove the distributor cap and visually inspect the armature. Ensure that the armature pin is in place, and that the armature is on tight and rotates when the engine is cranked. Make sure there are no cracks, chips or rounded edges on the armature.	If the breaker points are intact, clean the contact surfaces with fine emery cloth, and adjust the point gap to specifications. If the points are worn, replace them. On electronic systems, replace any parts which appear defective. If condition persists:	**3.4**

Test and Procedure	Results and Indications	Proceed to
3.4—On point-type ignition systems, connect a dwell-meter between the distributor primary lead and ground. Crank the engine and observe the point dwell angle. On electronic ignition systems, conduct a stator (magnetic pickup assembly) test. See Chapter 3.	On point-type systems, adjust the dwell angle if necessary. **NOTE:** *Increasing the point gap decreases the dwell angle and vice-versa.*	**3.6**
	If the dwell meter shows little or no reading;	**3.5**
	On electronic ignition systems, if the stator is bad, replace the stator. If the stator is good, proceed to the other tests in Chapter 3.	

Dwell is a function of point gap

3.5—On the point-type ignition systems, check the condenser for short: connect an ohmeter across the condenser body and the pigtail lead.	If any reading other than infinite is noted, replace the condenser	**3.6**

Checking the condenser for short

3.6—Test the coil primary resistance: On point-type ignition systems, connect an ohmeter across the coil primary terminals, and read the resistance on the low scale. Note whether an external ballast resistor or resistance wire is used. On electronic ignition systems, test the coil primary resistance as in Chapter 3.	Point-type ignition coils utilizing ballast resistors or resistance wires should have approximately 1.0 ohms resistance. Coils with internal resistors should have approximately 4.0 ohms resistance. If values far from the above are noted, replace the coil.	**4.1**

Check the coil primary resistance

Section 4—Secondary Electrical System
See Chapters 2–3 for service procedures

Test and Procedure	Results and Indications	Proceed to
4.1—Check for spark: Hold each spark plug wire approximately ¼″ from ground with gloves or a heavy, dry rag. Crank the engine, and observe the spark.	If no spark is evident:	**4.2**
	If spark is good in some cylinders:	**4.3**
	If spark is good in all cylinders:	**4.6**

Check for spark at the plugs

Test and Procedure	Results and Indications	Proceed to
4.2—Check for spark at the coil high tension lead: Remove the coil high tension lead from the distributor and position it approximately ¼″ from ground. Crank the engine and observe spark. **CAUTION: This test should not be performed on engines equipped with electronic ignition.**	If the spark is good and consistent:	**4.3**
	If the spark is good but intermittent, test the primary electrical system starting at 3.3:	**3.3**
	If the spark is weak or non-existent, replace the coil high tension lead, clean and tighten all connections and retest. If no improvement is noted:	**4.4**
4.3—Visually inspect the distributor cap and rotor for burned or corroded contacts, cracks, carbon tracks, or moisture. Also check the fit of the rotor on the distributor shaft (where applicable).	If moisture is present, dry thoroughly, and retest per 4.1:	**4.1**
	If burned or excessively corroded contacts, cracks, or carbon tracks are noted, replace the defective part(s) and retest per 4.1:	**4.1**
	If the rotor and cap appear intact, or are only slightly corroded, clean the contacts thoroughly (including the cap towers and spark plug wire ends) and retest per 4.1: If the spark is good in all cases:	**4.6**
	If the spark is poor in all cases:	**4.5**

CORRODED OR LOOSE WIRE

EXCESSIVE WEAR OF BUTTON

HIGH RESISTANCE CARBON

ROTOR TIP BURNED AWAY

Inspect the distributor cap and rotor

CHILTON'S
AUTO BODY
REPAIR TIPS

Tools and Materials • Step-by-Step Illustrated Procedures
How To Repair Dents, Scratches and Rust Holes
Spray Painting and Refinishing Tips

2 Grind away all traces of rust with a 24-grit grinding disc. Be sure to grind back 3-4 inches from the edge of the hole down to bare metal and be sure all traces of paint, primer and rust are removed.

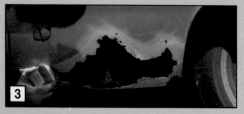

3 Block sand the area with 80 or 100 grit sandpaper to get a clear, shiny surface and feathered paint edge. Tap the edges of the hole inward with a ball peen hammer.

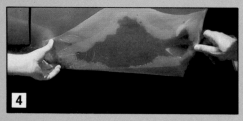

4 If you are going to use release film, cut a piece about 2-3″ larger than the area you have sanded. Place the film over the repair and mark the sanded area on the film. Avoid any unnecessary wrinkling of the film.

5 Cut 2 pieces of fiberglass matte to match the shape of the repair. One piece should be about 1″ smaller than the sanded area and the second piece should be 1″ smaller than the first. Mix enough filler and hardener to saturate the fiberglass material (see Body Repair Tips).

6 Lay the release sheet on a flat surface and spread an even layer of filler, large enough to cover the repair. Lay the smaller piece of fiberglass cloth in the center of the sheet and spread another layer of filler over the fiberglass cloth. Repeat the operation for the larger piece of cloth.

7 Place the repair material over the repair area, with the release film facing outward. Use a spreader and work from the center outward to smooth the material, following the body contours. Be sure to remove all air bubbles.

8 Wait until the repair has dried tack-free and peel off the release sheet. The ideal working temperature is 60°-90° F. Cooler or warmer temperatures or high humidity may require additional curing time. Wait longer, if in doubt.

9 Sand and feather-edge the entire area. The initial sanding can be done with a sanding disc on an electric drill if care is used. Finish the sanding with a block sander. Low spots can be filled with body filler; this may require several applications.

10 When the filler can just be scratched with a fingernail, knock the high spots down with a body file and smooth the entire area with 80-grit. Feather the filled areas into the surrounding areas.

11 When the area is sanded smooth, mix some topcoat and hardener and apply it directly with a spreader. This will give a smooth finish and prevent the glass matte from showing through the paint.

12 Block sand the topcoat smooth with finishing sandpaper (200 grit), and 400 grit. The repair is ready for masking, priming and painting (see Painting Tips).

Materials and photos courtesy Marson Corporation, Chelsea, Massachusetts

PAINTING TIPS

Preparation

1 SANDING — Use a 400 or 600 grit wet or dry sandpaper. Wet-sand the area with a 1/4 sheet of sandpaper soaked in clean water. Keep the paper wet while sanding. Sand the area until the repaired area tapers into the original finish.

2 CLEANING — Wash the area to be painted thoroughly with water and a clean rag. Rinse it thoroughly and wipe the surface dry until you're sure it's completely free of dirt, dust, fingerprints, wax, detergent or other foreign matter.

3 MASKING — Protect any areas you don't want to overspray by covering them with masking tape and newspaper. Be careful not get fingerprints on the area to be painted.

4 PRIMING — All exposed metal should be primed before painting. Primer protects the metal and provides an excellent surface for paint adhesion. When the primer is dry, wet-sand the area again with 600 grit wet-sandpaper. Clean the area again after sanding.

Painting Techniques

Paint applied from either a spray gun or a spray can (for small areas) will provide good results. Experiment on an old piece of metal to get the right combination before you begin painting.

SPRAYING VISCOSITY (SPRAY GUN ONLY) — Paint should be thinned to spraying viscosity according to the directions on the can. Use only the recommended thinner or reducer and the same amount of reduction regardless of temperature.

AIR PRESSURE (SPRAY GUN ONLY) — This is extremely important. Be sure you are using the proper recommended pressure.

TEMPERATURE — The surface to be painted should be approximately the same temperature as the surrounding air. Applying warm paint to a cold surface, or vice versa, will completely upset the paint characteristics.

THICKNESS — Spray with smooth strokes. In general, the thicker the coat of paint, the longer the drying time. Apply several thin coats about 30 seconds apart. The paint should remain wet long enough to flow out and no longer; heavier coats will only produce sags or wrinkles. Spray a light (fog) coat, followed by heavier color coats.

DISTANCE — The ideal spraying distance is 8″-12″ from the gun or can to the surface. Shorter distances will produce ripples, while greater distances will result in orange peel, dry film and poor color match and loss of material due to overspray.

OVERLAPPING — The gun or can should be kept at right angles to the surface at all times. Work to a wet edge at an even speed, using a 50% overlap and direct the center of the spray at the lower or nearest edge of the previous stroke.

RUBBING OUT (BLENDING) FRESH PAINT — Let the paint dry thoroughly. Runs or imperfections can be sanded out, primed and repainted.

Don't be in too big a hurry to remove the masking. This only produces paint ridges. When the finish has dried for at least a week, apply a small amount of fine grade rubbing compound with a clean, wet cloth. Use lots of water and blend the new paint with the surrounding area.

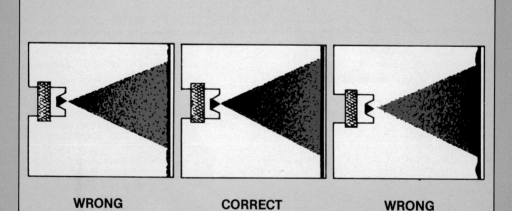

WRONG

Thin coat. Stroke too fast, not enough overlap, gun too far away.

CORRECT

Medium coat. Proper distance, good stroke, proper overlap.

WRONG

Heavy coat. Stroke too slow, too much overlap, gun too close.

Test and Procedure	Results and Indications	Proceed to
4.4—Check the coil secondary resistance: On point-type systems connect an ohmmeter across the distributor side of the coil and the coil tower. Read the resistance on the high scale of the ohmmeter. On electronic ignition systems, see Chapter 3 for specific tests.	The resistance of a satisfactory coil should be between 4,000 and 10,000 ohms. If resistance is considerably higher (i.e., 40,000 ohms) replace the coil and retest per 4.1. **NOTE:** *This does not apply to high performance coils.*	

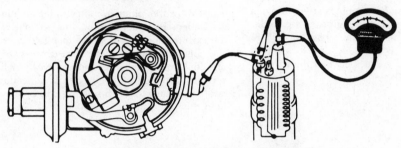

Testing the coil secondary resistance

| **4.5**—Visually inspect the spark plug wires for cracking or brittleness. Ensure that no two wires are positioned so as to cause induction firing (adjacent and parallel). Remove each wire, one by one, and check resistance with an ohmmeter. | Replace any cracked or brittle wires. If any of the wires are defective, replace the entire set. Replace any wires with excessive resistance (over 8000 Ω per foot for suppression wire), and separate any wires that might cause induction firing. | **4.6** |

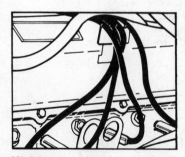

Misfiring can be the result of spark plug leads to adjacent, consecutively firing cylinders running parallel and too close together

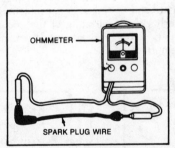

On point-type ignition systems, check the spark plug wires as shown. On electronic ignitions, do not remove the wire from the distributor cap terminal; instead, test through the cap

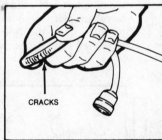

Spark plug wires can be checked visually by bending them in a loop over your finger. This will reveal any cracks, burned or broken insulation. Any wire with cracked insulation should be replaced

| **4.6**—Remove the spark plugs, noting the cylinders from which they were removed, and evaluate according to the color photos in the middle of this book. | See following. | **See following.** |

Test and Procedure	Results and Indications	Proceed to
4.7—Examine the location of all the plugs.	The following diagrams illustrate some of the conditions that the location of plugs will reveal.	**4.8**

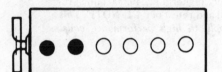

Two adjacent plugs are fouled in a 6-cylinder engine, 4-cylinder engine or either bank of a V-8. This is probably due to a blown head gasket between the two cylinders

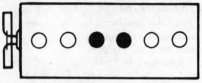

The two center plugs in a 6-cylinder engine are fouled. Raw fuel may be "boiled" out of the carburetor into the intake manifold after the engine is shut-off. Stop-start driving can also foul the center plugs, due to overly rich mixture. Proper float level, a new float needle and seat or use of an insulating spacer may help this problem

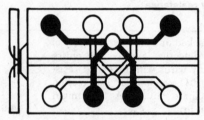

An unbalanced carburetor is indicated. Following the fuel flow on this particular design shows that the cylinders fed by the right-hand barrel are fouled from overly rich mixture, while the cylinders fed by the left-hand barrel are normal

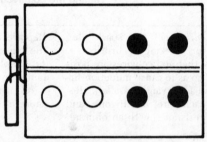

If the four rear plugs are overheated, a cooling system problem is suggested. A thorough cleaning of the cooling system may restore coolant circulation and cure the problem

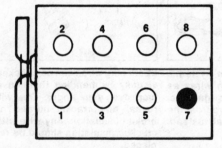

Finding one plug overheated may indicate an intake manifold leak near the affected cylinder. If the overheated plug is the second of two adjacent, consecutively firing plugs, it could be the result of ignition cross-firing. Separating the leads to these two plugs will eliminate cross-fire

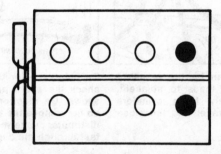

Occasionally, the two rear plugs in large, lightly used V-8's will become oil fouled. High oil consumption and smoky exhaust may also be noticed. It is probably due to plugged oil drain holes in the rear of the cylinder head, causing oil to be sucked in around the valve stems. This usually occurs in the rear cylinders first, because the engine slants that way

Test and Procedure	Results and Indications	Proceed to
4.8—Determine the static ignition timing. Using the crankshaft pulley timing marks as a guide, locate top dead center on the compression stroke of the number one cylinder.	The rotor should be pointing toward the No. 1 tower in the distributor cap, and, on electronic ignitions, the armature spoke for that cylinder should be lined up with the stator.	4.8
4.9—Check coil polarity: Connect a voltmeter negative lead to the coil high tension lead, and the positive lead to ground (**NOTE: *Reverse the hook-up for positive ground systems***). Crank the engine momentarily. **Checking coil polarity**	If the voltmeter reads up-scale, the polarity is correct: If the voltmeter reads down-scale, reverse the coil polarity (switch the primary leads):	5.1 5.1

Section 5—Fuel System
See Chapter 4 for service procedures

Test and Procedure	Results and Indications	Proceed to
5.1—Determine that the air filter is functioning efficiently: Hold paper elements up to a strong light, and attempt to see light through the filter.	Clean permanent air filters in solvent (or manufacturer's recommendation), and allow to dry. Replace paper elements through which light cannot be seen:	5.2
5.2—Determine whether a flooding condition exists: Flooding is identified by a strong gasoline odor, and excessive gasoline present in the throttle bore(s) of the carburetor. **If the engine floods repeatedly, check the choke butterfly flap**	If flooding is not evident: If flooding is evident, permit the gasoline to dry for a few moments and restart. If flooding doesn't recur: If flooding is persistent:	5.3 5.7 5.5
5.3—Check that fuel is reaching the carburetor: Detach the fuel line at the carburetor inlet. Hold the end of the line in a cup (not styrofoam), and crank the engine. 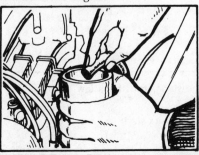 **Check the fuel pump by disconnecting the output line (fuel pump-to-carburetor) at the carburetor and operating the starter briefly**	If fuel flows smoothly: If fuel doesn't flow (**NOTE: *Make sure that there is fuel in the tank***), or flows erratically:	5.7 5.4

Test and Procedure	Results and Indications	Proceed to
5.4—Test the fuel pump: Disconnect all fuel lines from the fuel pump. Hold a finger over the input fitting, crank the engine (with electric pump, turn the ignition or pump on); and feel for suction.	If suction is evident, blow out the fuel line to the tank with low pressure compressed air until bubbling is heard from the fuel filler neck. Also blow out the carburetor fuel line (both ends disconnected):	**5.7**
	If no suction is evident, replace or repair the fuel pump: NOTE: *Repeated oil fouling of the spark plugs, or a no-start condition, could be the result of a ruptured vacuum booster pump diaphragm, through which oil or gasoline is being drawn into the intake manifold (where applicable).*	**5.7**
5.5—Occasionally, small specks of dirt will clog the small jets and orifices in the carburetor. With the engine cold, hold a flat piece of wood or similar material over the carburetor, where possible, and crank the engine.	If the engine starts, but runs roughly the engine is probably not run enough. If the engine won't start:	**5.9**
5.6—Check the needle and seat: Tap the carburetor in the area of the needle and seat.	If flooding stops, a gasoline additive (e.g., Gumout) will often cure the problem:	**5.7**
	If flooding continues, check the fuel pump for excessive pressure at the carburetor (according to specifications). If the pressure is normal, the needle and seat must be removed and checked, and/or the float level adjusted:	**5.7**
5.7—Test the accelerator pump by looking into the throttle bores while operating the throttle.	If the accelerator pump appears to be operating normally:	**5.8**
	If the accelerator pump is not operating, the pump must be reconditioned. Where possible, service the pump with the carburetor(s) installed on the engine. If necessary, remove the carburetor. Prior to removal:	**5.8**
Check for gas at the carburetor by looking down the carburetor throat while someone moves the accelerator		
5.8—Determine whether the carburetor main fuel system is functioning: Spray a commercial starting fluid into the carburetor while attempting to start the engine.	If the engine starts, runs for a few seconds, and dies:	**5.9**
	If the engine doesn't start:	**6.1**

Test and Procedure	Results and Indications	Proceed to
5.9—Uncommon fuel system malfunctions: See below:	If the problem is solved:	**6.1**
	If the problem remains, remove and recondition the carburetor.	

Condition	Indication	Test	Prevailing Weather Conditions	Remedy
Vapor lock	Engine will not restart shortly after running.	Cool the components of the fuel system until the engine starts. Vapor lock can be cured faster by draping a wet cloth over a mechanical fuel pump.	Hot to very hot	Ensure that the exhaust manifold heat control valve is operating. Check with the vehicle manufacturer for the recommended solution to vapor lock on the model in question.
Carburetor icing	Engine will not idle, stalls at low speeds.	Visually inspect the throttle plate area of the throttle bores for frost.	High humidity, 32–40° F.	Ensure that the exhaust manifold heat control valve is operating, and that the intake manifold heat riser is not blocked.
Water in the fuel	Engine sputters and stalls; may not start.	Pump a small amount of fuel into a glass jar. Allow to stand, and inspect for droplets or a layer of water.	High humidity, extreme temperature changes.	For droplets, use one or two cans of commercial gas line anti-freeze. For a layer of water, the tank must be drained, and the fuel lines blown out with compressed air.

Section 6—Engine Compression
See Chapter 3 for service procedures

6.1—Test engine compression: Remove all spark plugs. Block the throttle wide open. Insert a compression gauge into a spark plug port, crank the engine to obtain the maximum reading, and record.

	Proceed to
If compression is within limits on all cylinders:	**7.1**
If gauge reading is extremely low on all cylinders:	**6.2**
If gauge reading is low on one or two cylinders: (If gauge readings are identical and low on two or more adjacent cylinders, the head gasket must be replaced.)	**6.2**

Checking compression

6.2—Test engine compression (wet): Squirt approximately 30 cc. of engine oil into each cylinder, and retest per 6.1.

If the readings improve, worn or cracked rings or broken pistons are indicated:	**See Chapter 3**
If the readings do not improve, burned or excessively carboned valves or a jumped timing chain are indicated:	**7.1**

NOTE: *A jumped timing chain is often indicated by difficult cranking.*

Section 7—Engine Vacuum
See Chapter 3 for service procedures

Test and Procedure	Results and Indications	Proceed to
7.1—Attach a vacuum gauge to the intake manifold beyond the throttle plate. Start the engine, and observe the action of the needle over the range of engine speeds.	See below.	See below

INDICATION: normal engine in good condition

Proceed to: 8.1

Normal engine
Gauge reading: steady, from 17–22 in./Hg.

INDICATION: sticking valves or ignition miss

Proceed to: 9.1, 8.3

Sticking valves
Gauge reading: intermittent fluctuation at idle

INDICATION: late ignition or valve timing, low compression, stuck throttle valve, leaking carburetor or manifold gasket

Proceed to: 6.1

Incorrect valve timing
Gauge reading: low (10–15 in./Hg) but steady

INDICATION: improper carburetor adjustment or minor intake leak.

Proceed to: 7.2

Carburetor requires adjustment
Gauge reading: drifting needle

INDICATION: ignition miss, blown cylinder head gasket, leaking valve or weak valve spring

Proceed to: 8.3, 6.1

Blown head gasket
Gauge reading: needle fluctuates as engine speed increases

INDICATION: burnt valve or faulty valve clearance. Needle will fall when defective valve operates

Proceed to: 9.1

Burnt or leaking valves
Gauge reading: steady needle, but drops regularly

INDICATION: choked muffler, excessive back pressure in system

Proceed to: 10.1

Clogged exhaust system
Gauge reading: gradual drop in reading at idle

INDICATION: worn valve guides

Proceed to: 9.1

Worn valve guides
Gauge reading: needle vibrates excessively at idle, but steadies as engine speed increases

White pointer = steady gauge hand | Black pointer = fluctuating gauge hand

Test and Procedure	Results and Indications	Proceed to
7.2—Attach a vacuum gauge per 7.1, and test for an intake manifold leak. Squirt a small amount of oil around the intake manifold gaskets, carburetor gaskets, plugs and fittings. Observe the action of the vacuum gauge.	If the reading improves, replace the indicated gasket, or seal the indicated fitting or plug:	**8.1**
	If the reading remains low:	**7.3**
7.3—Test all vacuum hoses and accessories for leaks as described in 7.2. Also check the carburetor body (dashpots, automatic choke mechanism, throttle shafts) for leaks in the same manner.	If the reading improves, service or replace the offending part(s):	**8.1**
	If the reading remains low:	**6.1**

Section 8—Secondary Electrical System
See Chapter 2 for service procedures

Test and Procedure	Results and Indications	Proceed to
8.1—Remove the distributor cap and check to make sure that the rotor turns when the engine is cranked. Visually inspect the distributor components.	Clean, tighten or replace any components which appear defective.	**8.2**
8.2—Connect a timing light (per manufacturer's recommendation) and check the dynamic ignition timing. Disconnect and plug the vacuum hose(s) to the distributor if specified, start the engine, and observe the timing marks at the specified engine speed.	If the timing is not correct, adjust to specifications by rotating the distributor in the engine: (Advance timing by rotating distributor opposite normal direction of rotor rotation, retard timing by rotating distributor in same direction as rotor rotation.)	**8.3**
8.3—Check the operation of the distributor advance mechanism(s): To test the mechanical advance, disconnect the vacuum lines from the distributor advance unit and observe the timing marks with a timing light as the engine speed is increased from idle. If the mark moves smoothly, without hesitation, it may be assumed that the mechanical advance is functioning properly. To test vacuum advance and/or retard systems, alternately crimp and release the vacuum line, and observe the timing mark for movement. If movement is noted, the system is operating.	If the systems are functioning:	**8.4**
	If the systems are not functioning, remove the distributor, and test on a distributor tester:	**8.4**
8.4—Locate an ignition miss: With the engine running, remove each spark plug wire, one at a time, until one is found that doesn't cause the engine to roughen and slow down.	When the missing cylinder is identified:	**4.1**

Section 9—Valve Train
See Chapter 3 for service procedures

Test and Procedure	Results and Indications	Proceed to
9.1—Evaluate the valve train: Remove the valve cover, and ensure that the valves are adjusted to specifications. A mechanic's stethoscope may be used to aid in the diagnosis of the valve train. By pushing the probe on or near push rods or rockers, valve noise often can be isolated. A timing light also may be used to diagnose valve problems. Connect the light according to manufacturer's recommendations, and start the engine. Vary the firing moment of the light by increasing the engine speed (and therefore the ignition advance), and moving the trigger from cylinder to cylinder. Observe the movement of each valve.	Sticking valves or erratic valve train motion can be observed with the timing light. The cylinder head must be disassembled for repairs.	**See Chapter 3**
9.2—Check the valve timing: Locate top dead center of the No. 1 piston, and install a degree wheel or tape on the crankshaft pulley or damper with zero corresponding to an index mark on the engine. Rotate the crankshaft in its direction of rotation, and observe the opening of the No. 1 cylinder intake valve. The opening should correspond with the correct mark on the degree wheel according to specifications.	If the timing is not correct, the timing cover must be removed for further investigation.	**See Chapter 3**

Section 10—Exhaust System

Test and Procedure	Results and Indications	Proceed to
10.1—Determine whether the exhaust manifold heat control valve is operating: Operate the valve by hand to determine whether it is free to move. If the valve is free, run the engine to operating temperature and observe the action of the valve, to ensure that it is opening.	If the valve sticks, spray it with a suitable solvent, open and close the valve to free it, and retest. If the valve functions properly: If the valve does not free, or does not operate, replace the valve:	**10.2** **10.2**
10.2—Ensure that there are no exhaust restrictions: Visually inspect the exhaust system for kinks, dents, or crushing. Also note that gases are flowing freely from the tailpipe at all engine speeds, indicating no restriction in the muffler or resonator.	Replace any damaged portion of the system:	**11.1**

Section 11—Cooling System
See Chapter 3 for service procedures

Test and Procedure	Results and Indications	Proceed to
11.1—Visually inspect the fan belt for glazing, cracks, and fraying, and replace if necessary. Tighten the belt so that the longest span has approximately ½″ play at its mid-point under thumb pressure (see Chapter 1).	Replace or tighten the fan belt as necessary:	**11.2**

Checking belt tension

11.2—Check the fluid level of the cooling system.	If full or slightly low, fill as necessary:	**11.5**
	If extremely low:	**11.3**

11.3—Visually inspect the external portions of the cooling system (radiator, radiator hoses, thermostat elbow, water pump seals, heater hoses, etc.) for leaks. If none are found, pressurize the cooling system to 14–15 psi.	If cooling system holds the pressure:	**11.5**
	If cooling system loses pressure rapidly, reinspect external parts of the system for leaks under pressure. If none are found, check dipstick for coolant in crankcase. If no coolant is present, but pressure loss continues:	**11.4**
	If coolant is evident in crankcase, remove cylinder head(s), and check gasket(s). If gaskets are intact, block and cylinder head(s) should be checked for cracks or holes.	
	If the gasket(s) is blown, replace, and purge the crankcase of coolant:	**12.6**
	NOTE: *Occasionally, due to atmospheric and driving conditions, condensation of water can occur in the crankcase. This causes the oil to appear milky white. To remedy, run the engine until hot, and change the oil and oil filter.*	

11.4—Check for combustion leaks into the cooling system: Pressurize the cooling system as above. Start the engine, and observe the pressure gauge. If the needle fluctuates, remove each spark plug wire, one at a time, noting which cylinder(s) reduce or eliminate the fluctuation.	Cylinders which reduce or eliminate the fluctuation, when the spark plug wire is removed, are leaking into the cooling system. Replace the head gasket on the affected cylinder bank(s).	

Pressurizing the cooling system

Test and Procedure	Results and Indications	Proceed to
11.5—Check the radiator pressure cap: Attach a radiator pressure tester to the radiator cap (wet the seal prior to installation). Quickly pump up the pressure, noting the point at which the cap releases.	If the cap releases within ± 1 psi of the specified rating, it is operating properly:	**11.6**
	If the cap releases at more than ± 1 psi of the specified rating, it should be replaced:	**11.6**

Checking radiator pressure cap

Test and Procedure	Results and Indications	Proceed to
11.6—Test the thermostat: Start the engine cold, remove the radiator cap, and insert a thermometer into the radiator. Allow the engine to idle. After a short while, there will be a sudden, rapid increase in coolant temperature. The temperature at which this sharp rise stops is the thermostat opening temperature.	If the thermostat opens at or about the specified temperature:	**11.7**
	If the temperature doesn't increase: (If the temperature increases slowly and gradually, replace the thermostat.)	**11.7**
11.7—Check the water pump: Remove the thermostat elbow and the thermostat, disconnect the coil high tension lead (to prevent starting), and crank the engine momentarily.	If coolant flows, replace the thermostat and retest per 11.6:	**11.6**
	If coolant doesn't flow, reverse flush the cooling system to alleviate any blockage that might exist. If system is not blocked, and coolant will not flow, replace the water pump.	

Section 12—Lubrication
See Chapter 3 for service procedures

Test and Procedure	Results and Indications	Proceed to
12.1—Check the oil pressure gauge or warning light: If the gauge shows low pressure, or the light is on for no obvious reason, remove the oil pressure sender. Install an accurate oil pressure gauge and run the engine momentarily.	If oil pressure builds normally, run engine for a few moments to determine that it is functioning normally, and replace the sender.	—
	If the pressure remains low:	**12.2**
	If the pressure surges:	**12.3**
	If the oil pressure is zero:	**12.3**
12.2—Visually inspect the oil: If the oil is watery or very thin, milky, or foamy, replace the oil and oil filter.	If the oil is normal:	**12.3**
	If after replacing oil the pressure remains low:	**12.3**
	If after replacing oil the pressure becomes normal:	—

Test and Procedure	Results and Indications	Proceed to
12.3—Inspect the oil pressure relief valve and spring, to ensure that it is not sticking or stuck. Remove and thoroughly clean the valve, spring, and the valve body.	If the oil pressure improves: If no improvement is noted:	— **12.4**
12.4—Check to ensure that the oil pump is not cavitating (sucking air instead of oil): See that the crankcase is neither over nor underfull, and that the pickup in the sump is in the proper position and free from sludge.	Fill or drain the crankcase to the proper capacity, and clean the pickup screen in solvent if necessary. If no improvement is noted:	**12.5**
12.5—Inspect the oil pump drive and the oil pump:	If the pump drive or the oil pump appear to be defective, service as necessary and retest per 12.1: If the pump drive and pump appear to be operating normally, the engine should be disassembled to determine where blockage exists:	**12.1** **See Chapter 3**
12.6—Purge the engine of ethylene glycol coolant: Completely drain the crankcase and the oil filter. Obtain a commercial butyl cellosolve base solvent, designated for this purpose, and follow the instructions precisely. Following this, install a new oil filter and refill the crankcase with the proper weight oil. The next oil and filter change should follow shortly thereafter (1000 miles).		

TROUBLESHOOTING EMISSION CONTROL SYSTEMS

See Chapter 4 for procedures applicable to individual emission control systems used on specific combinations of engine/transmission/model.

TROUBLESHOOTING THE CARBURETOR

See Chapter 4 for service procedures

Carburetor problems cannot be effectively isolated unless all other engine systems (particularly ignition and emission) are functioning properly and the engine is properly tuned.

Condition	Possible Cause
Engine cranks, but does not start	1. Improper starting procedure 2. No fuel in tank 3. Clogged fuel line or filter 4. Defective fuel pump 5. Choke valve not closing properly 6. Engine flooded 7. Choke valve not unloading 8. Throttle linkage not making full travel 9. Stuck needle or float 10. Leaking float needle or seat 11. Improper float adjustment
Engine stalls	1. Improperly adjusted idle speed or mixture **Engine hot** 2. Improperly adjusted dashpot 3. Defective or improperly adjusted solenoid 4. Incorrect fuel level in fuel bowl 5. Fuel pump pressure too high 6. Leaking float needle seat 7. Secondary throttle valve stuck open 8. Air or fuel leaks 9. Idle air bleeds plugged or missing 10. Idle passages plugged **Engine Cold** 11. Incorrectly adjusted choke 12. Improperly adjusted fast idle speed 13. Air leaks 14. Plugged idle or idle air passages 15. Stuck choke valve or binding linkage 16. Stuck secondary throttle valves 17. Engine flooding—high fuel level 18. Leaking or misaligned float
Engine hesitates on acceleration	1. Clogged fuel filter 2. Leaking fuel pump diaphragm 3. Low fuel pump pressure 4. Secondary throttle valves stuck, bent or misadjusted 5. Sticking or binding air valve 6. Defective accelerator pump 7. Vacuum leaks 8. Clogged air filter 9. Incorrect choke adjustment (engine cold)
Engine feels sluggish or flat on acceleration	1. Improperly adjusted idle speed or mixture 2. Clogged fuel filter 3. Defective accelerator pump 4. Dirty, plugged or incorrect main metering jets 5. Bent or sticking main metering rods 6. Sticking throttle valves 7. Stuck heat riser 8. Binding or stuck air valve 9. Dirty, plugged or incorrect secondary jets 10. Bent or sticking secondary metering rods. 11. Throttle body or manifold heat passages plugged 12. Improperly adjusted choke or choke vacuum break.
Carburetor floods	1. Defective fuel pump. Pressure too high. 2. Stuck choke valve 3. Dirty, worn or damaged float or needle valve/seat 4. Incorrect float/fuel level 5. Leaking float bowl

Condition	Possible Cause
Engine idles roughly and stalls	1. Incorrect idle speed 2. Clogged fuel filter 3. Dirt in fuel system or carburetor 4. Loose carburetor screws or attaching bolts 5. Broken carburetor gaskets 6. Air leaks 7. Dirty carburetor 8. Worn idle mixture needles 9. Throttle valves stuck open 10. Incorrectly adjusted float or fuel level 11. Clogged air filter
Engine runs unevenly or surges	1. Defective fuel pump 2. Dirty or clogged fuel filter 3. Plugged, loose or incorrect main metering jets or rods 4. Air leaks 5. Bent or sticking main metering rods 6. Stuck power piston 7. Incorrect float adjustment 8. Incorrect idle speed or mixture 9. Dirty or plugged idle system passages 10. Hard, brittle or broken gaskets 11. Loose attaching or mounting screws 12. Stuck or misaligned secondary throttle valves
Poor fuel economy	1. Poor driving habits 2. Stuck choke valve 3. Binding choke linkage 4. Stuck heat riser 5. Incorrect idle mixture 6. Defective accelerator pump 7. Air leaks 8. Plugged, loose or incorrect main metering jets 9. Improperly adjusted float or fuel level 10. Bent, misaligned or fuel-clogged float 11. Leaking float needle seat 12. Fuel leak 13. Accelerator pump discharge ball not seating properly 14. Incorrect main jets
Engine lacks high speed performance or power	1. Incorrect throttle linkage adjustment 2. Stuck or binding power piston 3. Defective accelerator pump 4. Air leaks 5. Incorrect float setting or fuel level 6. Dirty, plugged, worn or incorrect main metering jets or rods 7. Binding or sticking air valve 8. Brittle or cracked gaskets 9. Bent, incorrect or improperly adjusted secondary metering rods 10. Clogged fuel filter 11. Clogged air filter 12. Defective fuel pump

TROUBLESHOOTING FUEL INJECTION PROBLEMS

Each fuel injection system has its own unique components and test procedures, for which it is impossible to generalize. Refer to Chapter 4 of this Repair & Tune-Up Guide for specific test and repair procedures, if the vehicle is equipped with fuel injection.

TROUBLESHOOTING ELECTRICAL PROBLEMS

See Chapter 5 for service procedures

For any electrical system to operate, it must make a complete circuit. This simply means that the power flow from the battery must make a complete circle. When an electrical component is operating, power flows from the battery to the component, passes through the component causing it to perform its function (lighting a light bulb), and then returns to the battery through the ground of the circuit. This ground is usually (but not always) the metal part of the car or truck on which the electrical component is mounted.

Perhaps the easiest way to visualize this is to think of connecting a light bulb with two wires attached to it to the battery. If one of the two wires attached to the light bulb were attached to the negative post of the battery and the other were attached to the positive post of the battery, you would have a complete circuit. Current from the battery would flow to the light bulb, causing it to light, and return to the negative post of the battery.

The normal automotive circuit differs from this simple example in two ways. First, instead of having a return wire from the bulb to the battery, the light bulb returns the current to the battery through the chassis of the vehicle. Since the negative battery cable is attached to the chassis and the chassis is made of electrically conductive metal, the chassis of the vehicle can serve as a ground wire to complete the circuit. Secondly, most automotive circuits contain switches to turn components on and off as required.

Every complete circuit from a power source must include a component which is using the power from the power source. If you were to disconnect the light bulb from the wires and touch the two wires together (don't do this) the power supply wire to the component would be grounded before the normal ground connection for the circuit.

Because grounding a wire from a power source makes a complete circuit—less the required component to use the power—this phenomenon is called a short circuit. Common causes are: broken insulation (exposing the metal wire to a metal part of the car or truck), or a shorted switch.

Some electrical components which require a large amount of current to operate also have a relay in their circuit. Since these circuits carry a large amount of current, the thickness of the wire in the circuit (gauge size) is also greater. If this large wire were connected from the component to the control switch on the instrument panel, and then back to the component, a voltage drop would occur in the circuit. To prevent this potential drop in voltage, an electromagnetic switch (relay) is used. The large wires in the circuit are connected from the battery to one side of the relay, and from the opposite side of the relay to the component. The relay is normally open, preventing current from passing through the circuit. An additional, smaller, wire is connected from the relay to the control switch for the circuit. When the control switch is turned on, it grounds the smaller wire from the relay and completes the circuit. This closes the relay and allows current to flow from the battery to the component. The horn, headlight, and starter circuits are three which use relays.

It is possible for larger surges of current to pass through the electrical system of your car or truck. If this surge of current were to reach an electrical component, it could burn it out. To prevent this, fuses, circuit breakers or fusible links are connected into the current supply wires of most of the major electrical systems. When an electrical current of excessive power passes through the component's fuse, the fuse blows out and breaks the circuit, saving the component from destruction.

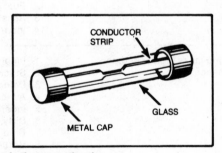

Typical automotive fuse

A circuit breaker is basically a self-repairing fuse. The circuit breaker opens the circuit the same way a fuse does. However, when either the short is removed from the circuit or the surge subsides, the circuit breaker resets itself and does not have to be replaced as a fuse does.

A fuse link is a wire that acts as a fuse. It is normally connected between the starter relay and the main wiring harness. This connection is usually under the hood. The fuse link (if installed) protects all the

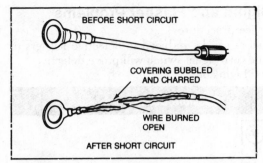

BEFORE SHORT CIRCUIT

COVERING BUBBLED AND CHARRED

WIRE BURNED OPEN

AFTER SHORT CIRCUIT

Most fusible links show a charred, melted insulation when they burn out

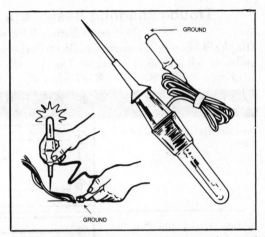

GROUND

GROUND

The test light will show the presence of current when touched to a hot wire and grounded at the other end

chassis electrical components, and is the probable cause of trouble when none of the electrical components function, unless the battery is disconnected or dead.

Electrical problems generally fall into one of three areas:

1. The component that is not functioning is not receiving current.

2. The component itself is not functioning.

3. The component is not properly grounded.

The electrical system can be checked with a test light and a jumper wire. A test light is a device that looks like a pointed screwdriver with a wire attached to it and has a light bulb in its handle. A jumper wire is a piece of insulated wire with an alligator clip attached to each end.

If a component is not working, you must follow a systematic plan to determine which of the three causes is the villain.

1. Turn on the switch that controls the inoperable component.

2. Disconnect the power supply wire from the component.

3. Attach the ground wire on the test light to a good metal ground.

4. Touch the probe end of the test light to the end of the power supply wire that was disconnected from the component. If the component is receiving current, the test light will go on.

NOTE: *Some components work only when the ignition switch is turned on.*

If the test light does not go on, then the problem is in the circuit between the battery and the component. This includes all the switches, fuses, and relays in the system. Follow the wire that runs back to the battery. The problem is an open circuit between the

battery and the component. If the fuse is blown and, when replaced, immediately blows again, there is a short circuit in the system which must be located and repaired. If there is a switch in the system, bypass it with a jumper wire. This is done by connecting one end of the jumper wire to the power supply wire into the switch and the other end of the jumper wire to the wire coming out of the switch. If the test light lights with the jumper wire installed, the switch or whatever was bypassed is defective.

NOTE: *Never substitute the jumper wire for the component, since it is required to use the power from the power source.*

5. If the bulb in the test light goes on, then the current is getting to the component that is not working. This eliminates the first of the three possible causes. Connect the power supply wire and connect a jumper wire from the component to a good metal ground. Do this with the switch which controls the component turned on, and also the ignition switch turned on if it is required for the component to work. If the component works with the jumper wire installed, then it has a bad ground. This is usually caused by the metal area on which the component mounts to the chassis being coated with some type of foreign matter.

6. If neither test located the source of the trouble, then the component itself is defective. Remember that for any electrical system to work, all connections must be clean and tight.

Troubleshooting Basic Turn Signal and Flasher Problems
See Chapter 5 for service procedures

Most problems in the turn signals or flasher system can be reduced to defective flashers or bulbs, which are easily replaced. Occasionally, the turn signal switch will prove defective.

F = Front   R = Rear   ● = Lights off   ○ = Lights on

Condition	Possible Cause
Turn signals light, but do not flash 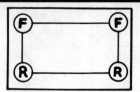	Defective flasher
No turn signals light on either side 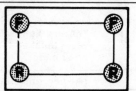	Blown fuse. Replace if defective. Defective flasher. Check by substitution. Open circuit, short circuit or poor ground.
Both turn signals on one side don't work 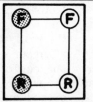	Bad bulbs. Bad ground in both (or either) housings.
One turn signal light on one side doesn't work 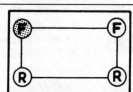	Defective bulb. Corrosion in socket. Clean contacts. Poor ground at socket.
Turn signal flashes too fast or too slowly 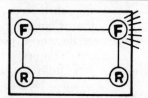	Check any bulb on the side flashing too fast. A heavy-duty bulb is probably installed in place of a regular bulb. Check the bulb flashing too slowly. A standard bulb was probably installed in place of a heavy-duty bulb. Loose connections or corrosion at the bulb socket.
Indicator lights don't work in either direction 	Check if the turn signals are working. Check the dash indicator lights. Check the flasher by substitution.
One indicator light doesn't light 	On systems with one dash indicator: See if the lights work on the same side. Often the filaments have been reversed in systems combining stoplights with tail-lights and turn signals. Check the flasher by substitution. On systems with two indicators: Check the bulbs on the same side. Check the indicator light bulb. Check the flasher by substitution.

Troubleshooting Lighting Problems
See Chapter 5 for service procedures

Condition	Possible Cause
One or more lights don't work, but others do	1. Defective bulb(s) 2. Blown fuse(s) 3. Dirty fuse clips or light sockets 4. Poor ground circuit
Lights burn out quickly	1. Incorrect voltage regulator setting or defective regulator 2. Poor battery/alternator connections
Lights go dim	1. Low/discharged battery 2. Alternator not charging 3. Corroded sockets or connections 4. Low voltage output
Lights flicker	1. Loose connection 2. Poor ground. (Run ground wire from light housing to frame) 3. Circuit breaker operating (short circuit)
Lights "flare"—Some flare is normal on acceleration—If excessive, see "Lights Burn Out Quickly"	High voltage setting
Lights glare—approaching drivers are blinded	1. Lights adjusted too high 2. Rear springs or shocks sagging 3. Rear tires soft

Troubleshooting Dash Gauge Problems

Most problems can be traced to a defective sending unit or faulty wiring. Occasionally, the gauge itself is at fault. See Chapter 5 for service procedures.

Condition	Possible Cause

COOLANT TEMPERATURE GAUGE

Gauge reads erratically or not at all	1. Loose or dirty connections 2. Defective sending unit. 3. Defective gauge. To test a bi-metal gauge, remove the wire from the sending unit. Ground the wire for an instant. If the gauge registers, replace the sending unit. To test a magnetic gauge, disconnect the wire at the sending unit. With ignition ON gauge should register COLD. Ground the wire; gauge should register HOT.

AMMETER GAUGE—TURN HEADLIGHTS ON (DO NOT START ENGINE). NOTE REACTION

Ammeter shows charge Ammeter shows discharge Ammeter does not move	1. Connections reversed on gauge 2. Ammeter is OK 3. Loose connections or faulty wiring 4. Defective gauge

Condition	Possible Cause

OIL PRESSURE GAUGE

Gauge does not register or is inaccurate	1. On mechanical gauge, Bourdon tube may be bent or kinked. 2. Low oil pressure. Remove sending unit. Idle the engine briefly. If no oil flows from sending unit hole, problem is in engine. 3. Defective gauge. Remove the wire from the sending unit and ground it for an instant with the ignition ON. A good gauge will go to the top of the scale. 4. Defective wiring. Check the wiring to the gauge. If it's OK and the gauge doesn't register when grounded, replace the gauge. 5. Defective sending unit.

ALL GAUGES

All gauges do not operate	1. Blown fuse
	2. Defective instrument regulator
All gauges read low or erratically	3. Defective or dirty instrument voltage regulator
All gauges pegged	4. Loss of ground between instrument voltage regulator and frame
	5. Defective instrument regulator

WARNING LIGHTS

Light(s) do not come on when ignition is ON, but engine is not started	1. Defective bulb 2. Defective wire 3. Defective sending unit. Disconnect the wire from the sending unit and ground it. Replace the sending unit if the light comes on with the ignition ON.
Light comes on with engine running	4. Problem in individual system 5. Defective sending unit

Troubleshooting Clutch Problems

It is false economy to replace individual clutch components. The pressure plate, clutch plate and throwout bearing should be replaced as a set, and the flywheel face inspected, whenever the clutch is overhauled. See Chapter 6 for service procedures.

Condition	Possible Cause
Clutch chatter	1. Grease on driven plate (disc) facing 2. Binding clutch linkage or cable 3. Loose, damaged facings on driven plate (disc) 4. Engine mounts loose 5. Incorrect height adjustment of pressure plate release levers 6. Clutch housing or housing to transmission adapter misalignment 7. Loose driven plate hub
Clutch grabbing	1. Oil, grease on driven plate (disc) facing 2. Broken pressure plate 3. Warped or binding driven plate. Driven plate binding on clutch shaft
Clutch slips	1. Lack of lubrication in clutch linkage or cable (linkage or cable binds, causes incomplete engagement) 2. Incorrect pedal, or linkage adjustment 3. Broken pressure plate springs 4. Weak pressure plate springs 5. Grease on driven plate facings (disc)

Troubleshooting Clutch Problems (cont.)

Condition	Possible Cause
Incomplete clutch release	1. Incorrect pedal or linkage adjustment or linkage or cable binding 2. Incorrect height adjustment on pressure plate release levers 3. Loose, broken facings on driven plate (disc) 4. Bent, dished, warped driven plate caused by overheating
Grinding, whirring grating noise when pedal is depressed	1. Worn or defective throwout bearing 2. Starter drive teeth contacting flywheel ring gear teeth. Look for milled or polished teeth on ring gear.
Squeal, howl, trumpeting noise when pedal is being released (occurs during first inch to inch and one-half of pedal travel)	Pilot bushing worn or lack of lubricant. If bushing appears OK, polish bushing with emery cloth, soak lube wick in oil, lube bushing with oil, apply film of chassis grease to clutch shaft pilot hub, reassemble. NOTE: Bushing wear may be due to misalignment of clutch housing or housing to transmission adapter
Vibration or clutch pedal pulsation with clutch disengaged (pedal fully depressed)	1. Worn or defective engine transmission mounts 2. Flywheel run out. (Flywheel run out at face not to exceed 0.005″) 3. Damaged or defective clutch components

Troubleshooting Manual Transmission Problems
See Chapter 6 for service procedures

Condition	Possible Cause
Transmission jumps out of gear	1. Misalignment of transmission case or clutch housing. 2. Worn pilot bearing in crankshaft. 3. Bent transmission shaft. 4. Worn high speed sliding gear. 5. Worn teeth or end-play in clutch shaft. 6. Insufficient spring tension on shifter rail plunger. 7. Bent or loose shifter fork. 8. Gears not engaging completely. 9. Loose or worn bearings on clutch shaft or mainshaft. 10. Worn gear teeth. 11. Worn or damaged detent balls.
Transmission sticks in gear	1. Clutch not releasing fully. 2. Burred or battered teeth on clutch shaft, or sliding sleeve. 3. Burred or battered transmission mainshaft. 4. Frozen synchronizing clutch. 5. Stuck shifter rail plunger. 6. Gearshift lever twisting and binding shifter rail. 7. Battered teeth on high speed sliding gear or on sleeve. 8. Improper lubrication, or lack of lubrication. 9. Corroded transmission parts. 10. Defective mainshaft pilot bearing. 11. Locked gear bearings will give same effect as stuck in gear.
Transmission gears will not synchronize	1. Binding pilot bearing on mainshaft, will synchronize in high gear only. 2. Clutch not releasing fully. 3. Detent spring weak or broken. 4. Weak or broken springs under balls in sliding gear sleeve. 5. Binding bearing on clutch shaft, or binding countershaft. 6. Binding pilot bearing in crankshaft. 7. Badly worn gear teeth. 8. Improper lubrication. 9. Constant mesh gear not turning freely on transmission mainshaft. Will synchronize in that gear only.

Condition	Possible Cause
Gears spinning when shifting into gear from neutral	1. Clutch not releasing fully. 2. In some cases an extremely light lubricant in transmission will cause gears to continue to spin for a short time after clutch is released. 3. Binding pilot bearing in crankshaft.
Transmission noisy in all gears	1. Insufficient lubricant, or improper lubricant. 2. Worn countergear bearings. 3. Worn or damaged main drive gear or countergear. 4. Damaged main drive gear or mainshaft bearings. 5. Worn or damaged countergear anti-lash plate.
Transmission noisy in neutral only	1. Damaged main drive gear bearing. 2. Damaged or loose mainshaft pilot bearing. 3. Worn or damaged countergear anti-lash plate. 4. Worn countergear bearings.
Transmission noisy in one gear only	1. Damaged or worn constant mesh gears. 2. Worn or damaged countergear bearings. 3. Damaged or worn synchronizer.
Transmission noisy in reverse only	1. Worn or damaged reverse idler gear or idler bushing. 2. Worn or damaged mainshaft reverse gear. 3. Worn or damaged reverse countergear. 4. Damaged shift mechanism.

TROUBLESHOOTING AUTOMATIC TRANSMISSION PROBLEMS

Keeping alert to changes in the operating characteristics of the transmission (changing shift points, noises, etc.) can prevent small problems from becoming large ones. If the problem cannot be traced to loose bolts, fluid level, misadjusted linkage, clogged filters or similar problems, you should probably seek professional service.

Transmission Fluid Indications

The appearance and odor of the transmission fluid can give valuable clues to the overall condition of the transmission. Always note the appearance of the fluid when you check the fluid level or change the fluid. Rub a small amount of fluid between your fingers to feel for grit and smell the fluid on the dipstick.

If the fluid appears:	It indicates:
Clear and red colored	Normal operation
Discolored (extremely dark red or brownish) or smells burned	Band or clutch pack failure, usually caused by an overheated transmission. Hauling very heavy loads with insufficient power or failure to change the fluid often result in overheating. Do not confuse this appearance with newer fluids that have a darker red color and a strong odor (though not a burned odor).
Foamy or aerated (light in color and full of bubbles)	1. The level is too high (gear train is churning oil) 2. An internal air leak (air is mixing with the fluid). Have the transmission checked professionally.
Solid residue in the fluid	Defective bands, clutch pack or bearings. Bits of band material or metal abrasives are clinging to the dipstick. Have the transmission checked professionally.
Varnish coating on the dipstick	The transmission fluid is overheating

TROUBLESHOOTING DRIVE AXLE PROBLEMS

First, determine when the noise is most noticeable.

Drive Noise: Produced under vehicle acceleration.

Coast Noise: Produced while coasting with a closed throttle.

Float Noise: Occurs while maintaining constant speed (just enough to keep speed constant) on a level road.

External Noise Elimination

It is advisable to make a thorough road test to determine whether the noise originates in the rear axle or whether it originates from the tires, engine, transmission, wheel bearings or road surface. Noise originating from other places cannot be corrected by servicing the rear axle.

ROAD NOISE

Brick or rough surfaced concrete roads produce noises that seem to come from the rear axle. Road noise is usually identical in Drive or Coast and driving on a different type of road will tell whether the road is the problem.

TIRE NOISE

Tire noise can be mistaken as rear axle noise, even though the tires on the front are at fault. Snow tread and mud tread tires or tires worn unevenly will frequently cause vibrations which seem to originate elsewhere; *temporarily, and for test purposes only*, inflate the tires to 40–50 lbs. This will significantly alter the noise produced by the tires, but will not alter noise from the rear axle. Noises from the rear axle will normally cease at speeds below 30 mph on coast, while tire noise will continue at lower tone as speed is decreased. The rear axle noise will usually change from drive conditions to coast conditions, while tire noise will not. Do not forget to lower the tire pressure to normal after the test is complete.

ENGINE/TRANSMISSION NOISE

Determine at what speed the noise is most pronounced, then stop in a quiet place. With the transmission in Neutral, run the engine through speeds corresponding to road speeds where the noise was noticed. Noises produced with the vehicle standing still are coming from the engine or transmission.

FRONT WHEEL BEARINGS

Front wheel bearing noises, sometimes confused with rear axle noises, will not change when comparing drive and coast conditions. While holding the speed steady, lightly apply the footbrake. This will often cause wheel bearing noise to lessen, as some of the weight is taken off the bearing. Front wheel bearings are easily checked by jacking up the wheels and spinning the wheels. Shaking the wheels will also determine if the wheel bearings are excessively loose.

REAR AXLE NOISES

Eliminating other possible sources can narrow the cause to the rear axle, which normally produces noise from worn gears or bearings. Gear noises tend to peak in a narrow speed range, while bearing noises will usually vary in pitch with engine speeds.

Noise Diagnosis

The Noise Is:	Most Probably Produced By:
1. Identical under Drive or Coast	Road surface, tires or front wheel bearings
2. Different depending on road surface	Road surface or tires
3. Lower as speed is lowered	Tires
4. Similar when standing or moving	Engine or transmission
5. A vibration	Unbalanced tires, rear wheel bearing, unbalanced driveshaft or worn U-joint
6. A knock or click about every two tire revolutions	Rear wheel bearing
7. Most pronounced on turns	Damaged differential gears
8. A steady low-pitched whirring or scraping, starting at low speeds	Damaged or worn pinion bearing
9. A chattering vibration on turns	Wrong differential lubricant or worn clutch plates (limited slip rear axle)
10. Noticed only in Drive, Coast or Float conditions	Worn ring gear and/or pinion gear

Troubleshooting Steering & Suspension Problems

Condition	Possible Cause
Hard steering (wheel is hard to turn)	1. Improper tire pressure 2. Loose or glazed pump drive belt 3. Low or incorrect fluid 4. Loose, bent or poorly lubricated front end parts 5. Improper front end alignment (excessive caster) 6. Bind in steering column or linkage 7. Kinked hydraulic hose 8. Air in hydraulic system 9. Low pump output or leaks in system 10. Obstruction in lines 11. Pump valves sticking or out of adjustment 12. Incorrect wheel alignment
Loose steering (too much play in steering wheel)	1. Loose wheel bearings 2. Faulty shocks 3. Worn linkage or suspension components 4. Loose steering gear mounting or linkage points 5. Steering mechanism worn or improperly adjusted 6. Valve spool improperly adjusted 7. Worn ball joints, tie-rod ends, etc.
Veers or wanders (pulls to one side with hands off steering wheel)	1. Improper tire pressure 2. Improper front end alignment 3. Dragging or improperly adjusted brakes 4. Bent frame 5. Improper rear end alignment 6. Faulty shocks or springs 7. Loose or bent front end components 8. Play in Pitman arm 9. Steering gear mountings loose 10. Loose wheel bearings 11. Binding Pitman arm 12. Spool valve sticking or improperly adjusted 13. Worn ball joints
Wheel oscillation or vibration transmitted through steering wheel	1. Low or uneven tire pressure 2. Loose wheel bearings 3. Improper front end alignment 4. Bent spindle 5. Worn, bent or broken front end components 6. Tires out of round or out of balance 7. Excessive lateral runout in disc brake rotor 8. Loose or bent shock absorber or strut
Noises (see also "Troubleshooting Drive Axle Problems")	1. Loose belts 2. Low fluid, air in system 3. Foreign matter in system 4. Improper lubrication 5. Interference or chafing in linkage 6. Steering gear mountings loose 7. Incorrect adjustment or wear in gear box 8. Faulty valves or wear in pump 9. Kinked hydraulic lines 10. Worn wheel bearings
Poor return of steering	1. Over-inflated tires 2. Improperly aligned front end (excessive caster) 3. Binding in steering column 4. No lubrication in front end 5. Steering gear adjusted too tight
Uneven tire wear (see "How To Read Tire Wear")	1. Incorrect tire pressure 2. Improperly aligned front end 3. Tires out-of-balance 4. Bent or worn suspension parts

HOW TO READ TIRE WEAR

The way your tires wear is a good indicator of other parts of the suspension. Abnormal wear patterns are often caused by the need for simple tire maintenance, or for front end alignment.

Excessive wear at the center of the tread indicates that the air pressure in the tire is consistently too high. The tire is riding on the center of the tread and wearing it prematurely. Occasionally, this wear pattern can result from outrageously wide tires on narrow rims. The cure for this is to replace either the tires or the wheels.

This type of wear usually results from consistent under-inflation. When a tire is under-inflated, there is too much contact with the road by the outer treads, which wear prematurely. When this type of wear occurs, and the tire pressure is known to be consistently correct, a bent or worn steering component or the need for wheel alignment could be indicated.

Feathering is a condition when the edge of each tread rib develops a slightly rounded edge on one side and a sharp edge on the other. By running your hand over the tire, you can usually feel the sharper edges before you'll be able to see them. The most common causes of feathering are incorrect toe-in setting or deteriorated bushings in the front suspension.

When an inner or outer rib wears faster than the rest of the tire, the need for wheel alignment is indicated. There is excessive camber in the front suspension, causing the wheel to lean too much putting excessive load on one side of the tire. Misalignment could also be due to sagging springs, worn ball joints, or worn control arm bushings. Be sure the vehicle is loaded the way it's normally driven when you have the wheels aligned.

Cups or scalloped dips appearing around the edge of the tread almost always indicate worn (sometimes bent) suspension parts. Adjustment of wheel alignment alone will seldom cure the problem. Any worn component that connects the wheel to the suspension can cause this type of wear. Occasionally, wheels that are out of balance will wear like this, but wheel imbalance usually shows up as bald spots between the outside edges and center of the tread.

Second-rib wear is usually found only in radial tires, and appears where the steel belts end in relation to the tread. It can be kept to a minimum by paying careful attention to tire pressure and frequently rotating the tires. This is often considered normal wear but excessive amounts indicate that the tires are too wide for the wheels.

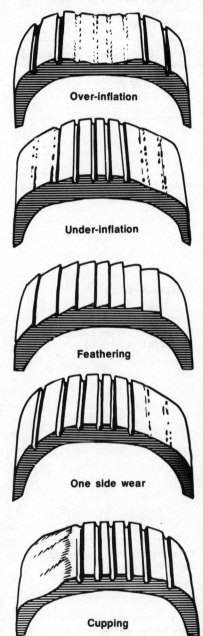

Over-inflation

Under-inflation

Feathering

One side wear

Cupping

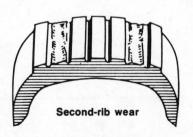

Second-rib wear

Troubleshooting Disc Brake Problems

Condition	Possible Cause
Noise—groan—brake noise emanating when slowly releasing brakes (creep-groan)	Not detrimental to function of disc brakes—no corrective action required. (This noise may be eliminated by slightly increasing or decreasing brake pedal efforts.)
Rattle—brake noise or rattle emanating at low speeds on rough roads, (front wheels only).	1. Shoe anti-rattle spring missing or not properly positioned. 2. Excessive clearance between shoe and caliper. 3. Soft or broken caliper seals. 4. Deformed or misaligned disc. 5. Loose caliper.
Scraping	1. Mounting bolts too long. 2. Loose wheel bearings. 3. Bent, loose, or misaligned splash shield.
Front brakes heat up during driving and fail to release	1. Operator riding brake pedal. 2. Stop light switch improperly adjusted. 3. Sticking pedal linkage. 4. Frozen or seized piston. 5. Residual pressure valve in master cylinder. 6. Power brake malfunction. 7. Proportioning valve malfunction.
Leaky brake caliper	1. Damaged or worn caliper piston seal. 2. Scores or corrosion on surface of cylinder bore.
Grabbing or uneven brake action— Brakes pull to one side	1. Causes listed under "Brakes Pull". 2. Power brake malfunction. 3. Low fluid level in master cylinder. 4. Air in hydraulic system. 5. Brake fluid, oil or grease on linings. 6. Unmatched linings. 7. Distorted brake pads. 8. Frozen or seized pistons. 9. Incorrect tire pressure. 10. Front end out of alignment. 11. Broken rear spring. 12. Brake caliper pistons sticking. 13. Restricted hose or line. 14. Caliper not in proper alignment to braking disc. 15. Stuck or malfunctioning metering valve. 16. Soft or broken caliper seals. 17. Loose caliper.
Brake pedal can be depressed without braking effect	1. Air in hydraulic system or improper bleeding procedure. 2. Leak past primary cup in master cylinder. 3. Leak in system. 4. Rear brakes out of adjustment. 5. Bleeder screw open.
Excessive pedal travel	1. Air, leak, or insufficient fluid in system or caliper. 2. Warped or excessively tapered shoe and lining assembly. 3. Excessive disc runout. 4. Rear brake adjustment required. 5. Loose wheel bearing adjustment. 6. Damaged caliper piston seal. 7. Improper brake fluid (boil). 8. Power brake malfunction. 9. Weak or soft hoses.

Troubleshooting Disc Brake Problems (cont.)

Condition	Possible Cause
Brake roughness or chatter (pedal pumping)	1. Excessive thickness variation of braking disc. 2. Excessive lateral runout of braking disc. 3. Rear brake drums out-of-round. 4. Excessive front bearing clearance.
Excessive pedal effort	1. Brake fluid, oil or grease on linings. 2. Incorrect lining. 3. Frozen or seized pistons. 4. Power brake malfunction. 5. Kinked or collapsed hose or line. 6. Stuck metering valve. 7. Scored caliper or master cylinder bore. 8. Seized caliper pistons.
Brake pedal fades (pedal travel increases with foot on brake)	1. Rough master cylinder or caliper bore. 2. Loose or broken hydraulic lines/connections. 3. Air in hydraulic system. 4. Fluid level low. 5. Weak or soft hoses. 6. Inferior quality brake shoes or fluid. 7. Worn master cylinder piston cups or seals.

Troubleshooting Drum Brakes

Condition	Possible Cause
Pedal goes to floor	1. Fluid low in reservoir. 2. Air in hydraulic system. 3. Improperly adjusted brake. 4. Leaking wheel cylinders. 5. Loose or broken brake lines. 6. Leaking or worn master cylinder. 7. Excessively worn brake lining.
Spongy brake pedal	1. Air in hydraulic system. 2. Improper brake fluid (low boiling point). 3. Excessively worn or cracked brake drums. 4. Broken pedal pivot bushing.
Brakes pulling	1. Contaminated lining. 2. Front end out of alignment. 3. Incorrect brake adjustment. 4. Unmatched brake lining. 5. Brake drums out of round. 6. Brake shoes distorted. 7. Restricted brake hose or line. 8. Broken rear spring. 9. Worn brake linings. 10. Uneven lining wear. 11. Glazed brake lining. 12. Excessive brake lining dust. 13. Heat spotted brake drums. 14. Weak brake return springs. 15. Faulty automatic adjusters. 16. Low or incorrect tire pressure.

Condition	Possible Cause
Squealing brakes	1. Glazed brake lining. 2. Saturated brake lining. 3. Weak or broken brake shoe retaining spring. 4. Broken or weak brake shoe return spring. 5. Incorrect brake lining. 6. Distorted brake shoes. 7. Bent support plate. 8. Dust in brakes or scored brake drums. 9. Linings worn below limit. 10. Uneven brake lining wear. 11. Heat spotted brake drums.
Chirping brakes	1. Out of round drum or eccentric axle flange pilot.
Dragging brakes	1. Incorrect wheel or parking brake adjustment. 2. Parking brakes engaged or improperly adjusted. 3. Weak or broken brake shoe return spring. 4. Brake pedal binding. 5. Master cylinder cup sticking. 6. Obstructed master cylinder relief port. 7. Saturated brake lining. 8. Bent or out of round brake drum. 9. Contaminated or improper brake fluid. 10. Sticking wheel cylinder pistons. 11. Driver riding brake pedal. 12. Defective proportioning valve. 13. Insufficient brake shoe lubricant.
Hard pedal	1. Brake booster inoperative. 2. Incorrect brake lining. 3. Restricted brake line or hose. 4. Frozen brake pedal linkage. 5. Stuck wheel cylinder. 6. Binding pedal linkage. 7. Faulty proportioning valve.
Wheel locks	1. Contaminated brake lining. 2. Loose or torn brake lining. 3. Wheel cylinder cups sticking. 4. Incorrect wheel bearing adjustment. 5. Faulty proportioning valve.
Brakes fade (high speed)	1. Incorrect lining. 2. Overheated brake drums. 3. Incorrect brake fluid (low boiling temperature). 4. Saturated brake lining. 5. Leak in hydraulic system. 6. Faulty automatic adjusters.
Pedal pulsates	1. Bent or out of round brake drum.
Brake chatter and shoe knock	1. Out of round brake drum. 2. Loose support plate. 3. Bent support plate. 4. Distorted brake shoes. 5. Machine grooves in contact face of brake drum (Shoe Knock). 6. Contaminated brake lining. 7. Missing or loose components. 8. Incorrect lining material. 9. Out-of-round brake drums. 10. Heat spotted or scored brake drums. 11. Out-of-balance wheels.

Troubleshooting Drum Brakes (cont.)

Condition	Possible Cause
Brakes do not self adjust	1. Adjuster screw frozen in thread. 2. Adjuster screw corroded at thrust washer. 3. Adjuster lever does not engage star wheel. 4. Adjuster installed on wrong wheel.
Brake light glows	1. Leak in the hydraulic system. 2. Air in the system. 3. Improperly adjusted master cylinder pushrod. 4. Uneven lining wear. 5. Failure to center combination valve or proportioning valve.

Mechanic's Data

General Conversion Table

Multiply By	To Convert	To	
		LENGTH	
2.54	Inches	Centimeters	.3937
25.4	Inches	Millimeters	.03937
30.48	Feet	Centimeters	.0328
.304	Feet	Meters	3.28
.914	Yards	Meters	1.094
1.609	Miles	Kilometers	.621
		VOLUME	
.473	Pints	Liters	2.11
.946	Quarts	Liters	1.06
3.785	Gallons	Liters	.264
.016	Cubic inches	Liters	61.02
16.39	Cubic inches	Cubic cms.	.061
28.3	Cubic feet	Liters	.0353
		MASS (Weight)	
28.35	Ounces	Grams	.035
.4536	Pounds	Kilograms	2.20
—	To obtain	From	Multiply by

Multiply By	To Convert	To	
		AREA	
.645	Square inches	Square cms.	.155
.836	Square yds.	Square meters	1.196
		FORCE	
4.448	Pounds	Newtons	.225
.138	Ft./lbs.	Kilogram/meters	7.23
1.36	Ft./lbs.	Newton-meters	.737
.112	In./lbs.	Newton-meters	8.844
		PRESSURE	
.068	Psi	Atmospheres	14.7
6.89	Psi	Kilopascals	.145
		OTHER	
1.104	Horsepower (DIN)	Horsepower (SAE)	.9861
.746	Horsepower (SAE)	Kilowatts (KW)	1.34
1.60	Mph	Km/h	.625
.425	Mpg	Km/1	2.35
—	To obtain	From	Multiply by

Tap Drill Sizes

National Coarse or U.S.S.

Screw & Tap Size	Threads Per Inch	Use Drill Number
No. 5	40	.39
No. 6	32	.36
No. 8	32	.29
No. 10	24	.25
No. 12	24	.17
1/4	20	8
5/16	18	F
3/8	16	5/16
7/16	14	U
1/2	13	27/64
9/16	12	31/64
5/8	11	17/32
3/4	10	21/32
7/8	9	49/64

National Coarse or U.S.S.

Screw & Tap Size	Threads Per Inch	Use Drill Number
1	8	7/8
1 1/8	7	63/64
1 1/4	7	1 7/64
1 1/2	6	1 11/32

National Fine or S.A.E.

Screw & Tap Size	Threads Per Inch	Use Drill Number
No. 5	44	.37
No. 6	40	.33
No. 8	36	.29
No. 10	32	.21

National Fine or S.A.E.

Screw & Tap Size	Threads Per Inch	Use Drill Number
No. 12	28	15
1/4	28	3
6/16	24	1
3/8	24	Q
7/16	20	W
1/2	20	29/64
9/16	18	33/64
5/8	18	37/64
3/4	16	11/16
7/8	14	13/16
1 1/8	12	1 3/64
1 1/4	12	1 11/64
1 1/2	12	1 27/64

Drill Sizes In Decimal Equivalents

Inch	Decimal	Wire	mm
1/64	.0156		.39
	.0157		.4
	.0160	78	
	.0165		.42
	.0173		.44
	.0177		.45
	.0180	77	
	.0181		.46
	.0189		.48
	.0197		.5
	.0200	76	
	.0210	75	
	.0217		.55
	.0225	74	
	.0236		.6
	.0240	73	
	.0250	72	
	.0256		.65
	.0260	71	
	.0276		.7
	.0280	70	
	.0292	69	
	.0295		.75
	.0310	68	
1/32	.0312		.79
	.0315		.8
	.0320	67	
	.0330	66	
	.0335		.85
	.0350	65	
	.0354		.9
	.0360	64	
	.0370	63	
	.0374		.95
	.0380	62	
	.0390	61	
	.0394		1.0
	.0400	60	
	.0410	59	
	.0413		1.05
	.0420	58	
	.0430	57	
	.0433		1.1
	.0453		1.15
	.0465	56	
3/64	.0469		1.19
	.0472		1.2
	.0492		1.25
	.0512		1.3
	.0520	55	
	.0531		1.35
	.0550	54	
	.0551		1.4
	.0571		1.45
	.0591		1.5
	.0595	53	
	.0610		1.55
1/16	.0625		1.59
	.0630		1.6
	.0635	52	
	.0650		1.65
	.0669		1.7
	.0670	51	
	.0689		1.75
	.0700	50	
	.0709		1.8
	.0728		1.85

Inch	Decimal	Wire	mm
	.0730	49	
	.0748		1.9
	.0760	48	
	.0768		1.95
5/64	.0781		1.98
	.0785	47	
	.0787		2.0
	.0807		2.05
	.0810	46	
	.0820	45	
	.0827		2.1
	.0846		2.15
	.0860	44	
	.0866		2.2
	.0886		2.25
	.0890	43	
	.0906		2.3
	.0925		2.35
	.0935	42	
3/32	.0938		2.38
	.0945		2.4
	.0960	41	
	.0965		2.45
	.0980	40	
	.0981		2.5
	.0995	39	
	.1015	38	
	.1024		2.6
	.1040	37	
	.1063		2.7
	.1065	36	
	.1083		2.75
7/64	.1094		2.77
	.1100	35	
	.1102		2.8
	.1110	34	
	.1130	33	
	.1142		2.9
	.1160	32	
	.1181		3.0
	.1200	31	
	.1220		3.1
1/8	.1250		3.17
	.1260		3.2
	.1280		3.25
	.1285	30	
	.1299		3.3
	.1339		3.4
	.1360	29	
	.1378		3.5
	.1405	28	
9/64	.1406		3.57
	.1417		3.6
	.1440	27	
	.1457		3.7
	.1470	26	
	.1476		3.75
	.1495	25	
	.1496		3.8
	.1520	24	
	.1535		3.9
	.1540	23	
5/32	.1562		3.96
	.1570	22	
	.1575		4.0
	.1590	21	
	.1610	20	

Inch	Decimal	Wire & Letter	mm
	.1614		4.1
	.1654		4.2
	.1660	19	
	.1673		4.25
	.1693		4.3
	.1695	18	
11/64	.1719		4.36
	.1730	17	
	.1732		4.4
	.1770	16	
	.1772		4.5
	.1800	15	
	.1811		4.6
	.1820	14	
	.1850	13	
	.1850		4.7
	.1870		4.75
3/16	.1875		4.76
	.1890		4.8
	.1890	12	
	.1910	11	
	.1929		4.9
	.1935	10	
	.1960	9	
	.1969		5.0
	.1990	8	
	.2008		5.1
	.2010	7	
13/64	.2031		5.16
	.2040	6	
	.2047		5.2
	.2055	5	
	.2067		5.25
	.2087		5.3
	.2090	4	
	.2126		5.4
	.2130	3	
	.2165		5.5
7/32	.2188		5.55
	.2205		5.6
	.2210	2	
	.2244		5.7
	.2264		5.75
	.2280	1	
	.2283		5.8
	.2323		5.9
	.2340	A	
15/64	.2344		5.95
	.2362		6.0
	.2380	B	
	.2402		6.1
	.2420	C	
	.2441		6.2
	.2460	D	
	.2461		6.25
	.2480		6.3
1/4	.2500	E	6.35
	.2520		6.
	.2559		6.5
	.2570	F	
	.2598		6.6
	.2610	G	
	.2638		6.7
17/64	.2656		6.74
	.2657		6.75
	.2660	H	
	.2677		6.8

Inch	Decimal	Letter	mm
	.2717		6.9
	.2720	I	
	.2756		7.0
	.2770	J	
	.2795		7.1
	.2810	K	
9/32	.2812		7.14
	.2835		7.2
	.2854		7.25
	.2874		7.3
	.2900	L	
	.2913		7.4
	.2950	M	
	.2953		7.5
19/64	.2969		7.54
	.2992		7.6
	.3020	N	
	.3031		7.7
	.3051		7.75
	.3071		7.8
	.3110		7.9
5/16	.3125		7.93
	.3150		8.0
	.3160	O	
	.3189		8.1
	.3228		8.2
	.3230	P	
	.3248		8.25
	.3268		8.3
21/64	.3281		8.33
	.3307		8.4
	.3320	Q	
	.3346		8.5
	.3386		8.6
	.3390	R	
	.3425		8.7
11/32	.3438		8.73
	.3445		8.75
	.3465		8.8
	.3480	S	
	.3504		8.9
	.3543		9.0
	.3580	T	
	.3583		9.1
23/64	.3594		9.12
	.3622		9.2
	.3642		9.25
	.3661		9.3
	.3680	U	
	.3701		9.4
	.3740		9.5
3/8	.3750		9.52
	.3770	V	
	.3780		9.6
	.3819		9.7
	.3839		9.75
	.3858		9.8
	.3860	W	
	.3898		9.9
25/64	.3906		9.92
	.3937		10.0
	.3970	X	
	.4040	Y	
13/32	.4062		10.31
	.4130	Z	
	.4134		10.5
27/64	.4219		10.71

Inch	Decimal	mm
	.4331	11.0
7/16	.4375	11.11
	.4528	11.5
29/64	.4531	11.51
15/32	.4688	11.90
	.4724	12.0
31/64	.4844	12.30
	.4921	12.5
1/2	.5000	12.70
	.5118	13.0
33/64	.5156	13.09
17/32	.5312	13.49
	.5315	13.5
35/64	.5469	13.89
	.5512	14.0
9/16	.5625	14.28
	.5709	14.5
37/64	.5781	14.68
	.5906	15.0
19/32	.5938	15.08
39/64	.6094	15.47
	.6102	15.5
5/8	.6250	15.87
	.6299	16.0
41/64	.6406	16.27
	.6496	16.5
21/32	.6562	16.66
	.6693	17.0
43/64	.6719	17.06
11/16	.6875	17.46
	.6890	17.5
45/64	.7031	17.85
	.7087	18.0
23/32	.7188	18.25
	.7283	18.5
47/64	.7344	18.65
	.7480	19.0
3/4	.7500	19.05
49/64	.7656	19.44
	.7677	19.5
25/32	.7812	19.84
	.7874	20.0
51/64	.7969	20.24
	.8071	20.5
13/16	.8125	20.63
	.8268	21.0
53/64	.8281	21.03
27/32	.8438	21.43
	.8465	21.5
55/64	.8594	21.82
	.8661	22.0
7/8	.8750	22.22
	.8858	22.5
57/64	.8906	22.62
	.9055	23.0
29/32	.9062	23.01
59/64	.9219	23.41
	.9252	23.5
15/16	.9375	23.81
	.9449	24.0
61/64	.9531	24.2
	.9646	24.5
31/32	.9688	24.6
	.9843	25.0
63/64	.9844	25.0
1	1.0000	25.4

Index